Education in Popular Culture

Education in Popular Culture explores what makes schools, colleges, teachers and students an enduring focus for a wide range of contemporary media. What is it about the school experience that makes us wish to relive it again and again? The book provides an overview of education as it is represented in popular culture, together with a framework through which educators can interpret these representations in relation to their own professional values and development. The analyses are contextualised within contemporary, historical and ideological frameworks, and make connections between popular representations and professional and political discourses about education.

Through its examination of film, television, lyrics and fiction, this book tackles educational themes that recur in popular culture, and demonstrates how they intersect with debates concerning teacher performance, the curriculum and young people's behaviour and morality. Chapters explore how experiences of education are both reflected and constructed in ways that sometimes reinforce official and professional educational perspectives, and sometimes resist and oppose them. The book addresses issues relating to:

- the characterisation of teachers
- sexual relationships in educational contexts
- race, gender and bullying
- resistance to educational processes and institutions
- lifelong learning.

Education in Popular Culture aims to stimulate critical reflection on the popular myths and professional discourses that surround teachers and teaching. It will serve to deepen analyses of teaching and learning and their associated institutional and societal contexts in a creative and challenging way.

Roy Fisher, Ann Harris and **Christine Jarvis** are at the School of Education and Professional Development, University of Huddersfield, UK.

D1461435

Education in Popular Culture

Telling Tales on Teachers and Learners

Roy Fisher, Ann Harris and Christine Jarvis

Routledge
Taylor & Francis Group

LONDON AND NEW YORK

First published 2008
by Routledge
2 Park Square, Milton Park, Abingdon, Oxon, OX14 4RN

Simultaneously published in the USA and Canada
by Routledge
270 Madison Ave, New York, NY 10016

Routledge is an imprint of the Taylor & Francis Group, an informa business

Typeset in Galliard by
Keystroke, 28 High Street, Tettenhall, Wolverhampton
Printed and bound in Great Britain by
MPG Books Ltd, Bodmin

British Library Cataloguing in Publication Data
A catalogue record for this book is available from the British Library
Library of Congress Cataloging in Publication Data
Fisher, Roy, 1953–
  Education in popular culture : telling tales on teachers and learners / Roy Fisher,
Ann Harris and Christine Jarvis.
       p. cm.
  Includes bibliographical references and index.
1. Education in popular culture. 2. Education–Social aspects. 3. Education in mass media.
I. Harris, Ann, 1951– II. Jarvis, Christine, 1955– III. Title.
  LC191.F525 2008
   306.43'2—dc22   2007044228

ISBN10: 0–415–33241–9 (hbk)
ISBN10: 0–415–33242–7 (pbk)
ISBN10: 0–203–08761–5 (ebk)

ISBN13: 978–0–415–33241–5 (hbk)
ISBN13: 978–0–415–33242–2 (pbk)
ISBN13: 978–0–203–08761–9 (ebk)

Contents

Acknowledgements

We are grateful to the many colleagues, friends, students and teachers who have either made suggestions as to material that we should consider in relation to this study or offered their advice in relation to other aspects of the project. We would specifically like to thank Professor Patrick Ainley, Tom Anderson, Professor Fen Arthur, Dr Elizabeth Atkinson, Trevor Austin, Professor James Avis, Sally Baines, Kim Bell, Dr Andy Bennett, Louisa Bostwick, Matthew Buckland, Dr Viv Burr, Martin Butterworth, Peter Cafferty, David Cross, Professor Cedric Cullingford, Duncan Dyson, Linda Eastwood, David Finch, Amy Fisher, Andrew Fisher, Dr Pamela Fisher, Martyn Gledhill, Alison Gorf, Becky Gregson-Flynn, Jenny Hankey, Katharine Harris, Keith Hartley, Andrew Harvey, Professor Terry Hyland, Ben Jarvis, Mike Jenkins, Adrian Johnson, Dr David Kitchener, Alan Laurie, Dr David Lord, Paul Lunn, Daryl Marples, Dr Ken Martin, Tony Nasta, Ros Ollin, Chris Ormondroyd, Kevin Orr, Michele Paule, Adrian Perkins, Nina Phillips, Celia Poole, Alan Quicke, Professor Jeffrey Richards, Denise Robinson, Dr Jocelyn Robson, Dr Pete Sanderson, Keith Shepherd, Robin Simmons, Andrea Sims, Linda Smart, Darren Storey, Ron Thompson, Dr Paul Tosey, Jonathan Tummons, Martyn Walker, Caroline Walker-Gleaves, Keith Webb, Dr Anthony Whitehead, Professor Sheila Whiteley and Andrew Youde. Particular thanks are due to Professor Kevin Brehony of the University of Surrey and Dr John Hodgson of the University of West of England for their encouragement of and enthusiasm for this project at the point when it was just an idea. Thanks are also due to the School of Education and Professional Development at the University of Huddersfield for generous administrative support, particularly with respect to the time-consuming (but in most cases ultimately futile) pursuit of copyright permissions, and to Jacqui Mellor for facilitating this. Our apologies go to anyone who has been omitted. Any errors in the text that follows are, naturally, our responsibility.

Attempting to gain copyright permissions has been a particularly frustrating task, as those involved in writing about popular culture will appreciate, and we are most grateful for the associated support that we have received in this work from Dr Sarah Bastow and Julia Downs. We have also been assisted in seeking out relevant details by Kim Cooper and David Close of the Mechanical Copyright Protection Society–Performing Rights Society Alliance, and by Nina Harding of the British Film Institute. Despite the help that we have received it is fair to say that this book would have looked very different – and, we must admit, would have been greatly enhanced – had we been able to obtain all the copyright permissions that we pursued. On many occasions our requests for permission were ignored or denied, or were granted subject to the payment of fees far beyond what a book of this kind might reasonably justify in terms of income generated. For those reasons, and because we recognise and respect the principle of copyright and the need for owners to protect their works, we are extremely grateful to those who have granted their permission for us to quote from their work or use their images. These are as follows:

- Home Box Office, Santa Monica, CA, for permission to quote from the film *Elephant*. The Home Box Office web address is <www.hbo.com>.
- Revolution Studios, Santa Monica, CA, for permission to quote from the film *Mona Lisa Smile*. The Revolution Studios web address is <www.revolution studios.com>.
- Twentieth Century Fox for permission to quote from *Buffy the Vampire Slayer* episodes. The Twentieth Century Fox web address is <www.foxmovies.com>.

   Excerpt from *Buffy the Vampire Slayer* (episode: 'The Pack') © 1997 Courtesy of Twentieth Century Fox Television. Written by Matt Kiene & Joe Reinkemeyer.

   Excerpt from *Buffy the Vampire Slayer* (episode: 'The Puppet Show') © 1997 Courtesy of Twentieth Century Fox Television. Written by Dean Batali & Rob Des Hotel.

   Excerpt from *Buffy the Vampire Slayer* (episode: 'Out of Mind, Out of Sight') © 1997 Courtesy of Twentieth Century Fox Television. Story by Joss Whedon. Teleplay by Ashley Gable and Thomas A. Swyden.

   Excerpt from *Buffy the Vampire Slayer* (episode: 'School Hard') © 1998 Courtesy of Twentieth Century Fox Television. Story by Joss Whedon & David Greenwalt. Teleplay by David Greenwalt.

   Excerpt from *Buffy the Vampire Slayer* (episode: 'What's My Line – Part 1') © 1998 Courtesy of Twentieth Century Fox Television. Written by Howard Gordon & Marti Noxon.

   Excerpt from *Buffy the Vampire Slayer* (episode: 'I Only Have Eyes for You') © 1998 Courtesy of Twentieth Century Fox Television. Written by Marti Noxon.

   Excerpt from *Buffy the Vampire Slayer* (episode: 'Dead Man's Party') © 1999 Courtesy of Twentieth Century Fox Television. Written by Marti Noxon.

   Excerpt from *Buffy the Vampire Slayer* (episode: 'Band Candy') © 1999 Courtesy of Twentieth Century Fox Television. Written by Jane Espenson.

   Excerpt from *Buffy the Vampire Slayer* (episode: 'Graduation Day – Part 2') © 1999 Courtesy of Twentieth Century Fox Television. Written by Joss Whedon.

   Excerpt from *Buffy the Vampire Slayer* (episode: 'Lessons') © 2003 Courtesy of Twentieth Century Fox Television. Written by Joss Whedon. All rights reserved.

The content of some sections of this book has been adapted from journal papers, and we should like to thank the publishers for permission to use them here. The papers in question are:

Fisher, R. (1997) '"Teachers' hegemony sucks": examining *Beavis and Butt-head* for signs of life', *Educational Studies*, Vol. 23, No. 3, pp. 417–428.
—— (2003) 'Gramsci, cyberspace and work-based learning', *Journal of Access and Credit Studies*, Vol. 4, No. 2, pp. 154–158.
Jarvis, C. (2001) 'School is hell: gendered fears in teenage horror', *Educational Studies*, Vol. 27, No. 3, pp. 257–267.
—— (2005) 'Real stakeholder education? Lifelong learning in the Buffyverse', *Studies in the Education of Adults*, Vol. 37, No. 1, pp. 31–47.

The website for *Educational Studies* journal can be found at <www.tandf.co.uk>. The websites for the *Journal of Access and Credit Studies* and *Studies in the Education of Adults* are at <www.niace.org.uk>.

If there are any copyright acknowledgements that have been erroneously omitted, or any copyrights that we have unwittingly infringed anywhere in this book, we offer our sincere apologies and will gladly correct the error in any future edition.

Finally, we should like to thank Anna Clarkson, Amy Crowle and Kerry Maciak at Routledge for their patience and support.

Roy Fisher, Ann Harris and Christine Jarvis

Note to readers on the web-interactive use of this book

In the Acknowledgements we have referred to the difficulties that we encountered in attempting to obtain copyright permissions in order to use quotations in this book. There are therefore many instances where we have been unable to quote from films and songs as we would have wished. As a result, we have chosen to refer readers to associated texts and/or visual resources available on the Internet by highlighting in **bold print**. Song lyrics, through artists' official sites as well as from other legitimate sources, can normally be accessed easily and quickly with the use of such search engines as Google and Yahoo. You should enter the name of the artist, the title of the song and the word 'lyrics'. In many instances, you can also hear songs and view associated videos or performances. In addition, it is often possible to access the scripts of films and episodes of television series as well as specific film and television programme-related promotional websites. Exploring such web-based resources will be a rewarding and pleasurable experience for most readers of this text.

1   Introduction

Education and popular culture

Education and popular culture are in some contexts considered to be almost antithetical concepts. Education is for enhancement and enrichment; it is about knowledge and learning. High culture might be spoken of in similar terms. But, for some, the notion of *popular* culture is still associated with the banal and trivial. Even those people who admit to enjoying popular culture can be dismissive of its value or significance. The assumption appears to be that if culture is popular then, by definition, it is likely to say little of note and to offer nothing that is educative. However, if you have decided to look at this book, it is unlikely that you subscribe wholeheartedly to the latter perspective, and more likely that you are among those who believe that popular culture is of interest and worthy of some serious consideration. Maybe as readers we should position ourselves where art teacher Katherine Watson, played by Julia Roberts in the film *Mona Lisa Smile* (2003), seeks to take her students: 'Do me a favour; do yourselves a favour. Stop talking and look. You're not required to write a paper. You're not even required to like it. You are required to consider it.'

Popular culture is part of our lives. With education, it forms a dynamic of contemporary existence. It appeals because it speaks to interests and anxieties that are widespread within the societies that produce it. It does not seek to impress; it seeks to entertain and to sell. In this book, however, what concerns us is not so much popular culture in general but rather the textual synthesis between education and popular culture. More specifically, we intend to explore how the people and places that are involved in education are represented in and through popular culture; how schools and colleges, teachers and students are portrayed in film, on television, in novels and through song lyrics. Each of us has been a pupil or a student, and, in school, we were the audience, producers and consumers of the multifaceted text that is contemporary education. Reading this book and study-ing the way in which education is represented in popular culture offers us an opportunity to be that audience again and, in doing so, to examine how society's and our own ideas about education are constructed and represented:

> The whole life of those societies in which modern conditions of production prevail presents itself as an immense accumulation of spectacles. All that once

was directly lived has become mere representation . . . The spectacle cannot be understood either as a deliberate distortion of the world or as a product of the mass dissemination of images. It is far better viewed as a *weltanschauung* that has been actualised, translated into the material realm – a world view transformed into an objective force . . .

The spectacle is capital accumulated to the point where it becomes image.
(Debord, 1995, pp. 12–13, 24)

What is this book?

Donnie Darko, Mean Girls, Grange Hill, School of Rock, Teachers, The Simpsons, Buffy the Vampire Slayer, Busted and Britney – images of and references to teachers, lecturers, trainers, pupils, students, schools, colleges, universities, teaching, learning and education abound throughout all genres of popular culture. What views of education and educators emerge from this wealth of material? What do such texts suggest about the educational concerns of the societies that produced them? What do they indicate about educational ideologies and priorities, about the tensions that might exist between different perspectives? How do popular cultural texts convey the effect and impact of education on individuals and communities? What do they suggest about our fears and expectations of education, about the challenges it offers, the desires and disappointments it creates? How do these texts relate to other educational discourses: for example, those of professionals, academics and policy-makers? These are the kinds of question this book aims to explore by its review and analysis of some relevant examples of popular culture.

There has always been an interface between fiction, art and educational ideas and practice. In 1965 Maxine Greene's classic work *The public school and the private vision* (republished 2007) examined the relationship between literary works and the writings of school reformers. Recently, there has been a growing body of academic work concerned with the representation of teachers, young people and education. This includes Brehony (1998); Cohen (1996); Dalton (1995); Daspit and Weaver (2000); Farber *et al.* (1994); Fisher (1997); Giroux (1993, 2002); Jarvis (2001, 2005); Joseph and Burnaford (2001); Judge (1995); Mitchell and Weber (1999); Paule (2004); Shary (2002); Warburton and Saunders (1996) and Weber and Mitchell (1995). Some of this work, such as that of Giroux (2002) and Daspit and Weaver (2000), has been concerned with 'decentring critical pedagogy' by exploring how popular culture embodies alternative voices about education and by considering the way in which popular culture itself has a pedagogical impact. There is an element of this in this book. That is, we are interested in the way popular texts offer constructions of reality that compete with those offered by academic, state and professional discourses about education, and we attempt to identify where there are contradictions and inter-sections between these perspectives. We also recognise that texts will not be read in the same way by everyone and therefore try to suggest some of the different ways they might be received. Nevertheless, we want to be quite clear about our own position, interests and perspectives. We are white, British teacher educators, with the typical educated working-class backgrounds that characterise many in the teaching profession. We share a commitment to critical pedagogy and emancipatory politics and a concern about the narrow conceptions of vocationalism that now dominate much of the UK educational agenda. Inevitably, this shapes our readings of texts, even when we try to consider and offer alternative perspectives.

The selection of texts discussed in this book is not meant to be comprehensive or representative. Our theoretical perspective assumes no single 'grand narrative' about education that can be derived from the study of popular culture. It does not aim to produce a history of education in popular culture. We believe, instead, that there is a range of narratives and competing discourses circulating through popular culture and about education. Our readers will bring their own agendas and apply what insights they can. Our selection of texts reflects the interests and preoccupations we have as academics, professionals and individuals. Alternative voices could have been explored; some quieter and less obvious than those we have identified. There are also significant themes which have not been considered here: for example, educational management and leadership as exemplified in films such as *Lean on Me* (1989) and UK television programmes such as *Hope and Glory* (2000) and *Ahead of the Class* (2005). We, however, have focused on other issues that we feel have been particularly dominant in the discourses about schools and education in the UK, USA and Australia. These include, first, in professional terms, a fixation with criticising competence and rooting out 'bad' teachers while at the same time proposing ever more precise and restrictive definitions of the 'good' teacher. Second, in relation to the curriculum, there has been a preoccupation, particularly in the UK, with the skills agenda and the status of vocational education. Third, on a more pastoral note, we have identified a focus on sex, including both an increasing anxiety about teachers as potential sexual predators and a moral imperative to curtail the sexual activity of pupils and students. Pastoral care is also emphasised in the regulation of children's and young people's behaviour and relationships within school by means of anti-bullying strategies and other intervention techniques. Finally, in policy terms, we are concerned with the development of a lifelong learning agenda and its generation of training and regulation, particularly in the UK, for teachers in the post-sixteen sector.

The texts explored in this book are primarily from the USA and the UK, with an occasional reference to other English-speaking cultures. These are texts we know and that have interested and influenced us. When we ask others about popular cultural representations of education, these are the ones which are cited. They are texts to which our students and colleagues in all educational sectors relate and which they recognise. US popular culture is global in its impact, and the bias of our selection reflects this. There are examples from a range of genres: popular music, television drama, popular fiction, television cartoons and film. Although we do not rate any genre above another, the final category receives most attention because films set in schools, colleges and universities are ubiquitous. As diverse communities, educational institutions provide a rich source of conflict and comedy, drama and dialogue. Furthermore, the widespread distribution and commercial consumption of film, resulting from the global dominance of the US industry, give additional impetus to questions about the role of popular culture in reflecting and constructing our perceptions about education.

The wider field

Major categories of cultural production where representations of education can be found and analysed include popular fiction, biography and autobiography, film, magazines, comics and cartoons, television and radio, cyberculture and popular music. While this book focuses on the representation of educational themes in a limited range of popular cultural texts, we have included below a brief synopsis of how some of the categories listed above might relate to a more general consideration of education in popular culture. Although this is not a book about ways of utilising popular culture in the classroom, we hope and expect that it will stimulate some ideas about how texts can both inform learning and be of value as pedagogical tools (see Gregson and Spedding (2003) for a discussion of the use of popular culture in post-compulsory teacher training).

Popular fiction

Popular fiction features its share of teachers and learners. Commercially successful young adult fiction series such as *Sweet Valley High*, *Point Horror* and *Point Crime* are set in schools or colleges, as are a number of murder mysteries, such as those by Antonia Fraser, Reginald Hill, Dorothy Sayers and Amanda Cross. On a different note, the extensive collection of *Miss Read* stories ('Miss Read' is the pen-name of novelist Dora Jessie Saint) exemplifies the potential for using school as the site for a nostalgic representation of childhood and rural life.

A significant genre of school-based literature is aimed specifically at children, including Enid Blyton's *St Clare's* and *Malory Towers* series, Angela Brazil's *Chalet School* books, Geoffrey Willans and Ronald Searle's *Molesworth* books and Anthony Buckeridge's *Jennings* series (set in an English prep school). More recently, J. K. Rowling's *Harry Potter* publishing phenomenon has demonstrated the commercial potential and individual appeal of school literature on the collective imagination of both UK and international readers. Popular fiction also has a capacity for transmogrification. To date there have been five very successful *Harry Potter* films (2001, 2002, 2004, 2005 and 2007), and more traditional literary texts have also been transmuted into cinema or television: for example, *Nicholas Nickleby* (films, 1947 and 2002; BBC TV series, 2001) and *Tom Brown's School Days* (films, 1916, 1940, 1951, 1971 and 2004).

Biography and autobiography

In the context of the current 'celebrity culture', biography and autobiography are key non-fiction categories in book sales, and the majority of these have some reference to the schooling and educational experiences of their subject. Such books either set out to recount the life experiences of ordinary people with extraordinary stories or, alternatively, they chronicle the life histories of 'the great and the good', often showing, among other things, how school shapes young ideas and influences the adults we subsequently become. Accounts can offer an insight into individuals' lived experiences of schooling and give space to alternative, even marginalised views of education. A number of autobiographical texts have also been produced around the experiences of teachers: for example, *Educating Esme: diary of a teacher's first year* by Esme Raji Codell (2003), recounting her experiences in Chicago; *I'm a teacher, get me out of here* by Francis Gilbert (2004), based on his work in a London school; and *Teacher man* (2005) by Frank McCourt, which describes his life and work in New York schools. In 1995, the autobiographical account *My posse don't do homework* by LouAnne Johnson (1992) was reissued under the title *Dangerous minds* after the film of the same name starring Michelle Pfeiffer proved a box-office success. Other autobiographical accounts, such as Roberta Guaspari-Tzavaras' *Music of the heart* (1999) and Marie Stubbs' *Ahead of the class* (2003), have also given rise to cinematic or television productions about their protagonists' experiences within school.

Film

Educational institutions, teachers and learners have all featured strongly in the cinema. Films ranging from high farce (*The Belles of St Trinian's*, 1954) to sentimental portrayals (*Goodbye, Mr Chips*, 1939, 1969 and 2002; *Mr Holland's Opus*, 1995) can tell us something about the way in which society represents teachers, learners and the educational process. Dalton (1995, pp. 23, 24) has discussed 'the way popular culture constructs its own curriculum in the movies through the on-screen relationship between teacher and student' and expresses a belief that 'general knowledge about the relationships between teachers and students, knowledge beyond the scope of the personal or anecdotal, is created by constructs of popular culture played out in the mass media'.

In recent years, owing to cinema's increasing popularity, film has intensified its focus on youth with a stream of 'teen flicks', including romantic comedies, road movies and comic horrors that offer celebrations of youthful jouissance and teenage angst while also exploiting adolescent humour. Examples include *Clueless* (1995), *The Faculty* (1998), the *American Pie* series (1999, 2001, 2003), *Ten Things I Hate About You* (1999), *Never Been Kissed* (1999), *She's All That* (1999), *Save the Last Dance* (2001), *Thirteen* (2003), *Mean Girls* (2004) and a host of others. Protagonists are generally at school or college, and the films cover themes such as: sexual experience; romantic relationships; friendships and school cliques; race and class issues; drug and alcohol abuse; parental control and oppression; grades and cheating; and music, dance and sport subcultures. Generally, however, despite dealing with some serious issues, these films offer a more comfortable and benign perspective on young people than the bleaker myths of previous generations and the brooding, intense performances of actors such as Marlon Brando in *The Wild One* (1953) and James Dean in *Rebel without a Cause* (1955). Nowadays, it is generally suggested that through insouciance, wit, energy and sheer good fortune, the young will triumph over adversity. See Pryce (2006) for a discussion of underlying moral messages and values in the *American Pie* series of films. Pryce (2006, p. 374) argues that these films seek to channel 'adolescent sexual behaviour into approved routes'.

Cyberculture

The late twentieth-century 'information explosion', with its associated processes of technologisation and globalisation, has created new cultural forms and virtual products as well as new audiences for popular culture through worldwide communities of computer users, chat rooms, discussion boards and websites. Friends Reunited, which enables former schoolfriends in the UK to make contact and also features school reminiscences, is a cyberspace representation of educational experience that, through nostalgic reconstruction, reveals underlying values, beliefs, desires and traumas relating to education. In a similar vein, the contemporary enthusiasm for 'blogging' also encourages individuals to detail the minutiae of their lives, including, potentially, their feelings about key experiences such as education and employment as well as other social and domestic events that have touched them. Websites such as YouTube, which enable people to present their own films, have controversially featured embarrassing or salacious clips of teachers filmed covertly in their classrooms by students; the once relative sanctity of the classroom as the dominion of the teacher has therefore been fatally breached.

Cyberculture creates a unique market place. It offers the potential for marginal alternative culture to be popularised through global communication, and it has helped to generate an environment in which education itself, through e-learning, is presented as a commercial and globally accessible commodity.

Comics and cartoons

Comics play a strong role in providing images of education to a young and impressionable readership. The *Beano*'s Bash Street Kids, for example, with their outrageous and anarchic classroom, are familiar to children in the UK. Japanese manga comics, generally aimed at a 'youth' market, have also become popular in the West and frequently incorporate school or college scenarios. A recent publishing success has been the manga series based on *Battle Royale*, the cult Japanese novel/film that depicts a future society where gangs of schoolchildren are made to fight to the death for entertainment. The cartoon genre, however, has increasingly moved from print-based comics to its animated form on television or in the cinema. Examples with significant educational representations include *Beavis and Butt-head* (Fisher, 1997), *Bromwell High*, *King of the Hill*, *The Simpsons* (Kantor *et al.*, 2001) and *South Park*.

The use of print cartoons in relation to an analysis of teachers' professional identity has been discussed by Warburton and Saunders (1996). Using a semiotic approach based on Barthes (1964), they focus on the meanings of three cartoons representing teachers that appeared in the *Daily Express* and *Daily Mail* newspapers and contributed to the 'Great Debate' on education launched by Prime Minister

James Callaghan's influential speech at Ruskin College, Oxford, on 18 October 1976. Warburton and Saunders (1996, p. 308) argue that such cartoons act as 'an indicator of public perception' and constitute 'evidence of myths and folklore, in the sense of publicly held stereotypes and "legends"'. The kind of cartoon animation represented by *Beavis and Butt-head* and *The Simpsons*, however, is markedly different to a 'static' newspaper cartoon in terms of how its messages are communicated, particularly if McLuhan's (1964) comment that 'the medium is the message' is believed.

Television and radio

Television is now a twenty-four-hour and global medium; it is also digital and interactive. In the UK and the USA, popular programming other than reality TV and news broadcasts tends to concentrate on dramas and documentaries that focus on crime and medicine. Yet, while the education scenario is not as common as police or hospital-based productions, it is none the less a staple of television. Teachers and learners often appear, for example, as characters in soap operas, though these rarely locate the action in educational institutions. UK viewers will be familiar with Ken Barlow's teaching years in the long-running Granada programme *Coronation Street* and the ascent to (and subsequent fall from) a career in teaching of former 'smackhead' Jimmy Corkhill in Channel 4's *Brookside*. Australian soaps, such as *Neighbours* and *Home and Away*, have focused on the lives of innumerable schoolchildren, and the series *Heartbreak High* realises the dramatic/melodramatic potential of adolescence. The BBC children's series *Grange Hill* has been both admired and criticised for what is perceived as its uncompromising engagement with some of the problems facing schools and young people, including, for example, drug abuse, bullying and teenage pregnancy. In contrast, the Channel 4 adult drama series *Teachers* takes a more surreal look at school life from the perspective of staff who are so self-absorbed they rarely notice the bizarre events that surround them. Less humorous views of education have been offered by the BBC drama *Hope and Glory* (1999), starring Lenny Henry, and the ITV drama *Ahead of the Class* (2005), starring Julie Walters, both of which focus on the recurrent myth of the 'superhead' whose dedication and charisma save a failing school.

'Spoken-word' radio in the UK is far less populist than television, but education-related fictions have included *King Street Junior*, a BBC Radio 4 light drama series depicting daily life in a provincial primary school, and *Night School* (also Radio 4), a comedy vehicle for Johnny Vegas, who plays a pottery teacher running an adult education class.

Popular music

Hundreds of songs have varying degrees of relevance to education and educational issues. Whatever claims have been made from time to time for popular music to be an 'art form', it has tended towards periodic decline and reinvention. Marcus (1992,

p. 752) observed more than a decade ago: 'In a time when it has been definitively pronounced that we have reached the end of history, the death of rock may appear to be a very small thing.' Yet the case for the cultural significance of popular music, at least as a cultural signifier, has been sufficiently well made to require no reinforcement here (see Hebdige, 1979, for example). More recently Bennett (2001, p. 1) has stated that: 'Without doubt, popular music is a primary, if not the primary, leisure resource in late modern society.' Since young people are among popular music's key consumers, it is not surprising that education and school figure among its concerns. Themes that can be found in pop songs about aspects of schooling include anti-school/anti-teachers; alienation and isolation; racism and violence; bullying and oppression; drugs in schools; idealisation and nostalgia for education; temporality; relationships and sex. The last of these, as we shall explore later, is often set against institutional repression and criticisms of conventional morality, as the **Pet Shop Boys** indicate in their song 'It's a Sin' (1987), where the narrator describes his experience of school as an environment that denies the pleasures of sexuality.

Representation: some useful concepts

Any study of representation in popular culture will draw on a set of theoretical perspectives, and, while this book is not a text on cultural theory, we do need to explore key definitions and introduce some relevant concepts, especially since we are working with two interdisciplinary fields – education and cultural studies – where the range of theories and disciplines can be almost infinite. Many people will be familiar with some of these underpinning ideas, but, since this book is aimed at a wide readership of intending teachers and current practitioners as well as at the interested general reader, some consideration of theory might be useful before engaging with popular cultural texts. What follows, therefore, is an attempt to define popular culture and then to present a brief summary of some theoretical perspectives relevant to representations of education in popular culture; these include feminism, hegemony, ideology, discourse, performativity and hyper-reality. We shall explore aspects of the work of, among others, Mulvey, Gramsci, Althusser, Foucault, Lyotard and Baudrillard. Our thinking has been strongly influenced by a range of thinkers who fall broadly within the body of scholarship that is often referred to as 'critical theory'. For those readers seeking an overview of critical theory we would strongly recommend Stephen Brookfield's (2005) *The power of critical theory for adult learning and teaching*. The following section will help the reader theoretically to situate the texts that are analysed later. Any readers who are primarily interested in the analyses of books, films, television and songs may choose to go directly to Chapter 2.

Popular culture

Culture has been defined in many ways. In this book, however, we are mainly concerned with what Williams (1983) offers as the third of his broad definitions of the concept, namely the 'works and practices of intellectual and especially artistic activity' (quoted in Storey, 2001, p. 2). Thus we have not attempted to analyse the process of watching television or visiting the cinema. Nor have we undertaken, or drawn extensively on, empirical work examining audience reception. Our focus is on the texts.

Our definition of 'popular' can be related to Storey's useful summary of six key approaches to defining popular culture. For example, our textual selections have mainly reached large audiences and, as such, they represent 'culture that is widely favoured or well liked by many people' and 'mass culture produced for mass audiences' (Storey, 2001, p. 6). Storey also notes that popular culture can be defined as what remains once high culture has been removed, but this definition is limited since the concept of a cultural canon has been extensively challenged, and, as a result, the boundaries between so-called high and low culture are somewhat blurred. Indeed, many cultural texts designed for mass consumption are both extremely popular and have received critical acclaim. So we do not take 'high' to be synonymous with 'elite'; nor do we define 'popular culture' necessarily as originating from 'the people'. Although some of the examples cited in this book (certain elements of popular music, for example) could be considered in this way, our position seeks to avoid an artificial distinction between mass and authentic culture. Commercial and creative interests interact in complex ways, and, we believe, it is not helpful to assume, simply because something is developed outside the mass culture industry, that it is of greater intrinsic worth or validity.

Storey (2001, p. 11) also notes that popular culture has been viewed as 'a site of struggle between the "resistance" of subordinate groups in society and the forces of "incorporation" operating in the interests of dominant groups in society'. This definition is based on the ideas of Gramsci, which will be discussed more fully later, especially the concept of 'hegemony' – a situation, or a process, in which a social group (or groups) exerts power over subordinate groups by shaping consent. This is characterised by Gramsci as a 'moving equilibrium' to be continually reproduced. The textual analyses which follow reflect an understanding that popular culture does indeed offer a site for this kind of struggle. Finally, Storey suggests it is possible to claim that the concepts of high culture and popular culture no longer have meaning, since, from a postmodernist perspective, distinctions have effectively collapsed under the weight of commercialism. While there is some truth in this, we would argue that there is still differentiation between products clearly designed to attract large audiences and those destined for minority consumption, and that this is marked out by the production and distribution processes, the intentions and preoccupations of creators and the expectations and interests of audiences.

Feminism

There are many feminisms and a wide range of feminist approaches to cultural studies. For a good introduction to feminism and popular culture, see MacDonald (1995), Hollows (2000) or Hollows and Moseley (2005); while, for a useful overview of feminist perspectives on education, see Weiner (1994) or *The Jossey-Bass reader on gender in education* (Jossey-Bass, 2002).

Feminist theorists have explored schools and colleges as sites where gendered identities are constructed, patriarchal power reinforced and girls' life chances constrained. In doing so, they bring differing perspectives of liberal, radical, socialist, psychoanalytical and postmodern thought to bear on analyses of education. Areas of particular relevance to representation in popular culture include the curriculum, girls' and boys' achievement, the impact of family on education, socialisation and social interaction, role models and the behaviour of teachers. The gendered nature of the curriculum – including a focus on male achievement, the privileging of subjects that are male dominated and the prevalence of learning and assessment methods that favour males – has often been analysed and has generated various attempts at reform. More recently, while family and social pressures still appear to constrain some female educational choices, the enhanced achievement of girls (not matched generally by subsequent higher earnings) has led to concern about boys' underperformance (Mac An Ghaill, 1994; McGivney, 2004) and a raft of educational initiatives to improve the boys' level of achievement. At the same time, there is continued pressure on girls to behave according to notions of femininity, particularly with respect to appearance and communication, and the oppression and intimidation that can result have also commanded attention. This can be extended to the complexity of interactions between teachers (male and female) and students (female and male), and the way in which gendered expectations and behaviours are reinforced through social practice: for example, the authority or vulnerability of female teachers and the feminisation or authoritarianism of men who go into teaching.

Popular culture has frequently been analysed in terms of its representation of women and girls. Early work focused mainly on stereotyping, sexist language and media presence, especially the dearth of serious, positive role models for women. More recently, popular culture has embraced the playfulness of postmodernism by producing images that subvert our expectations and undermine stereotypes. Examples include the UK advertisements for Boddington's beer, in which a glamorous woman adopts laddish behaviour, and a proliferation of violent female super-heroes such as Lara Croft, played by Angelina Jolie in the *Tomb Raider* films (2001 and 2003), or the Bride, played by Uma Thurman in *Kill Bill Volume 1* and *Kill Bill Volume 2* (2003 and 2004). Such subversions are entertaining, but their impact on the actual distribution of power between men and women is unclear. In this book, we are interested in the way the shifting representation of girls, particularly in much US popular culture (*Heathers* (1989), *Clueless* (1995), *Mean Girls* (2004)) both resists and reinforces gendered expectations; in the stereotyping of the female teacher in terms of her sex (sad, embittered spinster or schoolboy fantasy object); and in the problematic portrayal of women in positions of authority within education.

Psychoanalysis has played an important role in the development of feminist film theory. Mulvey's (1975) seminal work on the male perspective in film is one of the best-known examples. She argues that film prioritises the male perspective by shooting women in ways which emphasise that they are there to be observed. At the same time, viewers are drawn so closely into the film that they revert to the

Lacanian 'mirror phase', a stage of development characterised by a sense of wholeness and oneness with the world. Although there are further complexities, the essence of the argument is that film is constructed to ensure that the male perspective is dominant, and that, as a result, this is the perspective assumed by the audience. There have, however, been many challenges to this analysis from critics who argue, for example, that viewers are more sophisticated and creative in their responses than it implies. Mulvey was also writing over thirty years ago, and more recent developments in cinema and television production mean that it is possible to question the proposition that film is always constructed from a male perspective. There are now, for example, more women involved in the production of film, more central female characters and an increasing fetishisation of the male, as opposed to the female, body.

In looking at the representation of education in popular culture from a feminist perspective, we will be concerned with questions about points of view; the scope for reflexivity and openness; the range and nature of role models for women and girls; the construction of femininity and masculinity and the capacity of popular culture to offer a critique of a male-dominated educational system and a patriarchal society.

Hegemony and cultural studies

The ideas of Antonio Gramsci (1891–1937) have been influential in the fields of cultural studies and education. Gramsci formulated a rich conception of culture and a resolute opposition to crude forms of historical materialism. A committed activist who strongly adhered to the philosophical notion of *praxis*, his name is most commonly associated with the concept of hegemony. Much of his emphasis on the importance of education arises from this and the contingent problem of how to build a counter-hegemonic, and hopefully dominant, socialist culture.

This book draws on the notion of hegemony in two ways. The idea that popular culture might contribute to a set of hegemonic beliefs about education is implicit in the way we discuss texts and is one reason for believing they are worth analysing. Linked to this is the recognition that education is, in essence, a socialisation process which, by definition, sustains the current hegemony. Second, we are aware that the development of hegemony is always contested, and this is reflected in our desire to reveal some of the tensions and contradictions in the way in which popular culture represents education.

While some aspects of this discussion are grounded in a specifically British, and, in certain respects, English experience, the issues identified have international resonance in that they arise from global economic and cultural transformations. For Marxists, there is a strong link between the economic base of society and its 'superstructural' elements (i.e., politics, ideology, religion, culture, education and the legal system). Gramsci, however, developed a theory which recognised that a mature conceptualisation of societal change needs to account for the complexities of any historical moment and, inevitably, go beyond purely economic determinants.

Boggs (1976, p. 39) suggests that by 'hegemony' Gramsci 'meant the permeation throughout civil society . . . of an entire system of values, attitudes, beliefs, morality that is in one way or another supportive of the established order and the class interests that dominate it'. Hegemony refers to a world view, a set of assumptions, through which a social class is able to exert dominance, although, since this is always open to challenge, it has to be reproduced continually (Willis, 1977; Sarup, 1982). Here, then, is a theory of power relations that was enormously influential in shaping the intellectual landscape of the late twentieth century and which has been expressed as 'culture as praxis', a sense of reality 'as something flexible and fluid' (Bauman, 1992, p. 206). Gramsci (1971, p. 12) himself referred to:

> the 'spontaneous' consent given by the great masses of the population to the general direction imposed on social life by the dominant fundamental group; this consent is 'historically' caused by the prestige (and consequent confidence) which the dominant group enjoys because of its position and function in the world of production.

In this way, the ideas and values of the dominant group become accepted as 'common sense'. 'Hegemony' is a broad term, most properly used with regard to a 'whole society', while the related term 'settlement' has been employed specifically with regard to the inherently unstable balance of cultural/political forces within the sphere of education (Education Group, 1981; Avis, 1993a and 1993b). Educational philosophies, however, like the political philosophies to which they closely relate, are constantly in conflict and constantly in transition; and these conflicts and transitions can be identified, in part, by the ways in which education is represented in popular culture.

Ideology and education

Ideology is a much-discussed concept, and, although Louis Althusser's (1918–1990) significance is contested, his work is usually acknowledged as a point of transition between structural Marxism and the ascendance in social theory of non-Marxist modes (Elliott, 1994). As a result, his ideas are still current in discussions about education and are relevant to considerations of the nature, content and representation of education in popular culture. In particular, his discussion of ideology and education is important. This is perhaps best described in his essay 'Ideology and ideological state apparatuses (notes towards an investigation)' (Althusser, 1969).

Here, Althusser outlines Marx's conception of societies as consisting of an *infrastructure* (i.e., the 'economic base' of the forces of production) and a *super-structure*. In Althusser's schema, however, the superstructure has two levels or 'floors': the political-legal and the ideological (*ibid.*, p. 129), and he goes on to identify Repressive State Apparatuses (RSAs), comprising the government, army, police and penal system, and Ideological State Apparatuses (ISAs). The latter differ from RSAs in that they are generally identifiable as distinct institutions, and, unlike

RSAs, they can be private rather than public in nature. Furthermore, he suggests that, while RSAs function primarily by repression and, ultimately, violence, ISAs function 'massively and predominantly' (*ibid.*, p. 138) by ideology, and thereby manage to conceal and circumscribe any repression which might be present within them. Among the ISAs proposed by Althusser are the family, religion, communications and education. While he acknowledges that the religious ideological state apparatus has been historically predominant, he goes on to comment that:

> I believe that the ideological State apparatus which has been installed in the *dominant* position in mature capitalist social formations as a result of a violent political and ideological class struggle against the old dominant ideological state apparatus is the *educational ideological apparatus.*
>
> (*ibid.*, pp. 144–145)

Althusser credits schools and education with taking children as infants and inculcating them with the ruling ideology, then:

> Somewhere around the age of sixteen, a huge mass of children are ejected 'into production' . . . Another portion of scholastically adapted youth carries on . . . until it falls by the wayside and fills the posts of small and middle technicians, white collar workers, small and middle executives, petty bourgeois of all kinds. A last portion reaches the summit . . . the agents of exploitation (capitalist managers), the agents of repression . . . and the professional ideologists . . . Each mass ejected en route is practically provided with the ideology which suits the role it has to fulfil in class society: the role of the exploited (with a 'highly developed' 'professional', 'ethical', 'civic', 'national' and a-political consciousness); the role of the agent of exploitation (ability to give the workers orders and to speak to them: 'human relations').
>
> (*ibid.*, p. 147)

Altough Althusser's complex theoretical Marxism does not warrant further explanation here, his conception of education as a form of ideological state apparatus is directly relevant to some of the texts we will examine. Popular cultural representations of education can, to a greater or lesser degree, often be read as exposures of education as an ISA. Pink Floyd's 1979 hit '**Another Brick in the Wall Part 2**' offers a specific, if fairly crude, lyrical example of this, which, when combined with its accompanying video, makes a powerful statement about the repressive ideological power of education. The US television series *Buffy the Vampire Slayer* (*BtVS*) has also been analysed from a Marxist perspective and its critique of American capitalism noted by Wall and Zyrd (2002) and Pasley (2003). It could certainly be argued that Sunnydale High operates as a repressive ISA, in collusion with the more overt repression of the state, a collusion that is dramatically illustrated in 'Gingerbread' (the eleventh episode in the third series; from hereon, individual episodes will be referenced numerically, so 'Gingerbread' is 3.11), where police invade the school and raid the children's lockers. *BtVS*, however, is a complex and multilayered text, and, as such, is open to contradictory readings that might equally see it, for example, as supporting the status quo and celebrating consumerism.

Power and discourse

Michel Foucault (1926–1984), at least with respect to education, is associated primarily with notions of power and discourse, both of which have contemporary resonance in current debate. First, with respect to power, several texts in this book lend themselves to analyses of discipline and power relations, including, for example, such films as *Blackboard Jungle* (1955), *To Sir with Love* (1967), *Dangerous Minds* (1995) and *School of Rock* (2003). Traditionally, discipline in schools is founded on a level of compliance that is as much accepted by the students as it is enforced by the teachers. Foucault (1980, p. 39), who explored power both organisationally and as a process, describes power of this kind:

> In thinking of the mechanisms of power, I am thinking rather of its capillary form of existence, the point where power reaches into the very grain of individuals, touches their bodies and inserts itself into their action and attitudes, their discourses, their learning processes and everyday lives.

The idea that schools and educational processes are concerned with the construction of an obedient or governable subject can be explicated from the work of Foucault and, in particular, from *Discipline and punish: the birth of the prison* (first published 1975). In this study, Foucault (1991) charts how the eighteenth century saw a transition from public execution to penal retention as a societal control technique, and how, historically, a number of restraint methods and technologies developed as a result.

At the level of the human body, as opposed to the mind, a basic requirement for control was physical enclosure and the subsequent management of space and time. Educational establishments took on some characteristics of industrial environments whereby designs reinforced hierarchy, facilitated supervision and prescribed behaviour. Popular culture's focus on the conventional classroom and the traditional lecture theatre is indicative of the impact this has had on the collective imagination. Donald (1992) describes the English monitorial schools of the early nineteenth century as examples of the kind of architecture discussed by Foucault (1991, p. 172):

> an internal, articulated and detailed control – to render visible those who are inside it; in more general terms, an architecture that would operate to transform individuals: to act on those it shelters, to provide a hold on their conduct, to carry the effects of power right to them, to make it possible to know them, to alter them.

Foucault also refers to Jeremy Bentham's penitentiary design, the 'Panopticon', as an ideal model for control. This consisted of a central watch-tower from which a single person could observe a circle of tiered individual cells. The design meant that prisoners could be seen at all times but would be unaware when observation was taking place. In this way, control could become 'internalised' within the psyche of the individual. According to Sarup (1982, p. 20), panopticism is actually a kind of 'diagram' of how power functions:

> Panopticism appears to be merely the solution of a technical problem, but through it a new type of society emerges, a society not of spectacle but of surveillance. This is done through the disciplines, those tiny, everyday, physical mechanisms, those systems of micropower that are essentially non-egalitarian and asymmetrical. The disciplines characterise, classify, specialise; they distribute along a scale, around a norm, hierarchise individuals in relation to one another and, if necessary, disqualify and invalidate.

In education, the growth and increasingly diffuse nature of contemporary surveillance and accountability through inspection and quality assurance systems can be analysed in these terms (Ball, 1990).

In addition to managing the location or place of an individual, another important aspect of social control is the timetable. Time that can be planned, organised and circumscribed in increasing detail is likely to undermine subjects and diminish their individuality. According to Foucault (1991, p. 178), a process of control could be introduced by which:

> the workshop, the school, the army were subject to the whole micro-penalty of time (latenesses, absences, interruptions of tasks), of activity (inattention, negligence, lack of zeal), of behaviour (impoliteness, disobedience), of speech (idle chatter, insolence), of the body ('incorrect' attitudes, irregular features, lack of cleanliness), of sexuality (impurity, indecency).

Thus deviance from the 'norm' can be pathologised, and the systems through which people pass seen as a process of regulation and normalisation. A film such as *The Breakfast Club* (1985) shows how recalcitrant students are subject to discipline through a regime that exercises tight control over their time and physical location.

Normalisation and social acceptance require an exercise of observation and of judgement, the creation of norms and averages, of passes and fails, and the means by which this is most efficiently done in education is by examination and testing. Through this, an individual can be reduced to a grade, allocated a calculable value, and become, thereby, the object of a process of accountancy. Indeed, Hoskin (1990, p. 40), a researcher in the field of finance, dubbed Foucault a 'crypto-educationalist' because his concern with examination made him the 'grandmaster of pedagogic power'. Young people's anxiety, particularly in US popular culture, over grades and the grading process shows how closely this is linked to the construction and fulfilment of self. Students are obsessed not with learning but with grading because the latter determines what they can do and who they can be. They are even prepared, as in the films *187* (1997) and *Teaching Mrs Tingle* (1999), to resort to violence to achieve the grade they want or need.

Foucault's use of the term 'discourse' (a structured system of 'speech' and of 'signs') is also important for our analysis. Social phenomena and identities are constructed by discourses, and there are rules that govern discourse – who can say what, where and when. Different discourses have different rules: scientific discourse differs from political discourse, for example. At different times in history, there have been changes in what was accepted as meaningful discourse about specific topics, and Foucault uses the examples of madness and sexuality to illustrate this point.

Foucault does not, however, accept the concept of ideology. Instead, he argues that discourses carry their own power and do not need to be allied to modes of production (Sarup, 1993, p. 78). Hoskin (1994, p. 67) refers to discourse as a term which 'concerns what at a given era is said, written, thought out of all the things that could be said, written and thought: i.e. the historically specific *field* of what is said'. But discourse, as Foucault defines it, is not merely descriptive; it is productive. Thus power is not so much located with ruling elites as played out through discourses. Language, rather than material power, is emphasised. There are struggles and alliances between discourses, and, inevitably, discourses themselves change as a result. Thus, we would argue, it is important to delineate some of the discourses that produce and are defined by education, and, since some of these are located in popular culture, the latter inevitably affects what can and cannot be said about education.

Performativity

> [U]niversities and the institutions of higher learning are called upon to create skills, and no longer ideals . . . the transmission of knowledge is no longer designed to train an elite capable of guiding a nation towards its emancipation, but to supply the system with players capable of acceptably fulfilling their roles at the pragmatic posts required by the institutions.
>
> (Lyotard, 1984, p. 48)

Our analysis of post-sixteen education, in particular, shows how an economic vocationalism strives for status and dominance. For Jean-François Lyotard (1924–1998), concepts such as truth and falsehood in relation to questions of knowledge have been replaced by issues of efficiency and inefficiency; the term that he uses to describe this new focus is 'performativity'. In such circumstances, knowledge becomes a commodity which can be translated into quantities of information (Usher and Edwards, 1994, p. 166). It is a saleable product, the function of which is to augment power. Knowledge that does not fit into the game of performativity is effectively disqualified. A key factor in this has been the advent and extraordinary development of computer technology (Lyotard, 1984, p. 4). This phenomenon has had, and continues to have, significant implications for how

knowledge is researched and the ways in which it is learned. In particular, knowledge can be accessed and circulated through means that circumvent higher
education institutions. In response to this, universities have entered the 'information market place', selling educational products to individuals who want to
promote themselves within the economy (Cowen, 1996). This places the skilled
performance of economic activities – 'competence' – as a key notion within the
framing of educational processes and, specifically, in the design of curricula, not
only in universities but especially in the further education (FE) sector, which has
always been influenced by economic imperatives. Lyotard (1984, p. 4) referred to
a trend towards 'a thorough exteriorization of knowledge with respect to the
"knower" at whatever point he or she may occupy in the knowledge process'. It
may well be, in England, that the particular point at which this estrangement is
most intense is at the level of vocational education within the FE sector.

A curriculum based on competencies which emphasises skills, including
transferable ones, and focuses on 'student-centred learning' usefully illustrates
Lyotard's description of performativity in a postmodern context. As a result,
education is effectively shifted from its position as an aspect of social and moral
welfare to be situated instead as a means of economic productivity in a predominantly market-orientated enterprise culture. Lyotard (1984, p. xxiv) defines
postmodernism as 'incredulity towards metanarratives', and, in making a pre-
supposition that the age in which we live is subject to this sense of dissolution,
he points to a crisis in the status of knowledge and to the end of such 'universalist'
or totalising systems of thought as liberalism and Marxism. Following this approach,
we have not attempted in the conclusion to this book to argue that there is an
overarching metanarrative, an epic educational tale, to be found in popular culture.
Rather, we are concerned with the multiplicity of perspectives that emerges through
engagement and study.

In his work, Lyotard employs the concept of 'language games', in which different
types of 'utterances' are employed within narrative discourses, including science
and social science. He argues that 'Society as a totality is displaced by "flexible
networks of language games"' (Usher and Edwards, 1994, p. 157). The relationship between scientific and narrative knowledge is a particular concern of
Lyotard, and Sarup's (1993, pp. 136–137) account of his position explains:

> narrative knowledge certifies itself without having recourse to argumentation
> and proof. Scientists, however, question the validity of narrative statements and
> conclude that they are never subject to argumentation or proof. Narratives
> are classified by the scientist as belonging to a different mentality: savage,
> primitive, underdeveloped . . . Here there is an interesting twist in Lyotard's
> argument. He says that scientific knowledge cannot know and make known
> that it is true knowledge without resorting to the other, narrative kind of
> knowledge . . . In short, there is a recurrence of the narrative in the scientific.

Notwithstanding this presence of the narrative within science, the latter has itself
been the privileged discourse of the modern era and, as a consequence, has

dominated education and the associated processes of pedagogy and research methodologies. Narrative, on the other hand, is privileged in popular culture. It has a shaping power of its own, and in this book we have exploited the opportunity to explore how the narrative power of popular fiction focuses on teachers as heroes and villains, on education as a 'quest' and on the struggle towards enlightenment.

Hyper-reality

The term 'hyper-reality' was coined by Jean Baudrillard (1929–2007) to describe his perception of the contemporary blurring of boundaries between the material and the representational. Baudrillard argues that society in the late twentieth century increasingly lost its ability to distinguish between what was real and what was fiction. For example, how is our understanding of the world now constructed by material reality? To what extent is it created through representations – through stories, film, television, news images? Two of Baudrillard's examples are particularly well known. He talks about the way in which the America of Disneyland's American Pavilion is 'real' to us – and discusses whether we care about this. He also cites the first Gulf War, noting how the reality of that experience for those who were there was very different from the second level of reality for everyone who experienced it through the media. In fact, since all experiences are reconstructed through mass culture – education, relationships, politics, history, social issues – how can we distinguish what is real? Is reality a meaningful concept any more? How does technology impact on all of this, since it is no longer even possible to discern whether the images we see are made by filming people in specific situations and locations or if they are computer generated? The *Matrix* trilogy (1999, 2003 and 2003), in which reality as we know it is itself a computer program, has received a great deal of attention from Baudrillard enthusiasts for obvious reasons.

Popular culture can be self-referential and reproductive. For example, films from the eighties, such as *The Breakfast Club* and *Heathers*, depict school as a society divided into well-defined groups and cliques: nerds, princesses, jocks, computer geeks and so on. This is also reflected in later films, culminating in the *Mean Girls* map, which shows the physical location of each group in the school canteen and aligns geographical and social boundaries in a way that reifies the process of categorisation. The material reality of this, however, is less significant than the perceptual power of the parameters it identifies and the extent to which the social organisation and educational environment of schools has been affected by this categorisation process.

Education: values, purpose and professionalism

Many of the themes that recur in popular texts featuring education can best be understood within a social and historical context because they reflect and contribute to long-running concerns and debates. The nature and purpose of education for the masses and the relationship between education and social class are obvious examples. Similarly, an understanding of women's struggle for schooling can help readers to appreciate the gendered nature of contemporary images of education. Popular culture offers a range of perspectives on education for girls and boys, on a curriculum for the 'lower classes' and on the relationship between class and culture. This section includes a brief overview of some key historical developments which might inform our readings of these texts.

In 1993, the National Commission on Education (NCE) announced: 'In the United Kingdom, much higher achievement in education and training is needed to match world standards' (NCE, 1993, p. 43). Education in the UK was simply not performing well enough. This concern was subsequently reflected in New Labour's mantra of 'Education, Education, Education', which launched the party's agenda for raising standards and widening participation. A key factor in the debate over levels of achievement is the extent and purpose of education, yet this remains disputed territory, as it has been for over a century. Donald (1992), in a review of nineteenth-century approaches, presents an array of contradictory opinion, including the following from Davies Giddy, president of the Royal Society, who in 1807 felt that education for the working classes would inevitably be

> prejudicial to their morals and happiness, it would teach them to despise their lot in life, instead of making them good servants . . . instead of teaching them subordination, it would render them factious and refractory . . . it would enable them to read seditious pamphlets, vicious books, and publications against Christianity; it would render them insolent to their superiors; . . . if the bill [to establish parish schools] were to pass into Law, it would go to burden the country with a most enormous and incalculable expense, and to load the industrious orders with still heavier imposts.
>
> (Quoted in Donald, 1992, p. 20)

However, Leonard Horner, a factory inspector, pointed out in 1877:

> To put the necessity of properly educating the children of the working classes on its lowest footing, it is loudly called for as a matter of police, to prevent a multitude of immoral and vicious beings, the offspring of ignorance, from growing up around us, to be a pest and a nuisance to society; it is necessary in order to render the great body of the working class governable by reason.
>
> (Quoted in *ibid.*, pp. 22–23)

An inference that education might be wasted on certain groups of young people and an emphasis on individuals who 'better' themselves by using education to escape their working-class origins are readily apparent in popular culture. Socially, such divisive attitudes towards education are exemplified in the state/private schooling split, which, despite recent initiatives to 'widen participation', still tends to characterise education in the UK as essentially hierarchical and socially exclusive in terms of class, gender, age, ethnicity and academic achievement. For example, it is still generally the case that vocational education is more commonly experienced by the working classes, while academic, liberal education is much more the preserve of a social elite. (There are, however, complexities here, and hierarchies within hierarchies, since some extremely disadvantaged groups will find it easier to access a humanities degree at a non-prestigious higher education institution than to gain high-level vocational qualifications at a more well-regarded establishment.)

The historical background to English attitudes towards vocational subjects has been outlined by Weiner (1981), who suggests that the strongest antipathies have traditionally been found within the old English universities, with a less pronounced though similar situation in Ireland, Scotland and Wales. America, on the other hand, lacking the legacy of medievalism, has seemed more willing to embrace technocratic knowledge. The instrumental and applied nature of the vocational curriculum, however, remains sharply at odds with liberal traditions of higher education as envisaged by John Stuart Mill, Cardinal Newman or, more recently, Michael Oakeshott (Williams, 1989). Instead of providing students with the 'gift of an interval' in an exalted 'place apart', where ideas may be pursued regardless of extrinsic utility, vocational courses direct them to acquire skills to serve the needs of industry and commerce.

The education of women and girls has been a site of struggle for generations. Although concerns were expressed about the waste of women's ability as long ago as 1405 by Christine de Pizan (2005) in *The book of the city of the ladies*, even in the eighteenth century few girls received much education. Rousseau, whose educational philosophy is still credited in the development of child-centred education, excluded girls from the careful nurturing that would be offered to his imaginary pupil Emile. Instead, he suggested:

> A woman's education must therefore be planned in relation to man. To be pleasing in his sight, to win his respect and love, to train him in childhood, to tend him in manhood, to counsel and console, to make his life pleasant and happy, these are the duties of woman for all time and this is what she should be taught while she is young.
>
> (Rousseau, 1993, p. 393)

Although the nineteenth-century English writer John Ruskin, who argued that women should have access to a 'broad and noble' curriculum, could perhaps be regarded as liberal with respect to female education, in 1893 even he saw it wholly in terms of a wifely role:

> A man ought to know any language or science he learns thoroughly – while a woman ought to know the same language, or science, only so far as may enable her to sympathise in her husband's pleasures and in those of his best friends.
>
> (Ruskin, 2002, p. 118)

The majority of women, therefore, had almost no opportunity during the eighteenth and nineteenth centuries to learn anything that would have enabled them to be financially independent. Mary Wollstonecraft's 1787 pamphlet *Thoughts on the education of daughters* (1994) summarised concerns that women would be unable to develop fully as human beings or to learn anything useful if their struggle for education continued to be resisted. However, in the UK, it was not until the 1870 Education Act established free elementary schooling for all that girls were educated as a matter of right, and, even then, the education of boys continued to take priority in a system where secondary schools were fee paying.

The subsequent 1944 Education Act gave all boys and girls the right to a secondary education, but the nature of that education essentially differed, by enshrining women's domestic responsibilities in the post-war curriculum. As a result, throughout the fifties and sixties, many women were still expected to choose between education/career and marriage/family, whereas men could expect to have both. Katherine Watson in *Mona Lisa Smile* (2003) struggles to see a way round this when she pleads to her student: 'You can bake your cake and eat it too . . . You can study and get dinner on the table by five.' It was not until 1975 that it became illegal in the UK to discriminate on the grounds of sex, although even now more subtle forms of discrimination continue to be documented.

The image of teachers, their status in society and their ability, in particular, to control pupils and students have for some time formed part of social and political discourse in the United Kingdom. In the months preceding the British general election of May 1997, there was something approaching moral panic in relation to the issue of school discipline. A perceived undercurrent of violence and disruption within the school system had been dramatically and tragically thrown into stark relief by the murder outside his London school of the headteacher Philip Lawrence (the same school that Marie Stubbs was credited as reforming in the auto-biographical account and television production *Ahead of the Class*). More recently, school indiscipline and students' unruly behaviour have received further publicity as a result of the Channel 5 programme *Chaos in the Classroom* (2005), in which an ex-teacher and film producer went back into school as a supply teacher and secretly filmed her problems with classroom management and disruptive and aggressive pupils.

Education is a key site through which a modern state exercises power, acting, among other things, as a mechanism of socialisation and control for its young people. Yet, a significant proportion of students are visibly alienated from school and society, as evidenced by truancy, school exclusion units and antagonistic youth subcultures. There has also been a failure to sustain school improvement in the UK, as measured by government targets, examination performance and literacy levels. However, although alienation and failure are factors in the educational experience of some young people, it is nevertheless the case that, in general, students do not become rebels, but rather that the vast majority, at least on the surface, accept the process of schooling to which they are subjected. Popular culture, however, can be provocative. It seeks to sell, and therefore often exhibits a more confrontational, polemic slant on education.

For teachers and intending teachers, an understanding and examination of one's own beliefs and values about education, its significance and purpose are central to establishing an identity as a professional. Furthermore, conventional attitudes and assumptions can usefully be interrogated in relation to the historical and social context that has shaped the differing perspectives which underlie and have produced the current system. Yet, professionalism is not just an individual concept: it is not only a set of personal beliefs but an issue of public expectation and accountability. As a result, recent attempts to define professionalism for teachers in the UK have taken a more formal and directive approach. As a consequence, we anticipate this book will be a useful stimulus for teachers and trainee teachers reflecting upon the concept of professionalism. Hopefully, it will raise awareness, through an examination of popular representations, of the competing values that underpin social expectations of teachers. These will not, however, necessarily be the same as those that the government and its agencies wish the profession to adopt. The General Teaching Council for England (GTC) for schoolteachers, the Institute for Learning (IfL) for teachers in post-compulsory education, and the Higher Education Academy (HEA) for those teaching in higher education all publish codes of ethics and standards that anticipate the values of their respective professional groups. It may be useful to refer to the GTC *Statement of professional values and practice for teachers* (which can be found on the GTC website), since there is a sense in which its aspirational statements provide a template against which to examine and analyse some of the representations of teachers that are discussed in subsequent chapters. Another document, *Professional standards for qualified teacher status and requirements for initial teacher training* (TDA, 2007), sets out the standards which those training to teach in the UK must meet. Initial teacher training programmes and the discourse of both government departments and teachers' own organisations place great emphasis on the concept of 'professionalism', on the skills, attributes, qualities, thinking and philosophy which underpin the role. Perhaps this is not surprising, since the professionalism of teachers is under constant scrutiny and has been consistently questioned by policy-makers, inspection agencies, the news media and, finally, by the way in which, as we shall show in this book, it is represented by popular culture.

2 The good teacher

Class heroes and school saints

This chapter explores how teachers have been constructed as good and heroic in the classrooms of popular culture. It focuses on film and the equivocal way with which we deal with the notion of 'goodness' in Western society. It questions how we accommodate goodness and heroism when, as concepts, they do not seem to fit comfortably into a contemporary society where individual achievement and private enterprise dominate definitions of success. For many of us, goodness and heroism, especially when involving personal sacrifice, are difficult to comprehend, except perhaps in the exigencies of war, and, therefore, we are wary of them. Yet, the manifestation of goodness as heroism or saintliness is deeply embedded within Western mythology, legend, fairy tale and narrative. Notions of both heroism and saintliness permeate cultural and moral awareness, especially during childhood, when socialisation is crucial to development.

So how do we define a hero or a saint? What is it that distinguishes him or her? In the case of the hero, and some legendary saints like St George, physical prowess traditionally plays a part. It may be difficult to locate teachers in this mould (apart from Arnold Schwarzenegger as John Kimble in *Kindergarten Cop*, 1990), but heroes are also crusaders, leaders, individuals prepared to fight for the defence and salvation of others. It is this articulation of the hero, the notion of sacrifice for the greater good, that links the concepts of heroism and saintliness. Archetypal heroes, including those of Greek legend and medieval literature, have attributes of courage and strength tempered by nobility and integrity. Heroism is defined primarily as a moral concept, and the hero celebrated as:

> An individual of elevated moral stature and superior ability who pursues his goals indefatigably in the face of powerful antagonist(s). Because of his unbreached devotion to the good, no matter the opposition, a hero attains spiritual grandeur even if he fails to achieve practical victory.
>
> (Bernstein, 2002, p. 1)

'Elevated moral stature' was an essential aspect of the professional profile of a teacher. Joseph's (2001) review of early twentieth-century images of teachers describes how Avent (1931) claimed: 'The excellent teacher is forgetful of self. He thinks of others' comfort first. He is willing to labour on, spend, and be spent, even to be forgotten for the sake of others' (Joseph, 2001, p. 136). Teaching is seen as a vocation where one labours for a better world, selflessly serving humanity, and, according to Averill (1939), offers 'a way of life comparable with the way of the preacher or prophet' (Joseph, 2001, p. 137). Integrity, dedication, commitment, altruism and sacrifice are all words that litter the semantic field of the ideal teacher. Yet, in most *real* classrooms, teachers' strength is primarily psychological and emotional, creating 'A new form of pedagogical text – not simply reflecting culture but actually constructing it' (Giroux, 2002, p. 8). Good teachers are significant to that text, but require an environment in which to thrive. Heroes, like saints, are invariably products of crisis or conflict. They emerge when individuals find the strength to stand up for right and against wrong. They surface when self-interest is suppressed in deference to devotion and philanthropy or in defiance of oppression and subjugation. Heroes and saints are people who recognise injustice, identify need, and, careless of themselves, respond courageously and magnanimously. So, it is in this space that we can locate the figure of a teacher, assuming a heroic mantle in the face of adversity.

Andrew Bernstein (2002, p. 1), in his discussion of heroism, focuses on the dedication of heroes 'to the creation and/or defence of reality-conforming, life-promoting values'. Teachers have the potential to be heroes or saints because they deal in aspiration and ideals. In contemporary Western society, people can afford to have hopes for their children, and children to have hopes for their future. Education, as a conduit for achievement and success, situates hope, at least for a time, in the hands of teachers. Heroes and saints may not explicitly be part of our everyday lives, except in emergencies and crises, but hope is; and so are teachers. However, while this might reinforce the value and significance of teaching, it is also its blight because, where there is hope, inevitably, there is disillusion. In 1998 there was a UK recruitment campaign with the tag-line: 'Everyone remembers a good teacher'. Most people do, but they also remember bad teachers, those who were oppressive or had made derogatory or critical remarks. In a similar vein, Friends Reunited, the website which puts former school and college friends in contact, is inundated with both complimentary and critical (even libellous) comments about teachers on its bulletin boards. So, as a teacher, the chances are, if you are not anonymous or forgotten, you will have been constructed as either a hero or a villain by your former pupils and students.

As the previous chapter outlined, attitudes towards teachers are deeply embedded in socio-cultural context. Teaching is a very public profession of which almost everyone has had experience, and it seeks to develop individuals while also assimilating them into a hegemonic society. This is essentially a difficult and heroic struggle where teachers' personal beliefs and professional values may conflict. Schools and colleges by their nature and function are profoundly dialectical institutions. They represent a physical but also a psychological arena in which teachers, outnumbered on contested ground, seek to colonise students' intellectual, social and emotional space. The oppositional nature of schools and colleges is multifaceted. It is not just teachers and students in confrontation with each other:

there are teachers and senior managers; teachers and school boards/governing bodies; teachers and parents; teachers and government agencies and employers. Everyone has an opinion about education, creating a binary world where goodies and baddies, heroes and villains, saints and devils are defined and flourish. Popular culture, ever alert to dramatic tension, is attracted to this potential for confrontation and conflict.

Henry Giroux (2002, pp. 187–188) argues the case for a study of popular culture in relation to schooling through 'a pedagogy of representations' which examines the interdependency of education and culture:

> Struggles over popular culture, for instance, represent a different but no less important site of politics. For it is precisely on the terrain of culture that identities are produced, values learned, histories legitimated, and knowledge appropriated. Culture is the medium through which children fashion their individual and collective identities and learn in part how to narrate themselves in relation to others.

Giroux highlights a rich and diverse popular culture at the core of being and fundamental to identity. In 1997, the New Labour government identified as its priorities 'education, education, education' on the basis that young people were the nation's future. So, as we deconstruct the classrooms of popular culture to illuminate the pedagogy of representations, who are the teacher heroes, the classroom saints whom we might want to scrutinise and categorise? How are their achievements portrayed? How does an audience construct its narrative? What difference does having been pupils and students make? With whom do we identify? Where are the lines drawn between fiction and reality? What values and beliefs underpin notions of success?

Historically, schooling has offered a rich source of dramatic conflict. Prior to the 1950s, this was primarily manifest as a class struggle, with education providing intellectual liberation but also social discord. In Roy Boulting's 1948 film *The Guinea Pig*, Jack Read, played by Richard Attenborough, earns a scholarship to a prestigious private school despite his 'trade' background. His parents work hard to support him, but his working-class dialect and attributes are continually criticised, leaving him disillusioned and undermined. Ultimately, however, he adapts, acquiring appropriate manners, academic success and the ambition to be a teacher himself. This conclusion is in sharp contrast to that of the contemporary BBC1 programme *Class Apart* (2007, directed by Nick Hurran). When estate boy Kyle Jerome attends the exclusive Park Manor School as opposed to his local and failing comprehensive, the inference is that its begowned teachers have more to learn from Kyle and his working-class mother than the school can teach him. For Jack in *The Guinea Pig*, social mobility was desirable to enable him to mix with a 'better' set of people. Kyle interprets 'better' rather differently and eventually drops out of Park Manor to attend the local school. Meanwhile, Park Manor's headteacher resigns and, with new resolve, departs by walking disrespectfully across the school's hallowed lawns.

In the 1950s, teenagers, the demographic group most commonly sitting in the popular cultural classroom, emerged as a social and economic entity and as a deviant subculture:

> The 50s marked what can be called a Golden Age of juvenile delinquency, in terms of significant increases in its frequency, emergence of new types, and the concern and attention paid to it by the public and various media.
>
> (Miller, 2001, p. 63)

In school or college, students have the advantage of power in number, but in situations of conflict, against authority, resistance might be costly for an individual, if s/he is isolated and not supported by the majority. In dramatic terms, tension can emerge when individuals or groups of individuals are in opposition to the collective culture of the school. This is emphasised by the conceptualisation of 'teenagers' as a distinct sociological group with separate cliques and gangs, and by acknowledgement of a generation gap. Young people no longer aspired to maturity or adult mannerisms as in *The Guinea Pig*, where the boys had condoned their socialisation and indoctrination. Instead, in the 1950s, teenagers strived for difference. Revolution and rebellion were more exciting and sexier than conformity, and conflict with such authority figures as parents, police or teachers was relished. Inevitably, however, resistance means personal conflict with staff who represent physical manifestations of control in the classroom and a dialogic interface with the socio-political process of education. Yet, traditionally, as noted earlier, the power relationship between teachers and students is founded on a level of compliance accepted as much by the ruled as by those who rule. Foucault (1980, p. 39), exploring power both organisationally and developmentally, describes how it affects individuals:

> In thinking of the mechanisms of power, I am thinking rather of its capillary form of existence, the point where power reaches into the very grain of individuals, touches their bodies and inserts itself into their action and attitudes, their discourses, their learning processes and everyday lives.

In his earlier work *Discipline and punish* (first published 1975), Foucault (1991) had examined the institutionalisation of power whereby discipline was enforced by observation and surveillance, as in the panopticon, in order to regulate behaviour through minimal intervention and the acquiescence of those under scrutiny. Power is not simply hegemonic or hierarchical but rather transient and circulatory. For example, it is not defined so much by a teacher's role as by his/her professional engagement and interaction with students. Consequently, what might be construed as teachers' power becomes notional and fluid to such an extent that it can shift and even be transferred if circumstances permit. In the 2003 film *School of Rock*, Dewey Finn tries, when impersonating a teacher, to subvert classroom authority by asking what students really think of him. The children in *School of Rock* are not rebellious, but, when they persist in making derogatory remarks, Finn reverts to a hierarchical mode as teacher and adult, implying there will be disciplinary action if the critical comments continue. Thus, despite being an impostor and a putative anarchist, Finn's authority within the classroom remains intact through institutional control. As Foucault recognised, power is in the detail:

> Take, for example, an educational institution: the disposal of its space, the meticulous regulations which govern its internal life, the different activities which are organised there, the diverse persons who live there or meet one another there, each with his own function, his well-defined character – all these things constitute a block of capacity–communication–power.
>
> (Foucault, 1983, p. 218)

It is malleable and unstable, but not necessarily held by a dominant group or individual; indeed, where power exists or is assumed, resistance inevitably occurs. Students are primed for the sort of confrontation which provides teachers with a heroic struggle.

But, if this is the reality of education, how well does it equate with the classrooms represented in popular culture? Mary Dalton (1995, p. 24), in her account of the Hollywood curriculum, focuses, like this chapter, on teachers in film, and highlights how they are constructed as heroic figures: 'Good teachers are projected on the screen as bright lights in schools of darkness.' First, the good teacher, like most heroes, is an outsider, charismatic and inspirational, passionate about her/his subject. Heroic teachers challenge the system, daring to teach innovatively what is important (the inference being that a regular curriculum and pedagogy do not do this). Weber and Mitchell (1995, p. 80) highlight this, illustrating the point with reference to Ms Shepard in *Sweet Valley High*:

> We see a so-called subversion of conventional teaching practice that appears in many popular culture texts. Not only does Ms Shepard propose to dispense with the prescribed pedagogy, she introduces a counter curriculum that wins the admiration of her students.

Dalton (1995, p. 41) asserts that this combination of alternative curriculum and pedagogy comprises not just Hollywood's predominant model for a 'good' teacher, but its only model:

> Many Hollywood teachers jeopardise their jobs by tossing aside, if not openly flouting, school policies. Most try to transform their school's stated curriculum into a curriculum that better meets the needs of their students. Many take risks of one sort or another to try to connect to students on a personal level.

Yet, although creativity and interpretation are concepts within professional discourse, most good teachers know that students' success depends on focusing on what will be examined. Normal classrooms, therefore, give little opportunity for unconventional content although this is ubiquitous in popular culture. Mark

Thackery, for example, in *To Sir with Love*, is one of many teachers to dispense with the standard curriculum in favour of an alternative one. Instead of teaching mathematics, he explores life, love, sex, death, rebellion and so on, believing that lessons should be about life skills (maths, presumably, not being one of these). The implications of this will be dealt with more fully later.

However, it is not just what you teach but how you teach that makes a classroom special. Daring to be different pedagogically and creating a radical educational environment will impress students and audiences. These heroic classroom practitioners inspire through their teaching. They do battle for hearts and minds; and, like John Keating in *Dead Poets Society*, their teaching is passionate and exciting. Being in one of their sessions is like being in no other. It is not even confined by the classroom, and, for receptive students, it is an intoxicating experience. Keating, like Dewey Finn in *School of Rock*, at times purports to give power to the students; later in this chapter, we will explore his pedagogy in more detail.

So the good teacher is a charismatic and heroic figure, but, just as significantly, s/he is often constructed in popular culture as being empathetic and deeply compassionate, infinitely caring and giving. Teachers like Mark Thackery will go the 'extra mile', never counting personal cost, to encourage learning and help students. The dedication they reveal is not just heroic but saintly. This is a teacher-centred view of education, however. The emphasis is on the teacher's power as saviour, not on the students' autonomy or capacity for self-directed learning. In *To Sir with Love*, this is acknowledged in the lyrics of the title song, which celebrates the friendship, support and moral example provided by 'Sir'.

The philanthropic teacher dedicates his/her energies wholeheartedly to deserving but often difficult and demanding students. *Mr Holland's Opus*, *Dangerous Minds*, *Mona Lisa Smile* and *Freedom Writers* all merge the lines between professional and personal, school and home. The teachers' mission is not about curriculum, progress and assessment; it is about redemption, empowerment, giving hope to those who have none. This is an agenda located in discourses about trust, restoration and hope. It is a concept built on empathy and acceptance. Carl Rogers (1967, p. 311) explains:

> When the teacher has the ability to understand the student's reactions from the inside, has a sensitive awareness of the way the process of educa-tion and learning seems to the student, then the likelihood of significant learning is increased . . . When they [students] are simply understood – not evaluated, not judged, simply understood from their own point of view, not the teacher's.

This is the teacher identified in the early textbooks on teacher education, for example by Almack and Lang (1925), who stated: 'Altruism is the prevailing spirit' (Joseph, 2001, p. 136). It is a model of a teacher which is paternalistic, however, and, as Paulo Freire (1972, p. 36) points out, could be an excuse for imposition and coercion:

The pedagogy of the oppressed, animated by authentic, humanist (not humanitarian) generosity, presents itself as a pedagogy of humankind. Pedagogy which begins the egotistical interests of the oppressors (an egotism cloaked in the false generosity of paternalism) and makes of the oppressed the objects of its humanitarianism, itself maintains and embodies oppression.

Yet, Ayers (2001, p. 201) notes that, in an increasingly threatening society, it is comforting to think of teachers as saviours, protecting vulnerable children: 'Schools and teachers are in the business of saving children – saving them from the purveyors of drugs and violence who are taking over our cities, saving them from themselves, their own pursuits and purposes.' However, not all young people can be saved, and therefore teachers must be selective, focusing on the deserving few. Stories of dedicated teachers based on real-life accounts – such as *Lean on Me* (1989, directed by John Avildsen) about Joe Clark; and *Stand and Deliver* (1988, directed by Ramon Menendez) about Jaime Escalante – highlight this: 'The occasional teacher is a saint – he is anointed. His job is straightforward – he must separate the salvageable students from those beyond redemption and he must win them over to a better life' (*ibid.*). What 'salvageable' means, of course, is questionable.

Hear the music

The subjects taught in the popular cultural classroom vary, but two emerge as the most popular: English, especially literature; and music. The latter, like the former, is a cultural product which already has kudos, with classical music in particular having moral stature and cultural status. In the popular cultural classroom, music generates a multifaceted response: first, students listen while music teachers make music; second, the students themselves are usually aspiring musicians; and, third, there is an audience watching and hearing the film. Music, of course, is a fundamental aspect of cinematic discourse, evoking and communicating a movie's mood and message. Films about school or college where music is the curricular context simply make it a more explicit and instrumental element of the narrative. However, teaching is not just about talent but about discovery and development through dedication, determination and practice. Music teachers inspire by what they do and how they do it, as well as by what they say and how they teach. Students with the right encouragement will not only learn but eventually shine.

Madame Soustaka (1988, directed by John Schlesinger) features a piano teacher, played by Shirley MacLaine, who recognises the potential of her young student and then dedicates herself to him. Teaching him all she knows, however, she becomes expendable and is devastated when he leaves. Power is ultimately with the student, the possessor of the talent. The supposition is that those who can, do; while those who can't, teach. (The idea that nurturing talent is less worthy than expressing talent is a theme to which we will return.)

Music of the Heart (1999, directed by Wes Craven) is based on the life of Roberta Guaspari, a violin teacher from East Harlem. Played by Meryl Streep, she teaches out of necessity, and the absence of a career as a musician seems initially more significant than her actual employment as a teacher. However, being dedicated, Roberta inspires and over time realises, as she opens students' hearts to music, that she has also opened her own mind to the value and significance of teaching. Her role is especially heroic because, with cutbacks, she becomes a champion of the music curriculum, defending children's entitlement to music as part of their education.

Mr Holland's Opus

In *Mr Holland's Opus* (1995, directed by Stephen Herek), Glenn Holland, played by Richard Dreyfuss, also never planned to teach, merely obtaining a teaching qualification as something to 'fall back on'. Even the name of the film's school, John F. Kennedy High, enshrines lost hope. As a teacher, however, Mr Holland's first mistake is to assume that teaching is a day job which will give him free time for composing. His colleagues quickly dispel this illusion, pointing out no time is 'free'. So, initially, Mr Holland's heroic struggle is with himself, his dislike of teaching and his inability to communicate with children.

Pedagogically and ideologically, there is a gulf between Mr Holland and his students, and it is only when he rejects the conventional curriculum that communication and education can begin. In effect, he develops 'a border pedagogy' (Aronowitz and Giroux, 1991) that moves away from the notion of text in isolation to textuality and a wider framework for reading (or listening), interpretation and criticism. Mr Holland, like Dewey Finn in *School of Rock*, introduces rock 'n' roll into his classroom, despite being warned of its putative anarchic and disruptive qualities (explored in later chapters). What results is an epiphany for both the students and Mr Holland, and a classroom where there is enjoyment and engagement as well as education. The teacher finds inspiration, and, in the final scenes, his achievement is celebrated by a former student who highlights that Mr Holland's symphony is all around him, embodied in his students and former students. They are his life's opus. This sentimental finale is set, like that of *Music of the Heart*, against budget constraints and a real threat to music education.

School of Rock

The next film in the music portfolio is *School of Rock* (2003, directed by Richard Linklater). Dewey Finn, played by Jack Black, is in a band, and he lives and breathes rock music until his self-indulgent antics lead to his sacking. Dewey is unwilling to grow up, sponging off another ex-band member who has become a teacher. Desperate for money, Dewey poses as his friend, becoming a substitute teacher at a prestigious preparatory school where there are strict codes of conduct and teaching is carefully regulated and monitored. As Summer Hathaway points out, since her parents are paying $15,000 a year, she expects to learn from her teacher. Dewey tries, initially, to give the children perpetual recess, discharging the power and control normally associated with authority. Much to his chagrin, his students, used to teachers telling them what to do, resist until Dewey finds his way as a teacher by identifying a curriculum which he can teach: rock music. However, although his language is not conventional, his pedagogy essentially is: blackboard, question and answer, cognitive mapping, knowledge trees and so on. Also, when he takes the time to listen, Dewey is so impressed by the talent and dedication of his pupils that he signs them up for the lucrative Battle of the Bands competition. So, despite himself, Dewey develops a teacherly aspect. He learns the children's names and involves everyone in the music enterprise, encouraging progression and praising their achievements.

At the beginning of *School of Rock*, Dewey is motivated purely by financial gain, first to become a teacher and then to win the Battle of the Bands. During the film, however, he changes, just as the children, who are used to a more transmissive, less participative pedagogy, change. Power circulates around the group, shifting from one to the other, as the pupils, who are initially reserved, learn how to enjoy music and interact dynamically and creatively. Dewey brings his classroom to life by ignoring the traditional discourse of good teaching and instead employing a more personal, flexible and radical approach. He manifests increasing satisfaction and commitment to the job, delighting in positive student evaluations of his lessons. He has grown into the role of teacher to such an extent that at the Battle of the Bands when Freddy Jones, the drummer, joins another group in their van, Dewey quickly intervenes and indignantly castigates the adults for being irresponsible while, at the same time, berating Freddy and threatening to tell his parents. Dewey is so moved by his experience as a teacher that, even when he is revealed as an impostor, he wants to celebrate the children's achievements, telling their parents they are 'awesome' kids whom he is proud to know.

Like many teachers in popular culture – for example, John Kimble in *Kindergarten Cop* (1990) – Dewey does not require professional training because his innate ability sustains him. Weber and Mitchell (1995, p. 82) highlight this received notion that good teachers are born not made by describing an incident from the *My Little Pony Tales* cartoon in which a student, Starlight, takes over the class:

> Starlight has no formal teacher preparation; indeed she is a student herself. In the end her natural teaching evokes superhero powers since she is able to rescue her charges from being trapped in a cave. Thus not only is school deinstitutionalised (with most of the main action taking place on a school trip), but the work of teachers is also heroised, since schools are so boring, dreadful, so irrelevant and the learning so meaningless that only some superhero heroic deed can save the day.

Dewey's students have learned how to take initiative and assume responsibility. So, despite parental opposition and the principal's dissent, they galvanise a disheartened Dewey and make it through to the final of the Battle of the Bands for his and their final performance. The students, it seems, will continue rocking even after he has gone.

The message of *School of Rock* is quite ambiguous: on the one hand, rock music is presented as radical and anarchic, an articulation of young people's anger and alienation. On the other, it is perceived as a way of developing transferable skills, and as an after-school activity paid for by wealthy parents. However, a third reading might suggest that the idea of rich and privileged kids being politicised by the sound and lyrics of rock music represents in itself an intrinsically subversive message. In the end, however, maybe it is the exuberant Dewey who learns the most when he recognises that teaching is as heroic and radical as playing in a band because both are fundamentally about conveying messages that matter and carrying hope to the next generation.

Some elements of *School of Rock* were incorporated in the Channel 4 reality programme *Rock School* (2005, 2006). Fronted by Gene Simmons from the US band Kiss, the first series was filmed at Christ's Hospital, a private school in the south of England. Simmons worked with a group of classically trained Year 9 pupils who ostensively had no interest in rock or pop music. The second series involved less privileged Year 11 students from Kirkley Community High School in East Anglia and launched both songwriting and performance careers for some of those who took part.

Hard cases

The previous section described teachers who initially merely sought to earn enough money to survive but eventually learned to appreciate the importance and significance of their role. Next we focus on another teacher who ends up in a school because he has no other option. After eighteen months, he still cannot find employment as an engineer.

To Sir with Love

In *To Sir with Love* (1967, directed by James Clavell), Mark Thackery, played by Sidney Poitier, presents himself, according to a colleague, as 'a lamb to the slaughter'. He joins a tough inner-city London school redolent of the US vocational school in Evan Hunter's *The Blackboard Jungle* (filmed in 1955, directed by Richard Brooks), where a colleague told new recruit Rick Dadier:

> This is the garbage can of the educational system. Every vocational school in the city. You put them all together, and you got one big, fat, overflowing garbage can. And you want to know what our job is? Our job is to sit on the lid of the garbage can and see that none of the filth overflows into the streets. That's our job.
>
> (Hunter, 1955, p. 67)

The environment Mark finds is both intimidating and challenging (this synthesis of apprehension and difficulty dominates the lives of hard-case teachers, reaching its apotheosis in *187*). The students in *To Sir with Love* use their strength in numbers to daunt teachers and, as a result, they are outwardly powerful. Intimidation, not learning, preoccupies them in class, and they are seen by staff as devils incarnate.

However, as Mark knows, student power is illusory because it does not reflect their relative status in society. His initial reaction, therefore, is to be dismissive of them because they understand so little and to relish an easy time in terms of preparation and marking.

However, like Dewey Finn, Mark is eventually seduced by the role. He cannot be a mere babysitter because he is gifted and motivated, responding heroically to the challenge of disillusioned and discontented young people. In comparison, as his colleague observes, being an engineer would be child's play. His students are disadvantaged and brittle, aggressive and frustrated, apparently ill-equipped to deal with life. Mark, like other popular cultural teachers, therefore decides to jettison the curriculum in favour of one which he believes to be of more value: that is, social studies and life skills. Careless of his capitation budget, he throws textbooks into litter bins while setting out a culture of respect. He speaks the language of the sixties, articulating liberal humanism and a resistance to convention which reveal the dilemmas and prejudices of his own life. He vows to teach truths, but there is no opportunity for the students (or the audience) to interrogate these 'truths'. He is presented as a saviour, a teacher with answers, even though, in reality, he does not know the questions nor offer practical solutions to the pressing social problems of individuals' lives. Little or no credit is given in the film to the ways in which the students, their families and friends cope daily with deprivation. Instead, the dominant discourse implies that young people can gain status and self-esteem only from education and achievement. At a very basic level, Althusser (1969, pp. 162–163) suggests that even this acknowledgement of an individual is a form of recognition which identifies the ideological state apparatus of education: 'The existence of ideology and the hailing or interpellation of individuals as subjects are one and the same thing.'

Mark Thackery respects his students but, as a teacher, he unequivocally knows best and aims to be a 'transformative intellectual' (Aronowitz and Giroux, 1987, p. 23) in order to liberate and inspire them. He asks 'What if?' to explore the relationship between education, political power and individuals' social situations and to analyse how, even within established frameworks, people can interpret texts and create meanings. Giroux (1992, p. 199), discussing the social construction of knowledge, calls for the organisation of 'schools and pedagogy around a sense of purpose and meaning that makes difference' and an opportunity to 'grant public schooling a significant role in the ongoing process of educating people to be active and critical citizens capable of fighting for and reconstructing democratic public life'. Despite the rhetoric, however, Mark isn't really promoting a range of cultural or critical literacies because, ultimately, he remains in control. He is working towards and fighting for Sir's truths – his personal vision of democracy and liberatory education.

Dangerous Minds

Dangerous Minds (1995, directed by John Smith) is often cited in discussions about education and popular culture. Like *Dead Poets Society*, it is a seminal and controversial account of the 'heroic' teacher. Based on the book *My posse don't do homework* by real-life teacher LouAnne Johnson (1992), it follows an idealistic young English teacher, played by Michelle Pfeiffer, teaching in an inner-city US school, who endeavours to save her disaffected, bored students from themselves and the community and culture in which they exist. LouAnne arrives, enthusiastic and committed, to teach the 'academy' students, only to find that the unexpected vacancy and her emergency certification are both due to teacher attrition. Dressed conventionally, she finds herself faced with insurrection and chaos; within minutes, she retreats from the classroom to taunts of 'white bread' and with the rap music of her African-American and Chicano/Latino students ringing in her ears. As Giroux (2002, p. 149) points out in his analysis of the film: 'Framed by a racial iconography and musical score that constructs minority students as both the objects of fear and subjects in need of discipline and control, the audience is prepared for someone to take charge.'

However, for LouAnne Johnson to be that person, she needs a strategy. That night, following her friend Hal's advice, she determines to rewrite the curriculum and reconstruct herself as someone whom the students will respect. For LouAnne, this means offering to teach karate, wearing black leather and informing them that she *is* a US marine (using the present tense for her former occupation). She also tells them, contrary to policy, that everyone will start her class with an 'A', and that all they need to do is keep it. The demarcation lines of race, gender and power are systematically drawn. LouAnne has notional authority as a teacher, but this is not accepted within the context of the class, where her students have control. However, the latter are constructed as unstable and insecure. Their alienation, the street discourse and rap music with which they fill their lives are not presented as a coherent articulation of a subculture but rather as failure, an absence of any viable alternative. Consequently, when challenged, they are disconcerted, and several become susceptible to LouAnne's promise of redemption.

LouAnne is the 'great white hope' who brings order and sanity to a world of disorder and moral decay. She offers her largely minority students a model of colonialism expressed through solicitude and the promise of gifts and rewards. Giroux (*ibid.*, p. 148) calls this 'compassion and consumerism', the embodiment of caring capitalism, and explains: 'In both instances "whiteness" becomes a referent for not only rearticulating racially coded notions of teaching and learning, but also for redefining how citizenship can be constructed for students of colour as a function of choice linked exclusively to the marketplace.' The shifting nature of power is clearly defined in *Dangerous Minds*, leaving students susceptible to the wily, white words of Bob Dylan and Dylan Thomas and no longer needing Coolio or Aaron Hall to justify their lives. LouAnne's vision of the world assumes that the choices available to her are also options for her students if only they have courage and support. The fact that their lives are largely governed by social, cultural, political and economic circumstances beyond their (and her) control seems to carry little significance. Equally, LouAnne herself is completely assured of her right to interfere in the personal lives of students, including visiting them in their homes. For example, she visits Raul's family to tell them that, as a reward, she intends to take him out to a sophisticated restaurant, an occasion which only serves to emphasise difference and compel Raul to buy a jacket. Later, when LouAnne follows up two absentees, we meet their mother, an African-American who is dismissive of Johnson and her aspirations for the boys, pointing out the irrelevance of poetry to young men who have no hope of becoming doctors or lawyers. This parent is presented to the audience as obstructive and ignorant. It is what Giroux (*ibid.*, p. 153) calls the 'pedagogy of diversion', since from LouAnne's perspective poetry is its own reward.

Emilio, one of her more challenging students, is resistant to LouAnne's philosophy, pointing out that just saying 'no' will not be enough to save him. His words echo the anti-drugs campaign initiated by Nancy Reagan when she was US First Lady in the 1980s. Emilio is right: it doesn't save him. When he dies, LouAnne blames the unsympathetically portrayed African-American Principal Grandey, who had refused to speak to Emilio because he had not knocked on his door. So African-American parents and principal are presented negatively, without any acknowledgement of their efforts or achievements. LouAnne Johnson, in contrast, is the hero, the saviour. When, at the end of the film, distressed at Emilio's death, she considers leaving, her students demonstrate how well they have learned the lessons of colonialism and consumerism by telling her she cannot go because she has illuminated their lives. She is the light who can lead them from darkness, and in *Dangerous Minds* that is what being a teacher means.

187

If heroism is somewhat ambiguous in *Dangerous Minds*, it is even more so in the 1997 film *187* (directed by Kevin Reynolds), in which Trevor Garfield, played by Samuel L. Jackson, finds himself standing alone against both students and the establishment. In the opening scenes, Trevor is a science teacher bringing his classroom alive with animated experiments, but the Brooklyn high school where he works is a threatening and chaotic place, employing surveillance worthy of any panopticon. Discipline is about enforcement, although the teachers have limited resources on which to rely or with which to protect themselves. When Trevor discovers his book has '187' (the US police code for homicide) written all over it, he goes immediately to the principal, who reveals that a student and known gangster has been told that Trevor failed him. Offered no security, he is later stabbed repeatedly with a six-inch nail. This act and its legacy haunt the rest of the film, undermining the idealism and destroying the optimism with which Trevor once viewed his job. Fifteen months later, he is a substitute teacher in Los Angeles. Now a wounded saint, he asks God for courage because he still believes that teaching is his vocation, but it is not easy to face a class again, and the students, scenting frailty, prey upon him (despite Jackson's physical stature), taunting and probing for vulnerability. Trevor, however, survives and, like LouAnne Johnson, tells those students who will listen that his classroom can be a sanctuary and place of salvation.

The language throughout *187* incorporates metaphors of war and battle and of associated sacrifice and loss. Dave Childress, Trevor's colleague, talks of school like this, pointing out that nothing can be expected from an administration preoccupied with students' rights and fearful of litigation. When Dave hears Trevor's history, he is impressed, especially since, as the recipient of a certificate for teaching excellence, Dave sees himself as a fellow survivor. Trevor, however, is dismissive of the camaraderie, correctly identifying Dave as a morally bankrupt man who exploits students intellectually, emotionally and sexually. Dave even has a gun in his desk drawer just in case he is attacked, or feels like 'wasting' a student.

Trevor may not share Dave's world, but he does resort to violence, killing Benny, a particularly intimidating and vicious student, with the excuse being that death offers salvation for Benny as well as respite for his victims. Trevor believes in the greater good, and, perversely, assumes a moral position despite the immorality of what he does. Rather than reject violence, he appropriates it because the system does not offer any alternative:

> Educators need pedagogical strategies that move between dominant and oppositional appropriations of violence. These will enable them to develop alternative understandings of how violence is produced, framed aesthetically, circulated and ruptured. Violence may then be connected with broader considerations of critique, public discourse, and social engagement.
>
> (Stam and Shohat, 1994, p. 319)

Despite his experience and actions, Trevor is not motivated by self-interest or self-protection, but his view of the world and of his job as an educator is desperate and hopeless. He cynically explains to Ellen Henry, a young teacher who admires and likes him, that school is a place where anarchy rather than order rules and where righteousness is not rewarded.

Like LouAnne Johnson, Trevor Garfield is prepared to give extra time to students, even visiting them at home. Furthermore, although Trevor is African-American himself, the society inhabited by people of colour is again seen as dysfunctional and oppressive, a place where children rule their parents (usually single mothers) and where poverty and hopelessness give few options. Consequently *187* is a deeply racist film and it offers few solutions. Ellen, the only teacher with any shred of idealism, decides to leave teaching, while Trevor gives his life to teach his final lesson. Forced into a game of Russian roulette by a student, Cesar, Trevor argues that all Cesar appreciates is stupidity and machismo. In his defence, Cesar explains that is all he has. Trevor, however, has no time for a victim culture and, abruptly taking Cesar's turn in the 'game', shoots himself. Yet, it is a pointless sacrifice because Cesar, his manhood affronted, takes another turn and dies too. So it is left to Rita, the abused Chicano girl whom Trevor tutored, to suggest that there is something to be learned here. Her message at graduation is that students should not blame everything on their social environment, and that even good teachers can be pushed too far. Despite their superficiality, her words reinforce the fact that education is an interactive process and a negotiated space.

Freedom Writers

Freedom Writers (2007, directed by Richard la Gravenese) is based on the real-life experiences of Erin Gruwell and her students at Woodrow Wilson High School in Los Angeles during the 1990s. It forms an interesting link text between the preceding hard-case teachers and the charismatic individuals of the next section. Gruwell, played by Hilary Swank, a successful academic from an influential and radical family, decides to become a teacher rather than a lawyer after witnessing civil unrest in Los Angeles during 1992. Her career choice is considered perverse since, it is implied, being a teacher is not a sufficiently prestigious job for a high achiever. However, in a volatile socio-political environment where integration means young people are bussed across the city and where poverty, violence and racial tension are rife, Gruwell believes that teachers can make a real difference. She seeks to be a 'transformative intellectual' and to shape young minds while there is still hope for change.

Most teachers at the school, however, are disllusioned, believing that integration has undermined school values and academic standards. Yet Erin, full of anticipation and resolutely wearing her pearls and smart clothes, is determinedly optimistic when she meets her mixed-race first-year high school class. Like LouAnne Johnson, she is quickly frustrated by the hopelessness and negativity of her students (a fight breaks out before she has even registered her first class). However, she adopts a slightly different strategy from Johnson's to deal with the problem: rather than throwing away books, Erin determines to get more relevant and better-quality texts and to seek inspiration from the young people themselves. Instead of teaching, she is the one who is learning. She needs, initially, to be the student in order to find out more about the individuals in her class. When she asks how many have been shot at or lost friends or family members through violence, she is appalled that nearly everyone in the classroom raises a hand. Subsequently arguing that race is not an issue, she is told in no uncertain terms that it is *the* issue. Her romantic vision of herself bringing harmony and understanding to the classroom is eroded. People, she is told by her students, are teachers just because that is how they represent themselves. Education is worthless in a world where simply to get through a day alive is considered an achievement. As far as the students are concerned, the best Erin can hope for as a teacher is to survive and to maintain some semblance of order.

Erin listens but, when a gross caricature of an African-American student circulates in her class, she is forced to condemn her students' prejudice and racism, citing the effects of Nazi propaganda. The revelation, however, that these young people have never heard of the Holocaust gives her teaching new significance and meaning. She takes them to the Simon Wiesenthal Center and the Museum of Tolerance; she buys copies of Anne Frank's (1997, first published 1947) *The diary of a young girl*; and she invites some Auschwitz survivors into the class. She also suggests that the students write journals chronicling their hopes, feelings and frustrations which she will read only if they wish. It is this initiative which forms the cathartic and inspirational writing programme that, the film implies, makes Erin's classroom a place of salvation and change where young people can respect themselves and one another. Her dedication, predictably, is at the expense of her own personal life, with her single-mindedness resulting in divorce but also in the publication of her students' work as *The freedom writers' diary: how a teacher and 150 teens used writing to change themselves and the world around them.*

So what does *Freedom Writers* offer that is different from earlier films such as *Dangerous Minds* and *187*? Certainly, it provides a similiar view of the tribal loyalties and gang violence of American urban society. It also suggests that young people are dismissive of both education and the conventional social order and have more affinity with and respect for their own feral cultures. Conversely, however, *Freedom Writers* implies that, rather than anarchy, these offer internally regulated alternative societies in which people survive in the only way they can. The voice-over, taken from the young people's journals, reinforces the rationale and analytical depth with which they articulate their lives, but, all too often, it is set against a montage of gang violence and frantic attempts at self-preservation. Erin is motivated by a desire for change and, because she cannot easily change society or her colleagues, she aims to inspire her students so that they will change 'the world around them'. She has continued her work through the Freedom Writers' Foundation, aimed at promoting 'acceptance and innovative teaching methods across the country' (Gruwell, 2007), but the film does sentimentalise her achievements. Like other popular cultural teachers, she shows the way, the inference being that, with the right leadership, one good book, some visitors and a field trip will get things sorted.

Who knocks at the door of learning?

The charismatic and extraordinary teacher is both heroic and saintly, prepared to dedicate his/her life to education and to caring about the minutiae of students' lives. What these people have in common is commitment to a higher calling and devotion to their vocation. The nobility of the teachers in the next two films, both set in the 1950s, is highlighted by the social mores of the times and the privileged environments of the schools in which they work.

Dead Poets Society

Dead Poets Society (1989, directed by Peter Weir), like *Dangerous Minds*, is a significant film in the canon of popular cultural representations of teachers. The film is set in the fictional Welton Academy, an exclusive American institution of wealth and privilege founded on the cornerstones of tradition, honour, discipline and excellence (parodied by students as travesty, horror, decadence and excrement). In 1959, a new English teacher, alumnus John Keating, played by Robin Williams, comes into this rarefied environment. Keating, full of enthusiasm and energy, aims to reform both the school's curriculum and pedagogy. His whistling entry into his first class and his exhortations to the students are in marked contrast to the mathematics teacher who, minutes earlier, had begun his lesson with dire warnings. Keating, however, debunks authority, including his own. Looking at photographs of former Weltonians, he reminds everyone that youth is precious, encouraging the students to seize the day and make their lives extraordinary. Ironically, though, what is ordinary at Welton is for 75 per cent of its boys to go to Ivy League colleges and afterwards attain influential positions in society. The school's traditional curriculum and didactic pedagogy leave little room for the kind of independent thinking and personal expression celebrated by Keating.

In one session, Keating urges the students to rip out the introduction to their textbooks because it offers a mechanistic rating instrument for the greatness of poetry. For Keating, this is a battle against mediocrity and superficiality where defeat could cost hearts and souls. As in *187* and other films, the metaphor of war is used to indicate the Herculean nature of the teacher's task. What he suggests is initially seen by his students as sacrilegious because it is both a rejection of received opinion and a desecration of school property. Yet, Keating has two little secrets for them: humanity lives for passion; and poetry is passion. Along with beauty, love and romance, poetry, the teacher argues, is a reason for living. He is not simply justifying the study of poetry; he is repositioning it within the lives and loves of his students (Giroux, 2002), and to reinforce this he makes them reposition themselves physically, by standing on their desks and looking at the classroom from a different perspective. For Keating, this is why literature is important: it makes readers look at life in a different way.

Farber *et al.* (1994, p. 171) analyse the allure of this heroic and maverick stance in *Dead Poets Society*:

> For a while the message is conveyed that transformative action is possible, that action seems always to be the product of special heroes, working alone – often even entering from outside and never fitting in. Transformation is always a product of masculine charisma and unique interpersonal relationships . . . Nor is there any suggestion of shared work among adults of good will to achieve any transformative ends together.

However, Keating tells his students what to do and think much as other teachers do. It is simply the message that is different, as Giroux (2002, p. 95) points out: 'Resistance in Keating's pedagogy suggests a strangely empty quality . . . [It] serves to depoliticise and decontextualise, since it is only developed within a romanticised aesthetic.' As a consequence, when Neil Perry, an earnest and sensitive student, is faced with his father's implacable decision to transfer him to a military academy, instead of resisting he simply dons his theatrical head-dress like a crown of thorns and commits suicide. Neil is a somewhat ambivalent figure because the Perry family, like Jack Read's in *The Guinea Pig*, is not as affluent as others at Welton, so self-destruction confirms lack of privilege. This is despite the fact that the revival of the Dead Poets Society gives the boys opportunities for genuine self-expression as they smoke, listen to poetry and attempt, albeit rather weakly, to charm girls. Ultimately, however, the film reinforces class prejudice because it is the rich and influential, not the poor and aspiring, who assert their independence and individuality. The wealthy Charlie Dalton (nicknamed Nuwanda), who challenges the headteacher by pretending to receive a telephone call from God in assembly, is unlikely to be adversely affected by his subsequent expulsion. Even Keating himself is compliant in the face of censure and, when blamed for Neil's death, accepts his dismissal without demur, although he clearly appreciates the chant 'Oh Captain, my Captain' as the boys stand on their desks to commend him as he leaves.

John Keating is a charismatic and passionate teacher, dedicated to his career. As a student at Welton, he had been voted the man most likely to do anything. He chose to be a teacher. He is unconventional and original, fervent and committed, but he is a tarnished hero, a fallen saint, not so much because of Neil's death but because his message is insubstantial and partial. He does not radically challenge authority or power in Welton Academy, nor does he significantly share or negotiate the intellectual and emotional space in his classroom. For Keating, education is tutor-centred, and his pinnacle is to be borne triumphantly aloft on the shoulders of his students. While such a model of learning might have its place, it is not the only valid educational paradigm. Keating makes being a teacher important, not being a student important. However, despite everything, he does raise questions about the nature and process of learning which, in the context of the times, might be construed as a heroic, although ultimately pyrrhic, victory.

Mona Lisa Smile

Mona Lisa Smile (2003, directed by Mike Newell) takes place in a prestigious all-white US school, Wellesley College for Young Ladies, during the 1950s. The anachronistic setting evokes audience nostalgia, especially since it highlights fifties fashion as well as gender issues around stereotyping, sexism and social significance. From the beginning, Katherine Watson, the new art history teacher played by Julia Roberts, is identified as an outsider. According to the voice-over, she 'Made up in brains what she lacked in pedigree.' Katherine is a 'bohemian' from California (associated, presumably, with a more lax and liberal lifestyle), coming to teach at a conservative Eastern college: 'She didn't come to Wellesley because she wanted to fit in. She came because she wanted to make a difference.' Wellesley is an institution which appears to take learning and the education of its young ladies very seriously. The ritual prologue to the academic year reiterates its mission:

> Who knocks at the door of learning?
> I am every woman.
> What do you seek?
> To awake my spirit through hard work and dedicate my life to knowledge.

Katherine's students work hard. They are so familiar with the course textbook that they can even anticipate her slide schedule. Like John Keating, though, Katherine wants to challenge her students and encourage them to think for themselves. So she introduces modern art, including Chaim Soutine's 1925 expressionist painting *Carcass of Beef*: 'What is that? Is it any good? There is no wrong answer, no textbook telling you what to think . . . What is art? What makes it good or bad and who decides?' Betty Warren, a precocious, self-confident, soon-to-be-wed student, cannot resist answering: 'Art isn't art until someone says it is . . . the right people.'

Katherine has a mission at Wellesley, but it is not really about art history; rather, it is about questioning accepted values, including gender roles, in society. So much is constructed in repressive and patriarchal ways. For example, she observes a colleague telling students: 'A few years from now your sole responsibility will be looking after your husband and children – the grade that matters the most is the grade he gives you.' Although initially frustrated, Katherine decides as a 'progressive, forward thinker' that she must, like Johnson and Gruwell, find a way to work with the students. Rather radically, she gives lower grades for conventional responses: for example, to Joan Brandwell, a straight 'A' student who is interested in applying to Yale to do law. Joan has competing priorities, however, and Betty Warren's vision of their mutual future also appeals: 'We'll be best friends and our husbands will be best friends. And we'll have houses together, and we'll have babies together.' Like other 'good' teachers, Katherine decides to challenge her students by broadening their horizons. Through the auspices of a friend, she arranges a viewing of an original Jackson Pollock painting: 'Do me a favour; do yourselves a favour. Stop talking and look. You're not required to write a paper. You're not even required to like it. You are required to consider it.' Inevitably, however, this approach affronts parents and the Wellesleyan school board. Principal Carr tells Katherine: 'Your teaching methods are a little unorthodox for Wellesley. So, if you'd like to stay here . . . a little less modern art.' Incensed, Katherine decides to take on the system: 'Today you just listen,' she says as she bombards students with oppressive images of women in roles which construct them only in relation to and for others: 'A girdle to set you free – what does that mean? I give up. You win. The smartest women in the country . . . I didn't realise that, by demanding excellence, I would be challenging the roles you were born to fill. My mistake.'

Wellesley College is in fact nothing more than a finishing school, preparing young women for marriage, maternity, hostessing, dinner conversation and little else. Katherine Watson, who had believed she would be teaching 'tomorrow's leaders, not their wives', is disillusioned. However, as another teacher points out: 'Change needs time, you know. You've got to let them catch up with you.'

Katherine determines at least to rescue Joan from the thrall of matrimony and persuade her to go to law school, if not instead of, at least as well as marriage: 'You can bake your cake and eat it too . . . you can study and get dinner on the table by five.' Consequently, she is disconcerted when Joan elopes, rejecting the option of university. It is here that the feminist agenda is reversed, and Katherine, the advocate of women's rights, is forced to confront her own prejudices and the implications of choice. Joan explains: 'It was my choice not to go. He would have supported it . . . You stand in class and tell us to look beyond the image, but you don't. To you a housewife is someone who has sold her soul. You are the one who said I can do anything I want. This is what I want.' Like that of John Keating, LouAnne Johnson and Mark Thackery, Katherine's liberatory model of education is in fact constructed around a new orthodoxy: 'You didn't come to Wellesley to help people find their way. I think you came to help them find *your* way.' Katherine has no opportunity to ponder this, because, despite high enrolment figures, she is given an ultimatum: compromise or resign. She decides to leave.

Mona Lisa Smile is ambiguous in the way it constructs gender and class, and its title acknowledges this. These are women of privilege and education. If any woman had options in the 1950s, one would assume these women did; but, ultimately, choice is the product of our lives and conditioning. Privilege, with its social straitjacket, can in its own way be oppressive even if it does not overtly deny one the right to choose. Betty Warren, the film's narrator and editor of the college magazine, divorced and returning to school, in the end feels compelled to defend even Katherine Watson's choice to leave: 'Not all who wander are aimless, especially those who seek truth beyond tradition, beyond definition, beyond image.' She celebrates what she wants to see as a heroic gesture by dedicating her writing: 'To an extraordinary woman who lived by example and compelled us to see the world through new eyes.'

To teach or not to teach?

Popular culture offers varied representations of the good and heroic teacher. But these cinematic representations do not necessarily bring us closer to defining what a good teacher is because, in the construction of a media text, the demands of drama override those of authenticity. In reality, being a good teacher is not about having an impact on a few individuals because classes comprise twenty, thirty or more. It is not just about encouraging 'A'-grade students to excel because equity and differentiation are also important. Even when a teacher is deemed 'good', how is that judgement made? On the basis of which criteria? Students, parents, peers, senior/middle management might each want to emphasise and prioritise different things.

Whether we fully accept Althusser's (1969) claim that education is an 'ideological state apparatus', the purpose of school is clearly socialisation as well as education. The process of schooling within Western society is about conformity and order, integration and assimilation. For teachers, this means managing systems, addressing establishment expectations, school procedures, curricular demands, assessment regulations and government educational policies. This is the agenda that dominates professional discourse about teaching, but which is largely absent from popular cultural representations. Michael Eraut (1994, p. 200), reviewing professional knowledge and competence, cites the following as benchmarks for a good teacher:

- Underpinning knowledge and understanding of concepts, theories, facts and procedures;
- The personal skill and qualities required for a professional approach to the conduct of one's work; and
- The cognitive processes which constitute professional thinking.

In recent years, the professional agenda has been about interpreting such require-ments from a management perspective, and about establishing, maintaining and enhancing standards through internal quality assurance and external inspection. The political rhetoric, particularly in the UK during the 1990s, about identifying incompetent teachers focused on accountability, compliance and conformity, yet being heroic usually means stepping outside boundaries and paradigms. Good teachers in popular culture will often introduce their own curriculum, ignoring prescribed 'concepts, theories, facts and procedures'. His/her 'personal skills and qualities' are charisma and passion rather than professional expertise. Yet, in films, when more traditional staff criticise protagonists, the audience is encouraged to see them as outmoded and reactionary.

Heroism, because it is often about individuality, seems in many respects antithetical to theoretical notions of a good teacher because it actively subverts and challenges some of the principles commonly associated with professionalism. Popular culture constructs a model of good practice based on individual performance and qualities that suggest good teachers are born, not made: 'The Hollywood construction of the teacher and the aesthetic–ethical–political language spoken by that model is not unrepresented in the professional discourse of the curriculum, but it is virtually the only model present in popular culture' (Dalton, 1995, p. 39). So, while popular culture introduces an intriguing element into the debate about what makes a good teacher, it may seem a somewhat marginal one. Dalton (*ibid.*) suggests that teachers represented as good and heroic are distracted from the professional agenda in that they 'act as mediators who prepare students to meet the world that exists beyond the classroom', rather than 'working with students to affect [*sic*] lasting change' in administrative or institutional structures. 'Lasting change' is not a popular cultural priority because immediate impact and commercial success are what make culture popular. However, we may still usefully interrogate popular cultural images, and analyse and evaluate what is significant or how audiences and readers engage with different texts. If, by watching a film, we question the experience of students, the interplay of teaching and learning, the implications of intellectual, racial, gender and class chauvinism, or what it really means to be a teacher, then perhaps the cinematic experience will have some resonance for critical debate within the profession as whole. In doing this, however, we must acknowledge what is absent from images as well as what is present. Ayers (2001, p. 209) identifies very clearly what expectations he has of a good teacher, and, in doing so, describes the 'common cause' which should be at the centre of the profession's agenda because it offers not just hope for students but a validation of education:

> We need to take seriously the experiences of youngsters, their sense making, their knowledge, and their dreams; and particularly we must interrogate the structures that kids are rejecting. In other words, we must assume an intelligence in youngsters, assume that they are acting sensibly and making meaning in situations that are difficult and often dreadful – and certainly not of their own making. In finding common cause with youngsters, we may also find there our own salvation as teachers.

Education is a negotiated space, and students have a contribution to make to our understanding of how this space might be colonised and managed. Their expectations of teachers form the basis for this and are conditioned by what they see outside their immediate frame of reference and within media representations. A range of images of the good teacher emerges from popular culture and formulates a discourse that is meaningful personally and professionally. The films we have discussed in this chapter provide representations of teaching; they don't offer, even when based on true stories, authentic or documentary accounts of teaching. However, as representations, they do help us to analyse the values and beliefs we have about teachers and teaching, and contribute to the richness and diversity of thinking about professionalism. Thus, through challenging preconceived expectations, it might be possible to avoid disillusion and encourage good teachers to stay in the profession, accepting relentless and unheroic daily routines, while still finding satisfaction in classrooms. In doing so, they will be the real heroes of the profession, those who provide consistent and high-quality learning experiences for succeeding generations of children and young people.

3 The sad and the bad

Bad teachers: official definitions and public suspicions

Pathetic and monstrous teachers parade through popular culture and seem to reflect a deep-seated social mistrust of the profession. The history of the teaching profession in the UK may help to explain why teachers are regarded with such suspicion. Teaching emerged late as a profession and has not shared the status of traditional 'gentlemen's professions': the law, the Church and the armed services. The schoolmaster's role from the sixteenth century onwards was often taken by the less educated clergy unable to secure a parish living, or by lectors, low-paid lay readers employed by the Church (O'Day, 1982). Some schoolteachers combined their low-paid role with the humble job of parish clerk. The national schools used unqualified older children to teach younger pupils. Although the headteachers of the great endowed grammar schools had some standing in society, and despite attempts from the late sixteenth century onwards to provide training and education for some teachers, teaching in general remained poorly paid and of low status. Moreover, teaching, particularly of younger children, has often been the preserve of women and has therefore acquired the lower status associated with female work. It is concomitant with childminding and care work, particularly in dame and elementary schools, rather than with intellectual activity. As Miller (1996, p. 2) notes, women's qualification for the kinds of work they were expected to do 'usually rested on what they were thought to know and be able to do "naturally"'. This has led to many negative perceptions of teachers, including the assumption that those of young children are 'motherly but/and brainless' (*ibid*., p. 13).

Teachers today may be judged as achievers or as losers/failures, depending on the social and cultural capital and values of those in judgement. For example, families whose members have not previously entered the professions may be proud of their children's success in becoming teachers, although it is still often regarded as a less prestigious career for a man. Teachers may be perceived by less educated parents as people who have succeeded where they themselves have failed or were not interested. But they may also be seen as representative of a kind of labour that is not 'real work', and certainly not real manly work. By comparison, teachers working in wealthy middle-class areas among well-educated parents are likely to find that many parents earn far more than they do and that pupils expect 'better' jobs than teaching. These teachers may still be respected if those parents value education generally. Indeed, some of the parents will themselves be teachers. On the other hand, although associated with education, some parents will recognise that teachers deal with relatively low-level knowledge, suitable for children, and may regard them less as scholars than as a childcare facility that enables the parents to pursue their high-level careers. There are numerous permutations of these perspectives; the point is that the social status of the teacher is ambiguous.

Schoolteachers have authority and power, but these are located in the child's world, leading some to consider that they have not proved themselves as adults. Although teachers know this cosy view of schools is not a realistic representation of the social, political and economic complexities of life in modern teaching, it is a common perception and many teachers cringe at the use of the term 'in the real world'. Thus, some may perceive that teachers have no understanding of the harsh realities of life outside the school, but everyone believes they know all about teaching because they have been to school. Moreover, they have moved on from school, while teachers have not. The common experience of schooling also means that the job lacks the mystique attached to professions such as the law and medicine. Because everyone has observed teachers day in, day out for years, they believe they have seen the whole of the teacher's job, and some categorise it as easy and teachers as lazy. They do not see what goes on outside the classroom. After all, many pupils believe they do all the work and there are jibes about short working days (based on the assumption that the teacher's day is the same length as the pupils') and resentment at long holidays.

Even the most hard-working teachers will never satisfy the desires of some parents and some pupils; perhaps at some subconscious level they never satisfy anyone. The child's ego may well demand that s/he be the most important person in the world to the most significant adult in the room; the shock for those who move from a loving parental home to one in which you are just one person in thirty is considerable. Children may well feel ignored and dissatisfied by the quantity and quality of attention they receive at school. Parents are invited into schools, given lengthy written reports on their children and encouraged to discuss them with teachers. Yet, no teacher can ever care as much about one child, know as much about them, or have the time and take the infinite pains to ensure their progress above all others that his/her parent might wish. So, at some level, while parents and children may respect the teacher and accept at a rational level the constraints under which s/he is working, they are doomed always to be disappointed.

These ambiguities manifest themselves in two broad categories of teachers, both of which are commonly found in popular culture: the sad and the bad. An examination of a few texts shows how teachers are frequently portrayed either as objects of pity and derision or as sources of terror. Sometimes the categories overlap, through the use of dark humour in horror. The following texts serve to illustrate this: the animated television series *South Park* and the subsequent film of the same title (1999, directed by Trey Parker); the British Channel 4 television drama series *Teachers*; and several examples from the horror genre, namely the television series *Buffy the Vampire Slayer* (*BtVS*) (1997–2004, created by Joss Whedon), the films

Scream (1996, directed by Wes Craven), *The Faculty* (1998, directed by Robert Rodriguez) and *Cherry Falls* (1999, directed by Geoffrey Wright), and the *Point Horror* books. In most cases the categories of sad and bad are blurred, but it has still been possible to allocate each text to one or the other, with the exception of *BtVS*, which provides such fine examples from each category that it is included under both headings.

The sad

Miller (1990) notes that Hollywood tends to ridicule teachers. This convention has continued to the present day and can be seen in texts outside Hollywood. Teachers are often portrayed as people who cannot command respect or even operate as normal social beings. These representations fit the idea that teachers have low status in society and are often cowed by parents, students and authorities.

South Park

Unlike *The Simpsons*, which also repays analysis (Kantor *et al.*, 2001), *South Park* is not designed for family viewing. Its highly satirical script and storylines unmask racism, sexism, naked greed and lust as well as a sheer absence of affection for fellow humanity among all South Park citizens. Its extremely bleak, negative portrayal of family, religious, school and community life has attracted criticism. The humour is based on revealing the gulf between media idealisations of small town life and childhood innocence and exaggerated examples of the bigotry, cruelty and callousness that can also be found in such places. It features the lives of four children – Cartman, Kyle, Stan and Kenny – living in variously dys-functional families in the eponymous 'quiet, little, redneck, hoe-down, white trash, mountain town' celebrated in the opening song from the film *South Park: Bigger, Longer, Uncut* (written by Trey Parker, Matt Stone and Pam Brady).

Their school, South Park Elementary, provides a regular setting. The class teacher, Mr Garrison, is deeply socially inadequate. Unable to form proper relationships, he uses a glove puppet, Mr Hat, to communicate with the children and cannot function without it. His teaching style is utterly conventional: he works from a chalkboard using question-and-answer technique and little else. Throughout the series, his knowledge is shown to be poor: he misinforms the children and feeds them a ludicrous and inadequate version of American history that, for example, valorises the white man and erases the oppression of Native Americans. He is humiliated and outwitted by his small pupils but our sympathy for him is limited by his own lack of compassion for others. His foolishness and failures are rooted in a lack of concern for individuals and a spectacular disregard for issues of social and political equality. In the *South Park* film, we see him trying to get a response to a maths question he has written on the board at the beginning of the lesson, without preamble or explanation. 'Don't be shy, just give it your best shot,' he encourages, when there are no volunteers. Once a child has given the wrong answer, he cheerfully continues, 'Let's try to get an answer from someone who's not a complete retard.' Later in the same scene, Cartman calls Kyle a 'fucking Jew'. The class is silenced, horrified. Mr Garrison looks appalled, but we soon realise that he has not even noticed the racism or the bullying: 'Did you just say the "f" word?' he asks, sparking a torrent of foul language from the child.

Later in the film, Mr Garrison's weakness and lack of understanding of educational principles is shown when he abandons his lesson plans in order to teach an anti-swearing programme at the insistence of 'your moms'. His response to the children's queries about the reasons for their mothers' extreme concern is typical: 'They're probably all on their periods or something.' When accused of sexism by a politically aware child, we get a further insight into his disturbed psyche when he reveals: 'I just don't trust anything that bleeds for five days and doesn't die.' Parents are oblivious to his sexism and racism, just as they appear to ignore their children's apparently serious psychological disorders while literally waging war over their use of foul language. The film takes Mr Garrison's pusillanimity and lack of principle in the face of irate 'moms' to its logical and ludicrous conclusion, when he agrees to pull the lever activating the electric chair in which are seated the Canadian comedians who introduced the children to 'bad' language.

Although Mr Garrison is categorised here as 'sad', there is always a darker side to *South Park* humour. The border between sad and bad is blurred, when, following Mr Garrison's death in the ensuing war against Canada (whipped up by Kyle's mom), Mr Hat is found by Satan, who adopts the puppet as his own very special friend. Satan, like Mr Garrison, is shown to be lonely, and to have difficulty making relationships, so he uses Mr Hat as compensation. Mr Garrison's pathetic qualities seem fair game for the satirist, because they are rooted in serious character weaknesses. In effect, the movie gives the weak teacher Satan as his doppelgänger.

South Park's school counsellor, Mr Mackey, is another sad misfit who fails the children. He too merely carries out orders. The children are sent to him to be 'cured' of their swearing. He doesn't counsel, but lectures them on their bad behaviour, then entertains them with a totally inappropriate song, 'It's Easy MKay?', that parodies the 'Just Say No' anti-drugs campaign, revealing an equally unsubtle and ill-informed approach to a social problem. The ineffectual nature of his interventions is encapsulated by the fact that after joining in a rousing chorus of the song, the children go straight back to see the film that introduced them to the language in the first place. The film and the series offer a painful critique of approaches to education that focus on superficial rather than deep learning and which are undemocratic and complacent about wider social and political debates. No one talks to the children about the issues surrounding swearing, so they never understand. The final solution is an extreme version of the behaviourism that has operated so far: chips are implanted in all the children's heads that cause severe electric shocks if they swear. In the end, weak teachers are shown to be dangerous because they do not accept their professional responsibility to think critically and challenge the oppressive views of parents and authorities. In the iconoclastic *South Park* universe the 'jobsworth' teacher can help to bring about the apocalypse.

Buffy the Vampire Slayer

Apocalypses loom regularly in *BtVS*. The TV series begins in high school. Buffy Summers, played by Sarah Michelle Gellar, discovers she is the 'Chosen One', the Vampire Slayer, possessed of supernatural strength. The school library sits on the Hellmouth – an opening to various demon dimensions; a metaphorical representation of all the horrors haunting adolescents. Buffy and her friends (known as the 'Scooby gang'/'Scoobies') fight the vampires and demons that seek to feed on the inhabitants of Sunnydale. Core members are an academically gifted witch, Willow (Alyson Hannigan), a less enthusiastic scholar, Xander (Nicholas Brendon), and Rupert Giles (Anthony Stewart Head), who is the school librarian and also Buffy's Watcher, responsible for her training and supervision. Each season has a story arc encompassing all its episodes, in which the Scoobies thwart an apocalypse planned by that year's super-villain. Hence the inscription on Buffy's headstone: 'She saved world – a lot.'

The sub-genre of teen horror generally offers a particularly rich vein of sad teachers. *BtVS* uses the licence afforded by its horror/supernatural conventions to develop a range of humorous and hyperbolic metaphors that illustrate the damage to both students and teachers that results from poor teaching. The terrible fate of many of the teachers is one obvious example. Poor teachers do not simply fail to gain their merit increments. They are eaten. Some of these teachers are comic characters; others, discussed later in the 'Bad' section, are vicious and violent.

The first casualty is Principal Flutie (Ken Lerner), who displays twin weaknesses: hypocrisy and a lack of authority/charisma. As a new girl at Sunnydale High, Buffy is called to his office ('Welcome to the Hellmouth', 1.1, written by Joss Whedon, directed by Charles Martin Smith). Flutie parodies the radical teacher bent on changing relations of power with learners when he informs Buffy that he asks all the students to call him Bob. As she begins to do so, though, he hastily interjects to tell her that they do not actually follow this instruction. He dramatically tears up Buffy's report card from the previous school, claiming he likes everyone to start with a clean record, only to piece it together again in front of her when his eye catches some of the alarming details. Such insincere attempts at developing relationships with students are indicative of an incapacity to understand the young adults he teaches and a complete unwillingness to listen or empathise.

'The Pack' (1.6, written by Matt Kiene, directed by Bruce Seth Green) shows adult inability to combat bullying. Flutie makes an attempt to stop an incident of bullying on a school outing to the zoo, but he fails because he lacks the character and personality to see this through. The students in question ignore his ineffectual threat to watch them throughout the day and prove that his surveillance is insignificant, as they immediately break into a forbidden area of the zoo and become possessed by hyena spirits. The representation of these students as a gang of hyenas prowling around the school and its grounds, to the insistent soundtrack of Far's 'Job's Eyes', is a powerful representation of the menace of bullying and the insecurity of the school. This extended metaphor is taken to its limits when the hyena-possessed students eat first the school mascot, a piglet, which amounts to a symbolic devouring of the school, and then Principal Flutie himself in response to his nervous attempts to discipline them. It is difficult to evade the interpretation that many teachers are eventually destroyed by the cumulative and collective aggressions of students whose disaffection is at least partly the result of those teachers' incompetence.

Scream

Principal Himbry (Henry Winkler) in the horror movie *Scream* appears to be genuinely well meaning, which makes his fate even more disturbing. When murders begin on his school campus, he uses the PA system to urge students to take care walking home, telling them he loves them and cares for their safety. He is horrified by the behaviour of students who dress up as the killer to frighten others, insisting they make him sick and he would love to expel them. When the situation deteriorates, he suspends classes to try to keep students safe. There is no quarter for good intentions, however. He is unable to connect with the students. To some extent, the PA messages act as an exemplar of this: he is talking to the air, not directly to people, and is largely ignored. Like Flutie in *BtVS*, Himbry pays an extreme price for being unable to understand what is going on and for a complete inability to control the evil on his campus. He is murdered, gutted and hung from the goal post on the football field. When the students hear about this at a party, many of them cheer and most leave the party in excitement, delighted that school will be suspended indefinitely and keen to get to the scene of the crime and learn more gruesome details.

The cold humour of these scenes suggests chillingly that teenagers are not capable of seeing teachers as real people, as there is no suggestion that Himbry has victimised or bullied any of them. Like *South Park*'s children, they are locked into an entirely egotistical view of the world. Most of the young people in the film behave like psychopaths, unable to empathise or relate. Himbry is not bad, merely not quite up to the job. He is not even obviously foolish, like Flutie. At one point we see him, in a moment of silliness, unable to resist dressing up as the killer in the mask he has confiscated, but mostly he does his best, which just isn't good enough. This is a characteristic of teen horror. Teachers are vilified not just for actively harming students, but because they can never fulfil the expectation that they will protect them absolutely; and simply for being old, lacking grace, beauty and youth. The extreme nature of Flutie's and Himbry's punishment could be interpreted as a reflection of the anger and despair children experience as they come to realise that those they have trusted to protect them are incapable of doing so. Although this is expressed in terms of protection from murder, it is clearly linked in these dramas to protection from teasing, bullying, difficult relationships and personal angst. Schoolteachers symbolise the failure of the adult world to protect its young from reality.

Teachers

The UK Channel 4 television series *Teachers* is a comic drama, set in a secondary comprehensive school. It has a brief to represent schoolteachers with a degree of realism, noting their ordinary, human, flawed behaviour. It was always intended to be humorous and verges on the absurd. As the teachers go about their business, absorbed in their own concerns, outrageous and ludicrous events unfold in the background, caught on camera but unnoticed by the staff. The series presents the teachers as predominantly sad, cynical and inadequate characters; in spite of its supposed realism, it therefore offers a similar view of teachers and their weaknesses to Hollywood teen movies. The difference is one of perspective. In teen flicks like *Clueless* (1995, directed by Amy Heckerling), we see the sad teachers from the students' point of view. In *Teachers*, we see them from the inside – but they still present a sorry picture.

The teachers do not care about the children, or indeed even notice them much. Their neglect and lack of compassion do not have the vicious, sadistic edge that characterises some of the truly bad teachers in popular culture, but it is relevant that this casual neglect emerges repeatedly in popular texts about the profession. As they arrive at school in various episodes, they pass children fighting, falling from windows and collapsed on the floor. Strange creatures, like donkeys and zebra, wander around the school but the teachers show no interest, take no responsibility. In this respect the series seems to borrow from the conventions of such comic horror movies as *Scary Movie*, in which teachers hand out detentions but do not seem to notice that their students are being murdered. This lack of interest in the children as individuals is displayed by one teacher, Penny, when she says: 'I never look up during lessons.' The reason she gives is: 'I find it too depressing, all those hard little faces and cold eyes.' Any teacher or even trainee teacher knows that you lose control of the class without regular eye contact. Teachers are also aware that boredom results from a lesson in which they plough on regardless, not tempering their pace or content to the responses of the students. The series makes it clear that even her less than inspiring colleagues recognise that Penny is not suited to teaching. Her extreme behaviour, together with the indifference of her colleagues, is yet another example of a cultural representation reinforcing the popular view that teachers do not notice or respond to children as people. Penny sees only a sea of frightening faces.

Many teachers enter the profession from a genuine desire to help children learn and develop. Most at least pay lip-service to the idea that 'it's all about the kids'. But the entire staff in *Teachers* seems united in an understanding that this is the last thing that interests them. When Brian, the PE teacher, explains that he and Kurt, the IT teacher, have volunteered to supervise the school disco, he is faced by his other colleagues' incomprehension. He explains, 'It's for the kids'; that once a year he likes to put something back into the school community. We then see Brian and Kurt at the disco confiscating cigarettes and alcohol from the children and loading it into their car. This scam provides them with a substantial stash, reinforcing the cynical perspective of their colleagues. There are no examples of teachers going the extra mile to help a deserving child. On the other hand, unlike many programmes, we do not see much from the children's point of view, so we have no sense that any of them are deserving. They are all presented as troublesome or irritating in some way or other.

The series also suggests that teachers are sexually and socially inadequate. Many are shown to be physically repulsive or to have disgusting habits. One episode begins with a belching competition in the local pub, a contest they all take seriously. Most of them smoke, lurking in a quiet corner of the school for a cigarette just like the children. These unattractive qualities are concentrated in the person of Bob, the head of English. He is overweight and balding, with a red, blubbery face. He smells and his clothes are filthy. At one point he Tippexes out the stains on his jacket. Obviously a failure, he has been turned down three times for the headship and we learn that he has not had sex for twenty-three years. All of the characters have marked social weaknesses – Penny is self-centred; Max is adulterous and selfish; Kurt and Brian have no success with women and their friendship is presented as a symbol of their failure, not of an independent single lifestyle – but Bob is a truly tragic figure. He has been living rough since his wife kicked him out. Unable to sort out his life, first he sleeps in his car, then he takes to breaking into the school and making little nests in the gymnasium and the office. This works metonymically, representing the idea that teachers do not exist outside school. He is knocked downstairs by kids who do not even realise what they have done. Everything about him screams, 'Loser.' This quality is demonstrated to us when we see him visiting, as he does every night once the pubs close, his old home, to shout abuse at his wife and her new partner. He rants about his injustices – the time and money he spent decorating the house and garden, only to be excluded now. Although he has clearly been wronged, this fact in itself, combined with his lack of dignity in facing those wrongs, makes him look pathetic, a born victim. To compound this impression of teachers as people with very limited social options, the highlight of his colleagues' day is hiding and watching his humiliation outside his old home, something they find amusing rather than pitiful. Most episodes show them killing time in the pub, and suggest there is little in their lives that is fulfilling or challenging. In one scene, the ambitious teacher Karen joins them for a drink. The regulars are engaged in conversational activities so mind-numbing that she thanks them for 'the uncanny recreation of my auntie Margaret's funeral'.

The teachers are also presented as sexually deprived and inadequate, reinforcing most children's view of them as people who could not possibly have sex. Kurt's romantic experiences are doomed: even his encounter with Liz, the terrifying school administrator, ends when she decides he is too disappointing to take on a second time, and then lets everyone know. They all also know that Brian has not had sex in six months. Meanwhile, the cuckolded Bob takes hope from the fact that Liz decides to bestow her favours on him. For a time, he seems to be reinstated as a human being, but it soon transpires that Liz was only using him as a diversion and she dumps him without compunction once she realises he is serious.

The programme is entertaining and many teachers enjoy it, believing perhaps that by presenting them as far from strait-laced and virtuous it rehabilitates them in a society that generally sees them as dull and overly intellectual. However, in rejecting one stereotype of the teacher – that of the geeky, earnest academic – it merely confirms another, perhaps even more damaging one. It shows teachers, purportedly through their own eyes, as lazy, unsuccessful people, devoid of professional commitment, callous and unable to build a meaningful life within or without school. In its own way, *Teachers'* view of the profession is as negative as that shown in *South Park*.

The bad

Horror may offer several examples of sad teachers, but it is riddled with evil ones. The teacher who is a murderer or not human seems to represent our fears about the powers that teachers have and the way in which they use them. When we are in school, teachers have the power to affect our daily lives, making them satisfying or desperately miserable. They also classify us, grade us and make decisions that profoundly influence our futures. This section looks at a number of facets of the bad teacher that emerge from horror/sci-fi texts, specifically *Class of 1999* (1989, directed by Mark Lester), the *Point Horror* series, *BtVS*, *Cherry Falls* and *The Faculty*. These representations often show teachers who are obsessive conformists, preoccupied with control and standardisation.

Class of 1999

Made in 1989, *Class of 1999* features a world in which school indiscipline has become so severe that many are surrounded by free-fire zones in which young people in gangs use automatic weapons and drive armoured vehicles. It focuses on an experiment sponsored by the Department of Educational Defense and Megatech, a cybernetics corporation, with the cooperation of Kennedy High's desperate headteacher. Megatech develops three androids, programmed to teach history, chemistry and physical education and to keep discipline.

The new teachers keep discipline by violently beating any students who fall out of line. They are not interested in the children as individuals, nor concerned about where the responsibility for any indiscipline may lie. For example, the PE teacher beats the hero for fighting although he was doing so to rescue the headteacher's daughter from rape. This unfair behaviour mirrors the actions of the school security guards, who brutalise students indiscriminately. But the androids have super-human strength and they begin to kill students who break or seem to break the rules. Their actions are monitored by the headteacher and the scientists who produced them. We see through the androids' eyes, revealing computer-like screens showing the decision-making processes they follow. The screens offer a choice: 'Educate' or 'Discipline'. They usually select the latter. In later incidents options for 'Kill' and 'Exterminate' start to appear. The androids demonstrate a frightening combination of human and inhuman qualities: the director of Megatech is delighted that they are reacting in unexpectedly human ways, mainly by becoming vindictive; at the same time they show an inhuman disregard for the feelings, motivations and right to life of the students.

This indiscriminate brutality embodies our fears about the arbitrary and disproportionate nature of teacher sanctions. It also suggests that a dangerous psychological shift takes place when teachers find themselves repeatedly trying to work in disruptive and ill-disciplined situations. The androids' vision screens start to include a graphical target, which identifies all students as 'the enemy', just as teachers may come to regard their relationship with students as eternally combative. An exchange between the headteacher, who is trying to stop the experiment, and Forrest, the sinister director of Megatech, encapsulates this:

HEAD: So they've been waging war with my students?
FORREST: Isn't that what all teachers do?

The point of view in this film is overwhelmingly that of the students, especially the ex-convict, ex-gang leader hero. By presenting teachers as androids, the film evades the need to consider the human problems facing schoolteachers working in this kind of environment. We see classrooms in which teachers are ignored or verbally abused, where drug dealing and violence are common. All attempts to deal with this by teachers and police have failed; daily life must be desperate for any teacher in this situation and yet the only sufferers shown are students. When the hero tries to inform his girlfriend that 'There are teachers who kill people,' she replies: 'You have a problem with authority figures.' That familiar phrase is often addressed to rebellious young people. Here, though, we know that he is right: the teachers really are out to get him. This subtly suggests that maybe all youngsters on the receiving end of such dismissive comments have just cause for their attitudes.

The whisperer

The second text comes from the teen horror book series *Point Horror*. Many of these texts are set in school or college, and the horrors in question include supernatural monsters, ghosts and especially evil human agents. These horrors can frequently be seen to embody and represent the fears and anxieties of young people about their lives in general and about school in particular. In *The whisperer* (Hoh, 1997), the representation of Dr Mathilde Stark suggests that teachers stifle students' personalities and reveals students' fear and resentment about the demands of academic work. Her portrayal polarises academic achievement and mental good health, epitomising the strong anti-academic tendencies of *Point Horror*. Her murderous practices merely confirm her students' perceptions about the teaching profession. They see her as a witch/monster from the beginning: 'I heard she mixes up a kettle of lethal brew and conjures up the ghosts of dead scientists whenever she needs to come up with a new ever more terrifying exam' (*ibid.*, p. 4). Stark has the power to damage because she can give grades which mean students lose their scholarships, their credibility with parents, their chance of a job. Interestingly, she is seen to be unfair simply because she sets high standards and marks carefully. Because of this, the novel, not just its student characters, presents her as a sick, disturbed woman. Is the implication that a more reasonable teacher would not have been so concerned about ensuring students could do the work before getting the grades? *Buffy the Vampire Slayer* includes similar attitudes, but takes a characteristically ironic stance that recognises their absurdity: Xander's complaint that testing 'Discriminates against the uninformed' is typical

('Band Candy', 3.6, written by Jane Esperson, directed by Michael Lange). The portrait of Dr Stark is complicated by her resentment of pleasure, prettiness and sexual allure. At the end she rants: 'All the same . . . all of them . . . vain silly things, in college for a good time . . . just want to be pretty and cute and popular' (*ibid.*, p. 186). Her severe hairstyle, thin lips and old-fashioned clothes are mocked by the fun-loving students. The stereotype presented is that of the resentful spinster teacher, one who cannot bear to see the pleasures experienced by her young female students. The implication in attacking her strict standards is that academic work and effort have no value in themselves, and that teachers' insistence on them results from their own frustrations and perversities. A woman like Dr Stark, who is respected academically, is assumed to be compensating for other inadequacies.

The Faculty

The Faculty turns the idea of the inhuman teacher into an extended metaphor that shapes the whole film by presenting the teachers as people whose bodies have been taken over by aliens that want to colonise the whole human population. The metaphorical basis of the movie is grounded in two related concepts. First, teachers are 'other': they have unpleasant, even terrifying qualities that make them appear subhuman to young people. Second, they are engaged in a process of attempting to change young people into less than fully human creatures themselves; they want to erase the individual humanity of the young. The process is simultaneously resisted and desired by the students, the latter because life is easier once you conform, something these alien teachers exploit when they try to capture the students.

The teachers in *The Faculty* may have been taken over by aliens, but their alien selves are related to their flawed human selves. Among their number are examples of most of the unpleasant teacher stereotypes. The football coach is characterised by macho aggression and cruelty and is first encountered before the alien takeover, bellowing at his team. He swears at students, tells them he wants them under pressure and focused or off his team. This viciousness is unchecked once he has been possessed. When he tries to turn the school principal, Miss Drake, into a fellow alien, he corners her in the darkened school in a scene filled with sexual innuendo. When he disturbs the hero Casey Connor, played by Elijah Wood, on the sports field he comments on his lack of interest in team sports. Casey's calm statement that people should run only when chased signals the discomfort many children feel with respect to enforced physical activity. The coach's response lingers on the idea of being chased, thus conveying a certain menace. Throughout there is the suggestion that this is a teacher who will hurt you if he can.

The alien transformation renders all the teachers disgusting. They become slimy, tentacled, reptilian monsters who die in a disgusting pool of white body fluids. Their dismembered limbs and joints scuttle about by themselves. However, some of this repulsiveness is projected on to the other qualities the teachers possess. This is most apparent in the case of the old and doddery Mrs Brummell. Horror is to some extent based on fear and disgust with respect to age, sickness and decay; and the teen horror genre is particularly effective because it contrasts healthy, vigorous youth with these darker realities. McCarron (2000) argues that the absence of old people and natural deaths in *Point Horror* is indicative of the adolescent's desire to strengthen the divide between the living and the dead: to create a world in which death is always accidental or supernatural and therefore avoidable. *The Faculty* might seem to fit with this, by presenting death as a result of alien destruction, but it is also possible to argue that Mrs Brummell embodies the young man's fear of ageing female sexuality. When the young, athletic Stan is in the shower, she comes in naked, covered in sores, and throws herself on him, crying and incoherent. Her face is hideous with scabs, and when Stan tries to comfort her by stroking her hair it comes away in a huge matted and bloody mass. Although the primary explanation for this is that she has been invaded by the alien parasites and her body cannot cope, the fact that the principal tries to explain her collapse by saying she had cancer supports the interpretation that the alien invasion itself could be read as sickness – cancer as a terrifying and destructive parasite – with teachers and adults the creatures who embody these terrors and therefore disgust the young.

Miss Burke and Mrs Olsen represent the depressed, repressed teacher. In some ways they could therefore be placed in the category of 'Sad' rather than 'Bad', and Miss Burke could certainly feature in 'Hot for teacher' (Chapter 5). They are dealt with here because they both become murderous once their inhibitions have been removed, suggesting that even feeble teachers are evil underneath. We first see Mrs Olsen failing to secure resources for her students (only the football team gets any funding). She twitters and flutters, mounting no effective opposition. Later, however, she stabs the principal with relish. Her mumsy exterior is cast aside as she dresses elegantly and adopts a sleek new hairstyle. Miss Burke is the stereotypical spinster literature teacher, oversensitive and afraid of the class. She confronts Zeke Tyler, the drug dealer played by Josh Hartnett, as he sells home-made 'hits' in the school car-park. The confrontation is completely ineffective, and he is not at all perturbed. He uses her shyness and sexual inexperience against her, offering to sell her some magnum-sized, cherry-flavoured condoms. She expresses her shock and retreats. Later, as an alien, she gains her revenge. Dressed vampishly in red, with bright red lipstick, she strides across campus insults him crudely, casting aspersions on his manhood, while hitting him. She corners him in the school bus at night. Although it is an attempt to turn him into an alien, it is presented as a sexual advance in which she uses seductive language and refers to the fruit-flavoured condoms he offered to sell her earlier. In spite of her youth and beauty, her sexual advances are repugnant, suggesting the kind of deep-seated anxiety about adult sexuality discussed in Chapter 4. This disgust is made manifest when her head is cut off and grows tentacles before scuttling with a comical repulsiveness across the car-park.

Mr Tate is the middle-aged cynical teacher, trying to get through the day with the minimum of effort. He does not care about the students or his fellow workers. Like Bob in *Teachers*, he drinks too much and his wife has left him. He enters the classroom listlessly, drinks from a mug we assume contains alcohol and reveals his drunkenness, lack of interest, or both by transposing the words of the topic to be studied. He then starts reading out a chapter from a book. There is no attempt to explain or elicit interest and no indication that any preparation has been done. Stan, the school's football star and supposedly not academic, realises this is the chapter they read the previous week. Mr Tate only sighs and shows no embarrassment. The only difference in his behaviour once he has been 'turned' is that he drinks water, rather than whisky, as the aliens die if they become dehydrated.

Finally, Miss Drake, the principal, is neither as vindictive as *BtVS*'s Snyder (discussed below) nor as foolish as his predecessor Flutie. But, like them and indeed most of the other non-heroic heads in popular fiction, she is a cynical pragmatist. Her opening speech to the faculty at the staff meeting allows no dialogue. The committee is not there to debate but to accept reality. She has already given up the fight for education, but she will run an efficient school and pay due attention to public relations. The football team, she tells them, will get all the resources it demands because it raises the profile of the school, and the school board and parents want to prioritise it.

Buffy the Vampire Slayer

The unflattering portrayal of the superficially liberal Bob Flutie in *BtVS* may have given some comfort to the American right in its fight for discipline and standards, but his disciplinarian replacement, Principal Snyder, fares no better. (Paule (2004) offers an interesting comparison between the two, in which she argues that they exemplify different aspects of sovereign and disciplinary power as categorised by Foucault.) The series includes incidents that overtly demonstrate young people's anxieties about the ways in which teachers treat them and exercise their power. At the same time, it uses exaggeration and its supernatural context to add a figurative dimension that reinforces the damage that a vindictive teacher can do. Four facets of Snyder's behaviour characterise the man and his embodiment of everything young people loathe and fear in a schoolteacher.

First, he proves that students' suspicions that teachers do not like them are true. Young people often indicate their conviction that a particular teacher holds them in personal dislike. While it is difficult to know whether this is true in specific cases, the widespread nature of this conviction may be indicative of children's recognition that the teacher does not love them and place them at the centre of the universe in the way that previous carers (parents, for example) have done, or simply resentment at the imposition of discipline or lack of praise. The humour in Snyder's portrayal comes from his open expression of dislike for students. After all, as was suggested earlier, it is usually implied that schoolteachers are in the business because they like children. In his first appearance (in 'Puppet Show', 1.9, written by Rob Des Hotel and Dean Batali, directed by Ellen S. Pressman), Snyder states: 'Kids. I don't like 'em. From now on you're gonna see a very different Sunnydale High: tight ship, clean, orderly and quiet.' The fact that this is interrupted by a scream announcing the discovery of yet another dead body on campus points us to the inevitable failure of his determination to control using discipline rather than understanding. It has been pointed out many times (Little, 2003; Kaveney, 2001; Money, 2002; Robinson, 2001) that the monsters, murderers and demons of Sunnydale represent the horrors of teen life, but also the chaotic impulses of the teens themselves (Jarvis, 2001). The body count in school, read this way, can be seen as representative of everything Snyder hates about children, and above all their refusal to be entirely within his control. He is clear that there is no personal affection in his relationship with students: 'A lot of educators tell students, "Think of your principal as your pal." I say, "Think of me as your judge, jury and executioner"' ('What's My Line, Part 1', 2.9, written by Howard Gordon and Marti Noxon, directed by David Solomon).

His dislike is compounded by a total lack of respect for the students' achievements: 'She's a student, what does she know?' ('School Hard', 2.3, written by David Greenwalt, directed by John T. Kretchmer). This is revealed in his extreme use of the sarcastic critical and personal comments that children particularly fear and dislike. Rather than encourage Xander, a relatively weak student, he says: 'Whatever comes out of your mouth is a meaningless waste of breath. An airborne toxic event.' Even when the students have succeeded, he cannot bring himself to praise them graciously, still seeing them as despicable and disorderly. His speech to them on graduation begins: 'Congratulations to the class of 1999. You all proved more or less adequate. This is a time of celebration, so sit still and be quiet. Spit out that gum. I saw that gesture, you see me after graduation' ('Graduation Day, Part 2', 3.22, written and directed by Joss Whedon).

Second, Snyder epitomises what young people may well see as an excessive concern with control and order on the part of school staff. Teachers have to be concerned with order and routine to manage large numbers of young people and to guarantee some kind of learning. This can sometimes seem to younger children like an incomprehensible imperative that takes no account of their needs and wishes: to wander about the classroom; to have a break; to talk when they have something to say and to eat when they feel hungry. Similarly, it may not take account of what young adults perceive to be matters of overwhelming importance. Snyder's inability to differentiate between issues that interrupt routine because they are of vital concern and rebellion or indiscipline is evident in the comic juxtaposition of sins in this statement: 'There are things I will not tolerate: students loitering on campus after school; horrible murders with hearts being removed. And also smoking' ('Puppet Show', 1.9).

He is clearly meant to be a ludicrous example of a right-wing disciplinarian and sees the inability to control people as a weakness that can lead to destruction: 'Kids today need discipline. That's an unpopular word these days, "discipline". I know Principal Flutie would have said, "Kids need understanding. Kids are human beings." That's the kind of woolly headed, liberal thinking that leads to being eaten' ('Puppet Show', 1.9).

Ultimately, Snyder's obsession with control proves as dangerous for him as lack of it was for Flutie. He goes into denial when the world does not conform to his wishes. At graduation, the mayor transforms into a gigantic demon in the form of a snake and starts eating the students. A battle breaks out while Snyder blusters: 'This is not orderly, this is not discipline. (*To the mayor*) You're on my campus, buddy, and when I say I want quiet, I want . . . (*The mayor swallows him*)' ('Graduation Day, Part 2', 3.22).

This obsession with control fuels the third of his appalling characteristics: his disregard for justice and the pleasure he takes in punishment. Like the androids in *Class of 1999*, he is not interested in individuals' culpability. He labels people and holds them responsible without evidence. When Buffy stops a shooting at school, he turns on her, accusing her of inciting the fight. In response to her protests, he replies: 'I'm a truth seeker. I've got a missing gun and two confused kids on my hands. Pieces of the puzzle. And I'm gonna look at all the pieces carefully and rationally. And I'm gonna keep looking until I know exactly how all this is your fault' ('I Only Have Eyes for You', 2.19, written by Marti Noxon, directed by James Whitmore). However extreme the example may be, it echoes the concerns sometimes expressed by children and older students that teachers blame them for everything, even when it is not their fault. An unjust accusation results in Buffy's expulsion, something Snyder enjoys enormously. Indeed, his unjust behaviour seems to be caused in part by the sheer pleasure he enjoys from doling out punishment. When Buffy's mother challenges his right to expel her daughter he replies: 'I have not only the right, but also a nearly physical sensation of pleasure at the thought of keeping her out of school. I'd describe myself as tingly' ('Dead Man's Party', 3.2, written by Marti Noxon, directed by James Whitmore).

The fourth striking characteristic is that Snyder puts school, team and above all his and the school's prestige above the well-being of individuals, for whom he has no compassion. We see here the student's fear that his/her individuality is sacrificed at school. This is most noticeable in 'Go Fish' (2.11, written by David Fury and Elin Hampton, directed by David Semel), in which Snyder rebukes Willow, who has been standing in for the computer teacher and working extremely hard. In spite of this, he argues she has no school spirit because she has failed a member of the swimming team (who has shown neither application nor aptitude). Snyder does not even value swimming team members as individuals, however. When two of the boys appear to have been eviscerated, he insists it is a great tragedy but fails to remember one of their names while trying to disguise his obsession with the championship by claiming that continuing in it is what the boys would have wanted.

This is not an isolated incident. His desire to efface individuality is evident from his first appearance, when he labels Buffy and her friends as antisocial people who should integrate more with the rest of the school. Indeed, this emphasis on loss of individuality, while enforced by Snyder, is fundamental to the first three seasons of *BtVS*. They operate an extended metaphor that presents the educational system itself as vampiric. Institutionalised education serves only to destroy the individuality of the students, sucking the life from them. The actual vampires lurking beneath and around the school provide a physical representation of this. Students may end up dead as a result of their encounter with vampirism, alienated conformists; or they may be the undead, having transformed themselves into dangerous and destructive outsiders. The metaphor reaches its climax, fittingly, on graduation day. The consummation of their high school learning is turned into a literal consummation – of the students by the mayor, the epitome of civic power and authority, who, assisted by vampire aides, sets out to eat the entire year-group.

It is a powerful metaphor for the results of years of institutionalised learning. If this thought-quenching educational system has worked properly, then graduation will mean that these wayward, chaotic, rampaging teenagers will finally have their identities devoured and destroyed by the adult world, gobbled up by conformity and complacency. The Vampire Slayer and her allies, however, have worked at developing alternative knowledges that enable them to resist. They know how to destroy the mayor and the vampires and work together (a consistent feature of the resistance demonstrated in this programme) to put this into practice. The metaphor of consummation is subverted as they create an explosion that burns down the school, destroying the evil mayor and symbolically rejecting the school's approach to education.

Cherry Falls

This teen slasher/horror movie is set in a small town where a serial killer is preying on teenagers from the local high school. The killer targets only virgins (we know this because he carves 'virgin' on the inside of their thigh). The central character is Jody, the sheriff's daughter. A statement from her boyfriend, Kenny, brings a number of disparate ideas together: 'You lose your spiritual virginity when you realise your parents are even bigger hypocrites than your friends are.' An examination of the horror plot and the characterisation of the parents and teachers shows how this movie (in spite of its claim to be different) highlights the underlying disgust, fear and disappointment that can characterise young people's relationships with adults. The horror is in many ways a metaphor for the horrible and dangerous realities facing young people who cannot forgive the adults in their lives for their imperfections, particularly their sexual flaws. It is necessary to detail some of the plot to make the point clear.

Jody is apparently surrounded by caring adults, but the opening murder of two innocent lovers makes the viewer aware that the protective adults have failed these two and that, indeed, at least one adult is a murderer. Werndley (2003) shows how the *Point Horror* series depends on absent or inadequate parents and often features daughters' anger towards their mothers for getting old, and may incorporate incestuous desires for the father as a subtext. This thesis can, however, be applied to teen horror more generally. It is soon apparent in *Cherry Falls* that all the adults are flawed: Jody's mother smokes, drinks too much and flirts with Jody's boyfriend; her father is unreasonably strict; the school principal proves he is more interested in discipline than in saving students' lives when he refuses to reveal that virgins have been targeted. This focus on public relations above all else is a common trait in senior managers in horror (see also *Urban Legend* (1998, directed by Jamie Blanks), *The Faculty* and *BtVS*), perhaps reflecting a common belief that managers put the good of the school before the good of the students.

There are hints of desire/incest in Jody and the sheriff's behaviour, although there is always an innocent explanation for their actions. He comes to her bedroom late at night, asking her intimate questions about her love-life, which she answers in a husky voice. He gives her self-defence classes that result in him lying on top of her in a manner that is clearly meant to be evocative of a sexual encounter. Jody has refused to have sex with her long-term boyfriend Kenny and is clearly fixated on Daddy. When she learns that the killer looks like Laura, a woman her father and a number of other prominent citizens, including the principal, raped while they were all still at school, she turns to Kenny, to whom she offers her virginity. When he refuses because she is clearly doing this in a state of distress and anger, she runs to the sensitive teacher Mr Marleston.

Kenny has already noted that she has a crush on Marleston. He represents an alternative adult masculinity from that offered by her father. The latter is conservative, disciplined and conventionally masculine, while Marleston has spectacles, floppy hair, delicate features and can quote poetry. Unlike Snyder in *BtVS*, he is interested in the children's feelings and encourages them to share their thoughts and emotions in class after their friends are murdered. He is also, of course, the serial killer, the brutalised son of the rape victim, revenging himself on the hypocritical town that covered up his mother's tragedy and especially on the man he believes may be his father (and Jody's). Speaking about his villain, the director states: 'I think we have the first liberal psychopath in the history of the genre' (Roddick, 2000). This is one of the interesting features of a film that received very mixed reviews. Typically, villainous teachers are conservative bullies: Snyder and Maggie Walsh in *BtVS*; Mr Vernon in *The Breakfast Club*; Miss Trunchbull in *Matilda* (1996, directed by Danny de Vito); Mr Cleary in *School Ties* (1992, directed by Robert Mandes); Coach in *The Faculty*. By choosing an apparently gentle and liberal teacher and revealing him to be a brutal killer, the film suggests that *no* teachers can be trusted. Jody says, 'You're just about the only person I trust these days,' minutes before he punches her in the face. The sexual overtones in his relationship with Jody (the lingering eye contact in early scenes and the kiss he presses on her once she is strapped down and screaming) combine with the recapping of the rape story to indicate a strong suspicion of male sexuality. Indeed, this apparently liberal tale, which promoted its reversal of the standard 'punish the sexually active girl' motif with its whole-school 'Pop Your Cherry Ball', seems to suggest that male sexual desire is perverse, dangerous and indistinguishable from violence. The only male who comes out of it well is Kenny, the boy who refused to act on his desires. He is allowed to rescue Jody at one point, and we see them embracing after Marleston has been killed.

The film suggests that teachers, the adults who are *in loco parentis* and supposed to protect and care for you, are too weak and morally flawed to succeed. Moreover, it indicates that they have sexual desires that are violent, shocking and disgusting. (The principal is a rapist and Jody's admired Mr Marleston is a cross-dressing serial killer into bondage and disfiguring his victims.) This contrasts with many of the comically presented encounters between teenage partners, culminating in the 'Pop Your Cherry Ball', where sex is largely fun and girls, rather than boys, call the shots. Indeed, the film presents an uneasy tension between showing sexual initiation on the whole as a slightly comic event in which boys are fairly helpless and incompetent (the school's most sexually experienced female student calls all the girls together and explains that the boys will be pretty useless) and one in which the boys are seen as licensed by a hypocritical community to prey on girls from the wrong side of the tracks. This tension is part of the film's (relatively unsophisticated) feminist message. The distinction between nice middle-class girls and others that made it possible for Laura's rape to occur and then be concealed is presented as an injustice that has infected the whole community, because the whole community covered it up. Males are dangerous, and women must fight back because there won't be any men to save them. Jody, in spite of her girlishness, physically fights Marleston in the denouement and pushes him off a balcony, apparently to his death. The sheriff is dead, as is one of his male colleagues; but his female deputy saves the day when Marleston recovers from his fall.

Summary

There are various discourses concerning bad teachers and they cannot be brought together to make a single story. To some extent, particularly in texts aimed at young people, the sad or the bad teacher simply represents youth's fear of age and decay. The hairy nostrils, gross figures, wobbly jowls, poor dress sense, sexual predations and strong odours that characterise images of schoolteachers signal considerable disgust and anxiety with respect to maturity and adulthood. However, the extensive fear of, disgust and dissatisfaction with, and contempt for teachers that are manifest in popular culture go beyond anxiety about maturity. It is possible to interpret these portrayals as indications of individual, social and political concerns about teachers.

Conformity and cruelty

The idea that teachers seek to quell students' individuality and freedom is shown repeatedly in popular culture. As Principal Robin Wood in *BtVS* ironically states: 'Got to get back to deadening young minds' ('Lessons', 7.1). This repression of individuality often features as a metaphor underpinning the entire text. The teachers attempt to turn the students into automaton-like vessels for aliens (*The Faculty*); the school harbours vampires who suck the life from the pupils (*BtVS*); teachers would rather students were dead than rebellious (*Class of 1999*). Texts such as these and *South Park* contribute to a radical discourse in which the presentation of teachers repressing student individuality can be understood in the light of the work of such Marxist philosophers as Althusser (1969), who argued that while there are a few heroic individual teachers who struggle to encourage resistance in their pupils, the majority are unwitting servants of capitalism. The popular texts examined here, particularly *BtVS*, *South Park* and *The Faculty*, lend themselves well to these interpretations, in which teachers serve the interests of a capitalist hegemony, ensuring that children learn to become compliant workers, accepting the need to subjugate their own desires to those of the organisation.

Read from a more individualistic perspective, these questions of repression and control are also part of a liberal discourse, indicative perhaps of resentment in the Anglophone psyche concerning the individual repression and restrictions inevitably experienced in any mass education system. Focusing a fairly large group of people on a common purpose (learning something determined by the state, not the individual) requires the suppression of personal desires and preferences, regardless of the practice of 'differentiation' and the current interest in individual learning styles. A degree of discomfort and resentment is almost inevitable, as teachers are employed to make people do things they would not necessarily choose to do at that point in time, even where there is reasonable consensus about the general value of education.

Related to this repression is the widespread portrayal of teachers as vindictive, cruel and unjust. They are often portrayed as less than human, lacking the capacity for empathy. If teachers cause suffering, whatever their intentions, in a mass system that does not give them time or scope for understanding or responding to the desires, fears and needs of individuals, it is not surprising that, at an unconscious level at least, many people think of them as cruel or uncaring. Films like *Class of 1999* present an extreme version of these fears, in which the tensions between students' need to express themselves and teachers' need to control them leads to complete breakdown of communication and understanding until each side views the other as the enemy. Both radical and liberal discourses stand in opposition to much current policy, which seeks to increase rather than reduce standardisation in terms of curriculum and student performance. In the UK, the Training and Development Agency for Schools (TDA, 2007) has published standards which are detailed and itemised, and it can reasonably be assumed that the state has decreed that 'bad' teaching is teaching that fails to achieve these standards. They require teachers to be knowledgeable; sensitive to individuals and to cultural and ethnic differences; to respect pupils; and to communicate effectively not only with children but with parents and carers. In popular culture it is the bad teachers who stick rigidly to the rules and to the curriculum, rather than working flexibly and imaginatively in response to the interests of their students.

Failing teachers

There is another cluster of themes prevailing in popular texts. Rather than showing that teachers are the source of suffering and threat, they vilify them for failing to protect the young from such dangers. These representations form part of a larger discourse about childhood and child protection, and about the moral corruption of young people. The media is riddled with concerns about dangers to children and with anxieties that the young have fallen prey to the evils of drugs, sex and crime.

Teachers have a great deal to live up to: they are expected to prepare children for life and to enable them to succeed; to model good living and behaviour; to control children's destructive impulses towards themselves and others. In popular culture, we express our disappointment that they fail to be the charismatic heroes and the inspirational saints we want them to be; that they are human beings merely doing a job. The message pervading the television series *Teachers* is just this: teachers are doing a job like anyone else, and doing it with no more commitment, brilliance or enthusiasm than many other people do their jobs. The humour of the series is built entirely on the fact that we do not expect this; we think teachers, like priests and nurses, should be more dedicated to their work and less fallible than the average person.

Teachers are, of course, associated with knowledge, so it comes as a shock to some children to realise that their teachers may not be expert on everything they are expected to teach, particularly in a system that has shortages and understaffing. Popular culture suggests teachers fail young people by being ignorant. People who discover their teacher is wrong or has only a limited understanding of a topic and relies on the textbook may find it hard to respect the teacher for what they *do* know. Thus, we see *South Park*'s Mr Garrison presented as an ignoramus. In *The Faculty*, Mr Tate shows a complete lack of awareness of his subject; Miss Burke is unable to recognise multiple interpretations of the book they are reading in English; and Stan receives no encouragement for his desire to learn – the staff are happy for him to focus on football, even though his grades are poor.

Above all, perhaps, teachers never live up to the expectation that they will protect young people from harm. When children are small it may seem that the schoolteacher really can protect them from physical and mental danger. As dangers become more complex and social pressures more extensive, however, teachers are faced with an impossible task. Thus, they may be presented, like the teachers in *BtVS* or *Scary Movie*, as people who do not see the terrible dangers stalking children; people who are part of a conspiracy to deny the horrific realities of one's daily existence (*Urban Legend* or *The Faculty*). Or they may be shown as people whose efforts are pathetic in the face of the demands of the real world (Mr Garrison and Mr Mackie in *South Park*); who cannot control the terrifying, powerful, destructive urges that fuel young people (Principal Flutie in *BtVS*; Principal Himbry in *Scream*); or who simply do not care about danger (Principal Snyder in *BtVS*).

4   High school confidential

A secondary school is a kind of hormonal soup. All those bodies pressed in on one another – bubbling with puberty and low level adolescent fantasy – are bound to produce a certain *atmosphere*.

(Heller, 2003, p. 53)

Introduction

When the film *High School Confidential* (directed by Jack Arnold) was released in 1958 it reflected both anxieties and excitement within America. Lloyd (2002) states: '*Film Review* declared, "The film is itself a social evil" and decried its "ghastly nihilism" and the suggestion that "the primitivism of urban polyglots has become the American norm".' The film opened with Jerry Lee Lewis playing rock 'n' roll from the back of a truck. Its key ingredients were a high school setting, rebellious teenagers with 'difficult' backgrounds, cars, gangs, fights, knives and, daringly at the time, drugs. While it contains a lecture on the perils of 'marijuana addiction', its appeal would rest on its 'danger', and what Lloyd refers to as a 'vicarious unwholesomeness'. Indeed, as Lloyd points out, the US Commissioner for Narcotics required that a cautionary anti-drug prologue should accompany screenings. That school should be the context of 'sex 'n' drugs 'n' rock 'n' roll' made the film all the more outrageous to middle-aged Middle America, and all the more appealing to its teen audience.

Schools and colleges are places where peer relationships assume immense importance. Friendships (and enmities) are developed, hierarchies are established, groups and sports teams that support the ethos of the institution are formed, as are oppositional networks. These interactions, filled with complex feelings and emotions, including ambition and disappointment, achievement and anxiety, joy and despair, have long provided inspiration for film-makers.

The film *Blackboard Jungle* (directed by Richard Brooks) appeared in 1955 and is perhaps the best known of the 1950s high school dramas. The decade aw, co-terminus with the birth of rock 'n' roll, a glut of 'teen exploitation' movies, many of which naturally contained a school/education element. Often the school was the central focus, and *High School Confidential* was followed in America by *High School Hellcats* (1958, directed by Edward L. Bernds), *High School Big Shot*

(1959, directed by Joel Rapp) and *High School Caesar* (1960, directed by O'Dale Ireland).

A number of school/education-based or -related films had enjoyed commercial and critical success on both sides of the Atlantic prior to the 1950s, but many of these were light comedies. Although some suggested anxiety about young people, they also included productions such as *Goodbye, Mr Chips* (1939, directed by Sam Wood), based on James Hilton's 1934 novel of the same title (Hilton, 1984), in which youth is in many respects idealised. The post-war decades saw a succession of school-based dramas, romances and comedies. Most mainstream offerings included an element of romance. It is now possible for a film to be fairly explicit about sex between young people (*American Pie*, 1999, directed by Paul Weitz, for example) and still be regarded as a comedy. *Porkys* (1981, directed by Bob Clark) featured a group of students preoccupied by sex. *Clueless* (1995, directed by Amy Heckerling) provided social satire as a rich Beverly Hills schoolgirl learned that there was more to life than plastic surgery and shopping. Loosely based on the plot of Jane Austen's 1815 novel *Emma* (Austen, 2003), the film celebrates heterosexual romance as a medium for the redemption of shallow womanhood. In *Romy and Michele's High School Reunion* (1997, directed by David Mirkin), two young women travel to their high school reunion to 'show off' and confront their pasts (including the bullies), and discover that the sexual pecking order has reversed. *She's All That* (1999, directed by Robert Iscove) demonstrates the relationship between wealth and sexual popularity when a male student takes a bet that he can transform a girl from nerd to prom queen. *Mean Girls* (2004, directed by Mark Waters) reinforces this perspective, focusing on a new girl's efforts to join the 'in-crowd' with a view to subverting the 'top girl' and being accepted. It is clear that the 'top girls' are rich and upper-middle class. These films and others, such as *Ten Things I Hate About You* (1999, directed by Gil Junger), have light-hearted plots that function as frameworks for the romantic teen relationships that take centre stage. *American Pie*, however, with its predominantly male perspective, needs no such framework, taking as its narrative force the boys' desire to have sex before they leave high school. These films have different takes on particular issues, but all promote the importance of romance and heterosexuality for a secure and happy identity. Love and good character, they suggest, can overcome class, cultural and racial differences, promoting a worldview that fails to treat the material realities associated with these factors with much respect.

UK-produced school comedy films generally incorporate elements of romance, too, but not at the centre of the plot. They have included Frank Launder's classic *The Belles of St Trinian's* (1954) (and its sequels), which relies for its humour on the reversal of the stereotype of schoolgirl virtue and innocence, and *Carry On Teacher* (1959), an early offering in the bawdy series. *Please Sir* (1971) grew out of the British television situation comedy series (1968–1972) of the same title. *Bend It Like Beckham* (2002), unusually, features a British girl from an Indian family as the central character. Her romance with her football coach is significant, but not as important as the focus on her ambition and the challenges this creates for her family.

Drugs rarely feature in mainstream comedy fare, which underlines that the combination of schoolchildren and drug consumption is a serious matter. The underage consumption of alcohol, on the other hand, is often treated more lightly.

Sex and education: the social context

Young people's sexual practices are considered to be a matter for public scrutiny and control. They are not treated as private or apolitical. In the UK and the US, they are the subject of fierce debate in which schools are implicated as guardians of children's morals and sources of information about sex. The prominent voices in this debate are those of a liberal establishment (possibly more liberal in the UK than in the US) and the religious right (particularly, in the UK, Christian and Muslim groups). Liberal voices, epitomised by organisations such as the Brook Advisory Council, advocate discussion of sexual matters among young people and exposure to a range of information, coupled with the opportunity to access contraception and advice about safe sexual practices. They generally claim that sexual promiscuity and unwanted pregnancy are reduced by such information given in a context that stresses the importance of committed heterosexual relationships, particularly marriage. The religious right differs by seeing sex outside marriage as intrinsically wrong, rather than a matter for discussion: it is a sin; perpetrators are fornicators; and unmarried mothers are a source of shame. The 'Silver Ring' campaign, in which young people pledge to virginity before marriage, has received state funding in some parts of the US. The campaign has now spread to Europe, which already had its own 'family values' activists (such as Victoria Gillick in the UK, who has long opposed liberal sex education and access to contraception for young people).

A recent case in which a fourteen-year-old girl in the UK obtained an abortion without her parents' consent brought the tensions over teenage sexual activity into the spotlight. Pundits supporting the parents (who were outraged) and the medical practice appeared in the media to defend their respective positions. Although liberal groups differ from religious groups about the moral status of sexual acts and the way to educate young people, they often share, to some extent, their desire to promote marriage and the family, and usually profess a commitment to encouraging young people to locate their sexual behaviour within a committed heterosexual relationship. Alternative voices are muted in the educational context. The notorious Clause 28 of the Local Government Act (1988) made it illegal in the UK to 'promote homosexuality' in educational establishments, which in practice meant that many teachers were afraid even to discuss different sexual orientations, and felt unable to support young people coming to terms with their identity as homosexual. The clause was repealed in Scotland in 2002 and in the rest of the UK the following year. The pleasures of sex, too, are generally ignored in the official school curriculum, in favour of a focus on its dangers, or on reproductive biology. In practice, many teachers have been flexible in order to respond to the concerns of young people, but the official discourses are relatively narrow.

Popular culture and girls' identities

Society at large is very concerned with sex and the school pupil, seeing this as an issue that affects the moral well-being of everyone. It appears to restrict the range of sexual identities available to young people to those that are compatible with a social order built around marriage and the family. The role of popular culture in this process is particularly associated with Angela McRobbie (1982). Her early work on girls' cultural practices showed how magazines such as *Jackie* helped to perpetuate a view of girls' lives that saw a relationship with a boy as the main focus and essential to happiness. Girls' magazines were also implicated in the construction of a type of femininity that offered restrictive role models. Yet, even at that time, McRobbie noted a reaction against school disapproval of specifically feminine fun, such as wearing make-up and taking an interest in fashion. Similarly, Linda Christian-Smith (1993) noted that girls' consumption of teen romances (such as *Sweet Valley High* and *Point Romance* novels) often occurred in opposition to school culture. These are almost always 'school' stories, in so far as that is where they are set, yet school is a mere backdrop for the most important business of a girl's life: getting the right boyfriend.

Frith and McRobbie (1990) noted that counter-cultural music, such as rock, is associated with boys, whereas mainstream pop is associated with girls. This offers girls a limited interpretation of female sexuality. The persistent popularity of boy bands with young girls suggests that, to some extent, this phenomenon persists. It is possible for young people to construct different identities, however, and as Reay's (2001) study of primary school girls and boys has shown, there are many competing discourses that construct gender identities at an early age. Young people have influences from home and family, and may well participate in more transgressive counter-cultural activities. Walkerdine's (1997) analysis of the way young girls use popular culture indicates that this is a complex process. She notes, for example, that groups such as the Spice Girls offer models of power and friendship for girls, not just the more obvious sexual objectification. McRobbie's later work on this topic (1994) noted that contemporary girls' magazines offered a wider variety of opportunities for girls to express and reconstruct themselves through fashion. Our examination of the representation of sexual/romantic relationships between school students in popular culture suggests that there is still a limited range of sexual identities on offer to young people. It seems worthwhile to identify and analyse the mainstream images, however, simply because these discourses are so prominent and extensively distributed. They do not represent everyone's behaviour, or everyone's point of view, but they provide insight into some dominant ideas and concerns about relationships.

Film, television and popular music are accessible and ubiquitous media that confront us with a succession of representations of the 'private sphere' of relationships and moral choices in educational contexts. These are reproduced across genres. The analyses in this chapter focus first on teen horror, with particular reference to the first three seasons of *Buffy the Vampire Slayer*, and then on popular music.

Dangerous dates and daring daughters: love and sex in teenage horror

> They feel more in danger from having sex and being in school than from possible nuclear war.
>
> (McBride, 2000, pp. 10–11)

Teen horror seems to have adopted many features characteristic of an almost obsolete fictional form aimed at older women. Russ (1973) described a popular romantic sub-genre, the 'modern Gothic', in which a young woman, often married to a relative stranger and living in a remote house, finds her life and sanity mysteriously threatened. Invariably the young woman does not know whether the passionate stranger she has married loves her or is trying to kill her. The prime example is Daphne du Maurier's 1938 novel *Rebecca* (du Maurier, 2003).

This sub-genre had almost vanished by the mid-1970s (Thurston, 1987), but many of its features have resurfaced in teenage horror. This reappearance could be indicative of changes in the social and sexual behaviour of teenage girls that make their circumstances akin to those of their newly married foremothers. In modern Gothic, the mysterious mansion itself embodied the heroine's insecurities as she tried to adapt to her new life, community and emerging womanhood. The 'accommodation' represented the ambiguous nature, appealing and terrifying, of her 'accommodation' to her situation. The Gothic mansion the young woman entered was a private domestic space, the domain of a patriarch: guardian, husband or father. Her fears concerned her role in this community, and particularly her fears about sex and the dangers associated with desire and being desired. Analyses of the significance of the home in eighteenth-century or modern Gothic texts reveal understandable fears about male oppression manifest in these 'Gothic prisons' (Kilgour, 1995, p. 76). In the same way, detailed analyses of the location of teenage horror show teenage, particularly teenage girls', fears and preoccupations manifest in the physical location of the stories.

In teenage Gothic, these 'accommodation' anxieties are often translated into educational settings, schools that are resonant of Gothic mansions, with dark corridors, secret rooms and, especially, underworlds – mysterious basements or tunnels undermining the superficially secure institutions. Repeatedly, stories feature a new girl in school (see the first episode of *BtVS*). Schools are peculiar mixtures of public and private worlds. On the one hand, they are communities, with rules, hidden shared understandings, traditions and characters. On the other, particularly in the case of large, anonymous, US schools, such as Buffy's Sunnydale and those so often featured in the *Point Horror* series, they are places with unvisited sections and unknown fellow students. Their vastness is appealing, suggestive of possibilities open to the teenager, the space which is the future. These uncertainties can be frightening, too, but they lack the claustrophobic terror of the family home writ large which characterises the modern Gothic. They are mini-societies, not mini-families. The schoolgirl does not have a predetermined 'role' like the bride, daughter or dependent relative of the Gothic novel. She has instead to negotiate a role for herself: brainbox, cheerleader, athlete, social success. There are tensions between different friendship groups, anxieties about acceptance and uncertainty about where she fits and who she is. The terrifying school building, with its confusing, echoing corridors in which children get lost and face dangers, represents the teenager's fears of losing herself, of failing to 'find a place', of being 'out of place'.

We see, therefore, in *BtVS* and *Point Horror*, a reflection of some of the social changes affecting young women in the last forty years. Fears still focus on negotiating a gendered and sexualised place, but this is in a wider community, not a household. As Topping (2004) illustrates, *BtVS* is about being an outsider. It translates these concerns into specifically supernatural stories (for example, 'Out of Mind; Out of Sight', 1.11, deals with a girl so lonely and ignored that she becomes invisible), but the theme permeates the series. Buffy is an outsider, as a new girl and because of her special calling, and her friends are all marginalised in the school.

Moreover, this 'outsider' status is the context in which anxieties about relationships with the opposite sex are placed. The intensity of desire for the 'other' needs to be understood as a need to connect – you are judged by your ability to attract a girlfriend or boyfriend. At the same time, young people are rendered even more vulnerable by the strength of their sexual feelings and the possibilities of rejection, humiliation or physical harm. Anxieties about uncontrollable desires surface in teenage horror in a recurrent character – the dangerous, or apparently dangerous, hero. The modern Gothic, Modleski (1990) argues, builds on unequal power relations in traditional marriage. It deals, typically, with the early stages of married life. The young heroine has cause to suspect her new husband is dangerous, possibly a murderer. While Modleski, taking a psychoanalytical approach, links the heroine's search for the truth about her husband with women's ambivalence towards fathers, there are other possible explanations for the genre's appeal. The anxieties explored by the Gothic offered women the opportunity to work imaginatively through experiences which, although unconnected with their own literal realities, reflected the emotional relationships and psychological anxieties they experienced in the early married state. During the heyday of the modern Gothic, the sexual freedom of women was often curtailed, and men remained, for many, an unknown quantity, while the sexual act was shrouded in mystique, exciting but fearsome.

It is not surprising to encounter fictions in which these opposites of fear and attraction are juxtaposed in the person of the husband/hero. The heroine's task is to work out whether this man is her friend or her enemy – to get to know the mysterious 'other' just as newly married women had to get to know the husbands by whom they had been courted, but with whom they had not experienced sexual and domestic intimacy. First sexual experiences within these marriages might well be painful and/or frightening. The popular Gothic romance mirrors this dilemma: is the husband's sexual behaviour motivated by love or violent and aggressive intent? In teen horror, the focus moves to the boyfriend, suspected of being a monster or a murderer, a device used, for example, in such films as *Scream* and *Cherry Falls*.

Modern Gothic's renaissance in teenage television and books could be explained by shifting patterns in sexual experience. Today in the UK, for example, approximately 23 per cent of children claim to have had their first sexual experience before the age of sixteen (Channel 4, *Generation Sex*, June/July 2000). Girls and boys are educated together but keep socially separate at school (Renold, 1997; Skelton, 1997) until they begin to form romantic and sexual relationships. Thus, the opposite sex retains some mystique, and early sexual encounters take place amid the kind of unfamiliarity (see Ingham *et al.*, 1991, for an account of how little young people know about their sexual partners) that characterised some marriages during the period when the modern Gothic was popular.

The picture is complicated by the mix of hostility and seduction, sexual bullying and sexual desire, which comprises relationships between schoolboys and schoolgirls (Larkin, 1994; Channel 4, *Generation Sex*). Incidents of sexual harassment have been recorded even in primary schools (Skelton, 1997). Girls are therefore faced with situations in which they do not know whether the sexual advances of boys are indicative of attraction, affection, friendship, some genuine desire to build a relationship, or contempt and the wish to 'score'. This comment from a seventeen-year-old girl is telling: 'You're frightened . . . all the lads are there, shouting at you and calling you names like a slag. It's really bad. My mate got jumped on and they were lifting her skirt and everything and trying to put love-bites on her' (Wallace, 1992, p. 18). It does not take much imagination to see the vampires of Sunnydale, who also make you afraid to go outside, jump on you and bite you, as metaphors for this kind of male behaviour. When Buffy acquires telepathic powers ('Earshot', 3.18), her ears are bombarded by the sexualised, hate-filled wishes of the boys around her. Yet, these young men also constitute the young women's best hope of sexual pleasure. Aggression and desire are yoked together. It is not surprising, therefore, that Buffy is such an appealing character among girls. She has her cake and eats it. She walks the streets unafraid, repeatedly reminding everyone she can take care of herself, but she also has a relationship with Angel, one of the most powerful vampires.

Teen horror narratives often centre on the heroine's uncertainty about boys; they appear to suggest that forging relationships with boys should be the central concern of a girl's life, as do teen romances (Christian-Smith, 1993). A closer examination, however, reveals resistance to and anxiety about these relationships, grounded in girls' concerns about potential inequalities in the way relationships are constructed.

Buffy's relationship with Angel epitomises the horror story centred on the schoolgirl with the dangerous boyfriend. Angel tends to emerge broodingly from the shadows, say little and cast dark looks which suggest hidden knowledge, while lounging about provocatively. He is a schoolgirl's fantasy – a mysterious, attractive, mature (he is a couple of centuries old) man with whom to impress her friends. The vampire, of course, connotes forbidden sexuality in a multiplicity of ways (Dyer, 1988; Rickels, 1999; Wisker, 1998), which only serves to intensify the aura of sexual danger which surrounds Angel. He is the wolf to Buffy's Little Red Riding Hood. He fascinates and attracts her, but, ultimately, once she has had sex with him, he literally threatens to devour her, reverting to his vampiric habits.

Buffy's first sexual experience is romanticised, soft focus and discussed beforehand with her girlfriend. Jowett (2005, p. 153) notes that Angel's alienation, combined with 'his new man sensitivity', makes him a 'Romantic hero'. But he transforms after coitus from young girl's dream to callous vampire, fulfilling three fears: that sex is violence; that the boy will cease to value the girl after sex; and that the act itself will be much less important to him than to her. Angel's reversion to vampirism is accompanied by speeches asserting that this is just one of many encounters he has had, that Buffy was inadequate as a lover and that their relationship is unimportant. He changes from a caring, sensitive lover to a cold individual, disparaging Buffy to his fellow vampires. Thereby another common fear surfaces: that the girl will become the object of salacious gossip.

The Buffy story, as it appears in the first three seasons, might be read superficially as having the same message as Little Red Riding Hood: that girls will be damaged if they enter sexual relationships. But *BtVS* is more ambiguous and interesting than the earlier tale. For instance, Buffy never needs a woodcutter: she dispatches creatures of the night herself by combining supernatural powers and self-disciplined martial-arts training. Furthermore, Angel cannot kill her, but she could kill him (and does, eventually). The series conveys the message that the schoolgirl's fears about men may be realised in that they will prove predatory and cruel, but the girl should be able to fight back. The ambiguity is compounded by the emphasis placed on the reason for Angel's transformation after sex: he is subject to an ancient curse which robs him of his soul if he experiences one moment of complete happiness. So his transformation results from the pleasure of the sexual encounter he later disparages. The story therefore manages to have it all. The heroine is truly loved, sexually valued, powerful and able to look after herself. Yet, the hero remains an object of desire because he is unattainable. At the moment of consummation, his soul is stolen and he becomes metaphorically absent so the story can continue.

Buffy's status as a feminist icon has been much discussed: see, for example, Cocca (2003), Daugherty (2001), Early (2002), Marinucci (2003), Playden (2001), Vint (2002), Wilcox (2001). Although her consumerism, heterosexuality and use of violence have created difficulties for some feminists, she is generally seen as someone who offers a powerful alternative to the passivity of earlier heroines. Later seasons provide further material for the analysis of this question, but are not set when Buffy is a schoolgirl.

Stories focusing on dangerous heroes often reveal fears about inequality in male–female relationships. Although Buffy is capable of killing her hero, inequalities in age and experience leave her feeling insecure (see 'Enemies', 3.17, for example). *The phantom* (Steiner, 1994) offers an example of this from the *Point Horror* series. The hero, Garth, is suspected by the heroine, Lisa, of killing his team-mates to get the coveted role of football quarterback. Her suspicions that he may be the murderer grow alongside her suspicion that football may be more important to him than she is. Once Garth has secured the quarterback role, he seems to lose interest in Lisa: 'He became a distant stranger as he soaked up the praise, the hero worship, his new found fame. He seemed to forget she was sitting next to him' (*ibid.*, p. 104). Garth discovers a world beyond Lisa. What he is really accused of killing is their exclusive relationship, reflecting female fears about imbalances in relationships, where boyfriends are central to girls' lives but girlfriends are only a part of the boys' world.

It is possible to conclude that teen horror frequently intimates that sexual desire is so powerful it may be dangerous and destructive, a monster. Sex is both feared and desired. These contradictions are embodied in the person of the hero, who becomes an ambivalent figure – attractive, but possibly deceitful and deadly. His desirability is, of course, constituted by the absence created by this ambivalence. It is only possible to desire that which you lack; the boyfriend is desired because he is a chimera. In most *Point Horror* fiction, the stories have soothing and conservative resolutions. The heroes were good, caring characters all along, so girl readers may be reassured that relationships with the opposite sex will be successful, however insecure they might feel right now. *BtVS* has a more oppositional stance, in that it confirms that men may actually be hostile and dangerous, but suggests girls can cope with this.

Our comments here deal with Buffy's early romance as a schoolgirl, but Lorna Jowett (2005, p. 66), commenting on *BtVS* as a whole, notes that: 'All Buffy's relationships are failures in that they do not last. Yet her "failure" to find romantic fulfilment follows the serial pattern of deferment: it presents Buffy as capable of looking after herself and also shows her negotiating postfeminist romance.' This suggests that the way Buffy copes with her school romance helps prepare her for contemporary sexual and romantic negotiations.

Analyses of teen horror/romance suggest that the fear of boys conveyed in these stories is not only about the intensity of sexual desire but is grounded in anxieties about the social conventions surrounding sexual relationships and the imbalance of power between boys and girls. Girls fear that boys may have more loyalty to their male peer group. This leads to fears about being marginalised in boys' lives, having their sexual performance discussed and compared, being cheated on, and being the victim of moods they cannot understand. School is where girls get to grips with this for the first time.

Sex and students in popular music

Kevin Brehony's (1998) '"I used to get mad at my school"' provided an excellent overview of education in popular music up to that date, including some discussion of sexuality and schooling, and of teacher and pupil sex. Sex is a common theme of popular music, and since the genre is traditionally produced by young people for young people, it should be no surprise that schools, colleges and teachers are frequently linked to sex in popular song. Given the supposed superficiality of pop music, however, and the high-cultural view that the lyrics lack value, allied to the fact that they are often 'hidden' in the noise, it is equally unsurprising that the question of sex and education in popular music has attracted relatively little attention.

Overtly sexualised and fetishistic representations of school uniforms can be seen widely in popular culture. These images coexist with expressions of outrage when teachers (and others) are found guilty of sexual transgressions involving children and young people. The majority of teachers are conscious of the dangers that they can face from 'predatory' students. At the same time, there is a wider societal concern with paedophilia and the perceived danger of 'dirty old men' lurking around school gates. The popular culture representations of teacher–student relationships will be discussed in Chapter 5. The discussion below will focus on representations of relationships and sex in the context of schools as they have appeared in popular music from the 1950s. It should be noted that the stance of popular music is overwhelmingly male, and even more overwhelmingly hetero-sexual.

Schoolyard 'romance'

Many pop songs use school/learning as a metaphor for a relationship: for example, the Jackson Five's 1970 hit 'ABC', George Michael's 'One More Try' (1988), and, more recently, Avant's 'Love School' (2002). Sam Cooke's much-covered 1960 classic '(What a) Wonderful World' is narrated by a student who is trying to achieve 'A' grades to win the approval of a girl he loves. The Average White Band's 'School Boy Crush' (1975) relates to inept and furtive school-based boy–girl relationships. A more overtly sexual longing was crudely expressed in The Knack's 'Good Girls Don't' (1979). Chuck Berry's **'Lonely School Days'** (1965) evokes heartache for a boy when his girl finds a new boyfriend. Bobby Vee's **'Stayin' in'** (1961) has a boy agonising after punching his best friend for saying untrue things about his girl, only to find that they have formed a relationship. Like Berry's protagonist, Vee's endures the adolescent pain of seeing his girl and his friend walking home together, to a place free from the sexual restrictions of school.

Brehony (1998), following a discussion of the Hollies' **'Carrie Ann'** and 'Jennifer Eccles' as two late 1960s evocations of school as a site of romance, refers to the sexual status hierarchies that contribute to male sexual angst in school as well as to the genre convention of the walk to and from there as a time of opportunity that underlines the 'heavily gendered' aspect of these encounters, with the boy typically carrying the girl's books or satchel, as in Frankie Valli's 'My Eyes Adored You' (1974). Bobby Vinton's million-selling American number one, 'Roses Are Red (My Love)' (1962), is another song full of yearning for a past school love. Prince's 'Starfish and Coffee' (1987) offered a more surreal take on this. Several of these themes were explored in Billy Bragg's **'The Saturday Boy'** (1984), which narrates a schoolboy's romantic aspiration and his subsequent (from a mature perspective) realisation of his delusion. The song succinctly depicts the status hierarchies alluded to by the Hollies. The Arctic Monkeys' 'Bigger Boys and Stolen Sweethearts' (2005) explores similar territory, as a schoolboy laments his former girlfriend skipping classes to be picked up at the school gates by her new, older boyfriend in his car.

In **'May Queen'** (2002), the avant-garde English group Black Box Recorder ambiguously undermine genre conventions in the sinister refrain where a schoolgirl (or is it a female teacher?) pursues a schoolboy (or is it a girl?). Whereas some lyrics seem to relish the prospect of exposure, suggesting that status is associated with sexual/romantic activity, the lyrics of this song imply paranoia about discovery. This suggests there is something that would not be admired by the 'kids' and reminds us that sexual practices and sexual identities are subject to a wide range of informal controls and sanctions carried out by young people themselves. The relationship may be same-sex; it may be with someone who is not socially acceptable for other reasons; but it is a powerful indication that we do not live in as liberal a world as we might think. The more explicit rap offerings of **'Get Smart'** (2001) by Ghetto Fabolous contrast with this. The macho bravado of the song indicates that the persona delivering the lyrics is proud of his sexual practices. The song uses educational terms heavily, although it is not clear whether this is metaphorical. The sexual promiscuity of the central character and his exacting standards in terms of the oral sex he demands help to construct an identity in which a superior and sexist masculinity is central. The associations between school, sex and violence lurk constantly (not very far) below the glossy surface of popular culture.

Sexual violence

Far from the sentimental depictions of unattainable girls, loves remembered and loves gone wrong are songs that depict school-based violence (see Chapter 6 for more on this), and among these are narratives of sexualised violence. Rapper MC Ren's **'Behind the Scenes'** (1992) portrays a high-achieving schoolgirl who is 'punished' by a violent gang rape. The question of misogyny in rap music (which some see as an empowering oppositional musical form) has been widely debated: see, for example, Crenshaw (1991) and Armstrong (2001). The latter's analysis of 490 rap songs, including that mentioned above, identified 22 per cent as containing violent and misogynist lyrics. They are also often homophobic, constructing acceptable sexual identities grounded in the supremacy of the heterosexual male.

The issue of sexual abuse of schoolchildren by schoolchildren is one that has not featured prominently in public debate. The New York-based Human Rights Watch group issued a report in 2001 indicating that thousands of girls were suffering rape and sexual assault each year in South African schools, in a climate of violence that meant that the vast majority of cases were not prosecuted (Human Rights Watch, 2001).

It's a sin

One kind of pop song fixates on the concept of the schoolgirl from the perspective not of a contemporary schoolboy but of an adult from outside the educational institution. It is worth mentioning here that in the language of pop, with its numerous influences including traditional/folk dialect, youth argot and ghetto slang, not all is necessarily what it seems. Terms like 'girl', 'little girl' and 'baby' frequently refer to adults. The full context of such terms should therefore be considered. Notwithstanding this caution, however, Dee Clark's **'Hey Little Girl'** (1959) positively salivates with malicious intent. An ostensibly similar song is **'Good**

Morning Little Schoolgirl'. A minor success for the Yardbirds in 1964 and covered by many artists since, it is considered a blues classic and originates from a Sonny Boy Williamson recording in 1937. It should not be assumed, though, that the artist necessarily identifies with the words that are being sung, even if they are sung in the first person. Cheap Trick's '**Daddy Should Have Stayed in High School**' (1977) has been performed in concert in front of a backdrop film showing a sinister paedophile figure stalking a playground. The song, read simply as a lyric, appears reprehensible in the extreme, but, in the context of the video, it offers its own critique. The Red Hot Chili Peppers' '**Catholic School Girls Rule**' (1985), which tells of a schoolgirl with eyes like those of Marilyn Monroe, offers no obvious indication that there is meant to be any distance between lyric and singer, leaving this for the listener to interpret. The phrase 'Catholic school girls rule' and the general jubilant tone of the song locate it as a celebration of female sexual enthusiasm as much as an expression of male lust.

Where rock, rap and even pop appear outrageous or shocking, this may be in part a function of the fact that youth culture has, at least since the 1950s, purported at various times and in varying degrees to be rebellious. It is increasingly difficult to shock simply by dealing with sex. The discourses Foucault (1976) described in *The history of sexuality* did not ossify when the book was completed: sexuality continues to be normalised, regulated and held up to scrutiny. If rock wishes to use accounts of sex to shock, it is necessary to focus on sexual practices that are taboo. Moreover, sexual behaviour is so openly discussed that it ceases to be surprising – it is just something that happens all the time. First encounters and early experiences, therefore, such as those that take place between schoolchildren, have the power to interest young people because sex has not yet become commonplace. The outrageous and shocking are constantly incorporated by the entertainment business. There is a cycle in which notoriety is perpetually a ticket into the mainstream. The 'shocking' high school films discussed earlier in this chapter are now generally regarded as 'tame' or 'quaint'. A young person's natural interest in sex cannot be suppressed by the school, and popular culture expresses that interest, as the Pet Shop Boys observed in their quintessentially English way. '**It's a Sin**' (1987) was a number one hit for them in the UK and reached number nine in the US, but lyricist Neil Tennant was publicly denounced for his representation of education by one of his former teachers at St Cuthbert's Grammar School, Newcastle. For Tennant, his Catholic education was one of repression, initially denying his gay sexuality. During the 1990s, he came out, and he has subsequently been associated with gay rights campaigns. Interestingly, the lyrics of the song do not explicitly mention sexual sin or sexual practices.

Drugs and education: the social context

Concern about children and drugs can be found at all levels in society. Governments are concerned because of the links between substance abuse and criminality; health and social services are concerned; schools are concerned; parents are concerned because whatever care they take, it could be their child next. Schools in the UK are obliged by law to include drugs education in the curriculum, although, generally speaking, they have traditionally differentiated between alcohol, tobacco and illegal drugs. Their focus is usually educational programmes which recommend total abstinence from tobacco and illegal drugs, stressing physical dangers and addictive properties, and initiatives that point out the dangers of binge drinking. Many teachers, however, realise that drugs education needs to be more subtle and sophisticated than this. An adult, whatever their credentials, telling an adolescent not to do something because it is 'bad' may not have the desired outcome.

Pearson (2005, p. 94) looked at an innovative programme which confirmed the close relationship between drugs and identity formation and highlighted the need to take this into account when devising a drugs curriculum: 'Young people are presented with substances as another lifestyle choice where to partake is to create a particular identity for oneself and, conversely, to abstain is also to create an identity.' In Western society, ambivalent and contradictory messages are given to young people about drugs. First, many adults drink alcohol, which has life-threatening physical effects and is a contributory factor in violence. A significant number of adults, despite government initiatives and reminders that 'smoking kills', persist in smoking tobacco. Neither activity is illegal. Adults also make good and legitimate use of prescription drugs to deal with discomfort, pain, anxiety and depression. Furthermore, many adults have had at least passing contact with illegal drugs.

In the main, illegal drug use is classified as either instrumental or recreational. Instrumental use is when the drugs are taken for a reason other than mood elevation and getting 'high': for example, when steroids are used to enhance sports performance or amphetamines are taken to stay awake during revision for an examination. In Western society, individuals are often judged on a one-off performance, and, for many in an increasingly competitive and unpredictable world, it might be considered worth taking a risk to gain the edge. Pearson (*ibid.*, p. 93) alludes to this when he highlights the work of Dwyer and Wyn (2001), which examines the pressures of growing up and negotiating 'complex and often conflicting areas of risk' in contemporary society:

> The desire to conform and meet school and parental expectations is strong in many young people but so is the need to assert individuality and build self-identity. In the complexities of the risk society, where no courses of action are rarely unproblematically good or bad, this is especially difficult.

Equally, for young people, there is the appeal of recreational use, whereby drugs are taken purely for experience and enjoyment, which harks back to a tradition of hedonism and drug-induced euphoria. Particularly post-1945, however, drug use has become more accessible. This is illustrated by the fact that legal as well as illegal drugs have frequently featured in popular culture, especially linked to music and films. In the 1940s, 1950s and 1960s, smoking, or often sharing, a cigarette could be the prelude to a romantic evening, and, in more intimate situations, a metaphor for sex. Illicit drugs, although less prevalent, were closely associated with particular cultures. For example, throughout the twentieth century, part of the attraction of jazz was its radical edginess, its alternative otherness, so when some jazz musicians were revealed to be addicted to drugs or even died as a result of overdoses it rarely came as a surprise. During the 1960s and 1970s, illegal drugs, especially hallucinogens, were celebrated as vehicles either for searching for self or for losing self. As a result, for many young people, drugs were perceived as a rite of passage and an act of rebellion. Popular culture acknowledged this. The 1967 Lennon and McCartney song '**Lucy in the Sky with Diamonds**', from the Beatles album *Sergeant Pepper's Lonely Hearts Club Band*, for example, is conventionally seen as paean to LSD. What emerges is a complex picture of identity, resistance, pleasure and participation in relation to young people and drugs. The fact that their use constitutes a risk, or is disapproved of by adults, has never made recreational drugs less desirable to young people; predictably, rather the reverse. Indeed, in the 1980s, illegal substance use became less a cultural marker of the hippy or drop-out culture (except in the case of addicts) and more symptomatic, through the development and widespread availability of drugs such as cocaine, of material success and glamour.

When popular culture portrays illegal drugs as a threat to young people, the source, especially in US films, is often associated with ethnic minority supply and crime, so much so that in a film such as *Save the Last Dance* (2001, directed by Thomas Carter), it is implied that the white girl, Sara Johnson, played by Julia Stiles, is at risk of corruption from her association with African-American student Derek Reynolds, played by Sean Patrick Thomas. However, in reality, he is the one in jeopardy as a result of his association with friend and gang member Malakai. Other films, such as *187, Dangerous Minds* and *Freedom Writers*, suggest that Latino, Chicano, Asian and African-American students' home lives are so permeated with the violence endemic to gang and drug culture that only education can provide a lifeline to save them from themselves and the corruption of their society. Unsurprisingly, then, popular culture frequently constructs illegal drug use primarily as an ethnic minority problem, particularly in the United States. Evidence, however, from a University of Michigan survey (conducted annually since 1975 among 45,000 American students in the eighth, tenth and twelfth grades) indicates that drug use among African-American young people is consistently *lower* than that of white students in all categories except marijuana smoking. A comparison of African-American, Hispanic/Latino and white students at senior school level reveals that white young people generally have the highest annual prevalence rates in most, if not all, categories. Alcohol use is also particularly high among Caucasians (Levinthal, 2002, p. 12).

Although illegal drug use for recreational and experimental purposes is common among young people, its persistent and self-harming use, according to UK research, is more likely to occur among those who might be described as vulnerable: for example, because they have previously offended, or have been excluded from school, or are habitual school refusers or in the care of external agencies. Other groups likely to be at risk are those who:

- are homeless;
- have alcoholic or abusing parents;

- have learning difficulties;
- have been sexually abused or exploited through prostitution;
- have a history of family problems;
- have mental health problems.

(Standing Conference on Drug Abuse, 1997,
quoted in Melrose, 2000, p. 1)

Young people in these categories may be described as 'vulnerable', but they are not without self-determination. Trends in drug use, however, tend to alter over time, including, most recently, increasingly youthful users. Charles Levinthal (2002, p. 1) asked young people about the attractions of drug use:

> He was seventeen, a high school junior. He looked at me with amazement, telling me by his expression that either my question was ridiculous or the answer was obvious. Why do kids do drugs? Because it's cool, he said, that's why. Kids do drugs to fit in with the cool people. It's a way of acting older. If it weren't cool, kids wouldn't do it.

The reasons for taking drugs both instrumentally and recreationally are classified by Melrose (2000, p. 51) as follows:

- Oblivion seeking;
- Acceptance seeking;
- Thrill seeking;
- Seeking thrills and acceptance;
- Seeking oblivion and acceptance.

Each of these is potentially part of a young person's interactions in school or college. Number one, 'oblivion seeking', may be desirable to a young person when it means escape from personal, familial or social problems; when it constitutes avoiding oppression and rejection in school; or even when it simply means opting out of the system and rejecting the competitive culture of success and educational achievement. The consequences of this might be self-evident, but some young people are able to offer 'diverse narratives of self' (Giddens, 1991, p. 54), whereby they can have dissolute weekends, including the consumption of drugs and alcohol, but are then able to assume their 'normal' and conventional roles as compliant students on Monday. This is not, however, likely to be a hallmark of more vulnerable drug users because, for them, the construction of an alternative self through drug use is likely to make them feel that they have gained a level of credibility and status that would otherwise be denied. Drug use makes them 'cool' because nothing else can, and being cool is a desirable commodity. Also, in relation to their home situations, drugs offer young people a means of rejecting conventional values and opting out of familial responsibilities. They seek oblivion and distance from their parents through an alternative existence which is likely both to worry and affront the older generation.

Michael Eckman, talking to Cameron James at the beginning of *Ten Things I Hate About You*, describes the lines of demarcation in Padua High School in relation to students' consumption: everyone from the edgy coffee kids to the white Rastafarians, who, he suggests, while they might think that they are making a political statement, actually just smoke a lot of ganja. So whether it is consuming caffeine or cannabis, social acceptance is about being part of a gang and not being alone. This is as desirable in girls' society as it is in boys'. In the UK, official sources cite research – for example, Parker *et al.* (1988) – which has indicated the significance of friendship groups in drugs' use: 'It is indisputable that friendship networks are invariably the means by which people are introduced to drugs and that among young people the first steps in a drug using career might involve exploration amongst a group of friends' (Newport Community Safety Partnership, 2006, p. 48). Parker *et al.* (1988, p. 42) also comment on the significance of popular culture, explaining: 'The language and imagery of drug use have become deeply embedded within the contemporary popular culture.' This is not perceived, however, as a causal relationship, although it is suggested that the commercial power of popular culture could be harnessed to deliver alternative messages. Indulging in gratuitous thrill-seeking involves taking risks, injecting excitement into a life which may otherwise seem dull, routine and driven by adults. McMillan and Connor (2002) indicate that young people's attitudes to drug use become increasingly liberal if they go to university, suggesting that both pushing the boundaries of experience and searching for social acceptance figure highly in university life. For some, drug use is casual and unremarkable, although there are still those who may perceive it as exciting and sophisticated, not least because it can give them an image different from the reality of their apparently mundane everyday existence. The UK government drug strategy, however, remains focused on 'preventing drug misuse and the harm that results through effective drugs education, prevention and early intervention' (Home Office, 2006, p. 15). This is not something which preoccupies popular culture, or even high culture, too much, though:

> Beware! Beware!
> His flashing eyes, his floating hair!
> Weave a circle round him thrice
> And close your eyes with holy dread,
> For he on honey-dew hath fed,
> And drunk the milk of Paradise.
> (Coleridge, 2002 (first published 1816), 'Kubla Khan', ll. 49–54)

Drugs and alcohol in school movies

The teen movie is often upbeat. Many at the 'chick-flick' end of the genre, such as *Clueless, Ten Things I Hate About You* and *Mean Girls* are relatively wholesome, but even Paul and Chris Weitz's *American Pie* movies, which feature self-indulgence prominently, do not focus on drug use. This may seem surprising, given the high levels of drug use recorded among young people across the social spectrum. Nevertheless, the films render the practice invisible. This may be indicative that drug use is more uniformly condemned than teenage sex. Whereas there is a range of opinions about the latter, including a liberal voice that expects a degree of experimentation, most schools and parents are unequivocally opposed to the use of illegal drugs. It therefore becomes a difficult subject to treat in a light-hearted manner in a movie that wants to attract no more than a 15 rating. The spoofs *Scary Movie* (2000, directed by Keenan Ivory Wayans) and *Not Just Another Teen Movie* (2001, directed by Joel Gallan) point up this absence by showing excessive, gross and outrageous drug and alcohol abuse among schoolchildren. *Scary Movie* parodies the stereotypical close father–daughter relationship often seen in teen movies by making the father a drug dealer who says a loving farewell to his daughter when he has to lie low after a deal goes awry. His admonitions to her are delivered in tones that would usually be reserved for warnings about taking care while crossing the road, going out with boys and doing her homework, and she responds with the kind of loving tolerance teenagers show towards parental advice.

As these parodies operate by stringing together a series of gags based on other teen films, they tend to lack any coherent perspective on issues. Overall, however, they present American youth as sexually promiscuous users of large quantities of drugs and alcohol, which challenges the somewhat anodyne image of the films they appropriate.

On the whole, the consumption of alcohol is naturalised in the teen flick; it is not treated as a serious problem. There are instances of drunkenness – such as the scene in *Heathers* in which the heroine embarrasses herself and her friends by throwing up at a party – but these are treated as one-off incidents rather than endemic difficulties. Alcohol use features strongly in the *American Pie* trilogy, for example, but primarily as an opportunity for gags in which it is confused with other bodily fluids, while the consumption of spirits is associated with a degree of sophistication. It is not problematised by the films in the way that sexual relationships are. *Scary Movie* elides teen inebriation with the occult, in a joke that implies the extreme behaviour of the central character (which mirrors one of the most famous scenes in the 1973 film *The Exorcist*: masturbation with a crucifix and growing a long green tongue) results from drinking her first keg of beer. In this way it makes explicit the metaphorical basis of most teen horror, in which the supernatural threat represents the real dangers of adolescence by humorously suggesting it refers to the dangers of exhibitionist behaviour resulting from drunkenness.

In general, then, drug and alcohol consumption are not treated as serious issues in the teen movie, reflecting perhaps the high levels of consumption among young people and the fact that, for many of those from comfortable backgrounds, this is such a part of everyday life as to be a non-issue. The teen films also tend to ignore the problems of addiction faced by such young people as the homeless youngsters surveyed in Kidd's research (2004), for whom drugs were central to feelings of hopelessness and worthlessness that led to suicide. It is films aimed at older audiences that show these issues from adult perspectives. Here, drug use is seen to be shocking and threatening, reflecting either a general fear of out-of-control youth or a projection of parental anxieties about the dangers facing their offspring.

Two popular mainstream teen films, *The Faculty* and *Crazy/Beautiful* (2001, directed by John Stockwell) are worth considering in more detail. In *The Faculty*, drug use is important to the plot, though never problematised in its own right; in *Crazy/Beautiful*, the heroine's excessive use of alcohol is the most prominent of her transgressions. Although we discussed *The Faculty* in Chapter 3, it is worth revisiting because it is unusual in offering the use of illegal drugs as a central and positive metaphor. The school drug dealer, Zeke Tyler, is presented as an attractive figure. He stands apart from the violent, chaotic world of his fellow students. He is confident, cool and unfazed, possibly the only student in the school who looks happy and laid back. He is self-reliant: his wealthy parents are somewhere in Europe so he lives alone and makes money selling home-made drugs, fake IDs to under-age drinkers, and pornographic videos. Although he is repeating his senior year, his intelligence and knowledge are remarkable. His challenges to his English teacher are both offensive and clever, and his exceptional biological and chemical knowledge help him to understand the aliens. He is also an action hero, showing courage and a cool head under pressure. Taking Zeke's illegal 'scat' also appears to do relatively little harm. His middle-class school-mates have the income to pay for it, so they are not criminalised. It consists of a fair proportion of caffeine, and its main effect seems to be to render the user happy and giggly. Legal drugs, particularly alcohol, on the other hand, are shown to be more destructive. A mother is rejected as a confidante because she drinks; and a teacher's ability to do his job is ruined by alcohol. One student's parents learn all they know about drugs from television, and, believing that their child must have drugs stashed in the spines of books, they promptly tear them apart. When he witnesses an attack by the aliens at the school, they do not believe him, insisting he must be 'on drugs'. They offer a classic illustration of a generational tendency to blame young people's difficulties on some half-understood 'problem', like drugs, rather than attend to the reality and complexity of their experiences.

Most significantly, however, the drugs themselves save the children, the school and the planet. Zeke's illicit concoction has diuretic properties which destroy the water-loving alien parasites that have invaded the bodies of the staff and systematically and aggressively colonised the children. The 'scat' becomes a precious commodity that the remaining alien-free group of young people have to preserve and take risks to obtain. Certain qualities are commonly attributed to drug users: for instance, they are regarded as apathetic and stupefied. In *The Faculty*, the students who are taken over by the aliens develop these characteristics, while the drug dealer is the most alert person on campus. Drugs are coded positively in this film: they are associated with individuality and rebelliousness, with resistance to oppressive conformity. It is teachers who threaten to deaden the mind, not drugs. The language used by the alien-possessed teachers even echoes that often associated with drug pushing: the young people are encouraged to let the aliens invade them, too, because then they will feel better, and their fears and pain will disappear.

Crazy/Beautiful, starring Kirsten Dunst and Jay Hernandez, is set in a Los Angeles high school. It tells the story of Carlos, a Latino student participating in an exchange programme that enables bright students from poor districts to attend the prestigious Pacific High School. His romance with the hedonistic Nicole, a poor little rich girl and daughter of a liberal congressman, threatens both his grades and his chance to escape poverty. By contrast with *The Faculty*, alcohol and drug use are associated with decadence and instability. Illegal drugs receive only a passing mention. We hear, for example, that the police found 'drug paraphernalia' in Nicole's car, but we do not see anyone indulging. Instead, alcohol is the main symbol of transgression. Nicole's drunkenness becomes a metonym for the failings and the lack of moral backbone of the liberal elite. It is the rich girl from the politically liberal, educated family whose drinking and 'crazy' behaviour threatens her life and health, the stability of her family and the future of her boyfriend. We first see her when she is carrying out a community service order for drink driving. She and her girlfriend appear to be 'wasted' most of the time. At school she keeps alcohol in a soft-drink bottle and slips out of class to drink. She hates school and uses alcohol to escape. Carlos is presented as her opposite. A person of colour, he contrasts with her petite, blonde whiteness. His two-hour journey to school reflects his commitment. His close-knit, boisterous family is set in deliberate opposition to the cool, distant household in which Nicole lives. His hard work and aspiration are set against her lack of appreciation of education. When she offers him a drink at school, he spits it out when he realises it is alcohol, dramatically illustrating the difference between them.

Although Nicole turns to alcohol to escape personal and family trauma (her mother committed suicide while her father, who has a new wife and child, finds it difficult to show affection), it is associated directly with her wealth and class. Out of respect for her father, the police generally just take her home when she is found drunk, whereas we might assume they would be less considerate were she someone else's daughter. It is the rich boys, not Carlos, who attempt to take sexual advantage of Nicole when she is almost comatose through alcohol; Carlos's sexual relationship with her is consensual and instigated by her. The rich kids' party is a decadent, unchaperoned affair; the party at Carlos's house is a celebration of family which exudes suspicion towards the outsider Nicole, seeing her as a threat to their values and cohesion.

The film has a superficially radical message, representing immigrant communities positively, suggesting that the ruling white elites have lost touch with core values but can be saved by the decent (conservative) values of less privileged members of society. The producers' decision to cut a number of scenes which might have shown Carlos or the Latino community in a more negative light offers further evidence that this was intentional. It is easy to read this film against the grain, however, and suggest that it has more conservative undertones. Nicole's father is engaged in admirable social projects, but the film implies that such practices are superficial, ego-boosting activities, thereby undermining the value of positive social action by politicians. The restrictive and controlling behaviour of Carlos's family is presented as healthier than Nicole's liberal regime, sustaining a highly conservative view of child-rearing, family values and their effect on children's life chances. The film overtly subscribes to the American dream that anyone can do anything if they work hard; but, however much we admire Carlos's commitment, his achievements are ultimately dependent on the patronage he obtains only because he knows a congressman's daughter. Moreover, his ambitions will only reinforce the status quo, as he wants to join the military, and he accepts the given social order without question. In effect, the story shows that the deserving poor may climb a little higher on the social ladder, but their progress will not change conditions for the rest of the community. If the schoolchildren of the rich get drunk and take drugs, they will be forgiven, sent to therapists and eventually to a rehabilitation clinic. The children of the poor have to remain clean and clear-headed to have any hope of a decent life.

Both films offer an individualistic perspective on drug and alcohol use, featuring young people involved in drugs coming from rich but dysfunctional families. The 'blame' for the drug problem becomes one that can easily be resolved, therefore. It is shown to be about bad parenting and is the fault of individuals who do not love their children sufficiently. Although it is correct that drug use is widespread among middle-class children, focusing on this means that its hugely destructive effect on poor communities, especially the homeless, is completely ignored. So both films neglect to consider the economic and social factors that contribute to the drug industry, with its disproportionately damaging effects on poor and black communities. Instead, drug and alcohol abuse are located in a purely moral domain, in which schoolchildren merely have to say 'no' to be saved and the complex pressures of identity and economics are denied.

Summary: really not so dangerous?

Popular culture often presents fictionalised or metaphorical representations of the fears and constraints that surround early sexual experiences. The texts we have chosen here present a range of perspectives. They tap into widespread anxieties experienced by young people: fear of rejection, humiliation, physical harm; fears that recognise the extent to which identity and status are determined by sexual success and the choice of a sexual partner. Indeed, romantic and sexual affairs are often represented as the most important thing that happens at school, which is therefore primarily the site of sexual and social, rather than academic, education.

The big liberal public myth of freedom of sexual and romantic choice is much promoted and the class-based nature of sexual pairings ignored, while only the faintest hints of any alternatives appear in the mainstream. Same-sex relationships are not denigrated, but their absence speaks volumes. Whispers in popular song of 'forbidden' love at school are indicative of the extent to which 'choice' is constrained and constructed. These absences and limitations are exploited for humorous purposes in *Crazy/Beautiful*, where the macho, black football player reveals his gay leanings through his enthusiasm for the song 'It's Raining Men' and his desire to have his girlfriend dress in a football strip.

In general, then, in mainstream popular culture, far from being shocking, sexual freedom is portrayed in such a way that we are reassured that it will not undermine the status quo. Decent people will get together and all will be well. By contrast, some music that might more appropriately be defined as subcultural rather than mainstream presents a less comforting view of sex and young people. In these texts, sex is often a form of violence, used to enforce a sexist masculinity. It can carry overtones of revenge against girls for their academic success and social confidence, and appears to give voice to the male underachievers who have caused educationalists and academics such concern. Sex, for the schoolboys represented in these songs, becomes a vehicle for the reassertion of a heterosexual male dominance that has diminished in society at large as well as in schools, where sexual equality is actively promoted. Yet, these views, while not comforting, are hardly revolutionary. Rather, they are conservative in their sexual politics. We also noticed that there appears to be a tendency towards the fetishisation of schoolgirls. This tends to remain mild in popular culture, however – anything else would verge on the illegal – so it is difficult to analyse in depth.

Treatment of drug use in popular culture is limited and clearly problematic. There is a reluctance to present either the commonplace reality of recreational drug use among the young – that is, to present it as something that is part of normal development rather than indicative of psychological trauma – or to analyse the economic and social conditions that make the drugs trade such a destructive phenomenon for some impoverished communities. Instead, it is often treated as an individual problem. The problems it can create are laid at the door of weak or vicious characters while decent young people can simply say 'no'. Good parents' children will not use drugs. Nice young people do not sit down with their friends and smoke a joint. We can only assume that this tendency towards simplistic representation is to some extent constrained by the film industry's awareness of censorship and by recognition that hard-line attitudes towards drugs are sufficiently widespread to affect the consumption of popular texts.

5 Hot for teacher

[T]he educational process involves an emotionally suffused link between human beings. Its intimacies form a tangled web of intellectual aspiration and erotic desire. In our culture, the idea of education is inextricably bound up with constructions of power, governance, and an erotically charged allegiance or submission to the father- (or . . . mother-) teacher.

(Barreca and Denenholz Morse, 1997, p. vii)

The claim that teaching and learning are erotic acts is based on a conception of Eros as a life force that pervades human interactions both with other people and with the environment. Alison Pryer (2001, p. 80) argues that pedagogy involves an initiation in which 'the teacher breaks the student, bringing the student into the death space in order to give new life'. This metaphor is unsettling. Pryer believes that the power relations explicit in technical/rational schooling constitute a violent imposition and points to the way in which schooling is concerned with disciplining the body and suppressing desire but contends that, given the power of Eros and desire, it cannot succeed in such a project.

Elizabeth Atkinson (2003, p. 1) has referred to the

sexual anonymity demanded of teachers and researchers within all phases of education [which] is representative of a wider silencing, or neutralising, of identity for those involved in the teaching profession, which contrasts oddly with discourses of sexuality embedded in the interactions of children and young people within and beyond the context of schooling.

Outside sex education, and to some extent even within it, there is little talk of sex in formal debates about educational practice, except in the context of regulation, transgression and abuse. However, popular culture is suffused with sex, so talking about representations of education in popular culture inevitably leads to discussions about sex.

Johnson (2005, p. 134) has characterised popular culture as being 'saturated with warnings to teachers who conflate passion and teaching'. She warns of the dangers of denying that a sexual dynamic can exist in relationships between teachers and students and urges the development of an understanding of '. . . the difference between what McWilliam (1996) terms pedagogical eroticism and pedagogical abuse' (*ibid.*). In other words, mature recognition of sexual dynamics enables them to be managed in socially, morally and ethically responsible ways. 'The Maginot line is clearly breached when teachers physically act on their desires by engaging in a sexual relationship with students' (*ibid.*, p. 146).

For young people in co-educational secondary education, school is often experienced as an arena of sexual competition, tension and opportunity. This is an assertion that could be underlined by a study not only of the commercial products of popular culture (for example, teen magazines, teenage fiction and pop music), but by any sample of graffiti in any school. There is a complex mix of emotional exploration and maturation that is acknowledged within the formal curriculum through 'sex education' and informally through peer cultures. (See Epstein and Sears (1999) for a series of papers discussing, *inter alia*, sexism, homophobia, abortion and HIV as issues in pedagogy. Mitchell and Weber (1999) consider pedagogy and conceptualisations of the teacher's body. Keroes (1999) focuses on novels and films in her insightful discussion of teacher–student relationships.)

Key components of sex in popular culture are the hegemonic dominance of heterosexual identities and of patriarchal gender roles. There is a relative absence of 'otherness'. Atkinson (2002, p. 125) has referred to a 'tyranny of silence' in relation to non-heterosexual identities. These characteristics are particularly acute in popular music, as will be evident in the song extracts that appear below. As Atkinson (2003, p. 3) has pointed out, even in the academic sphere, where 'gender' has found its place as a legitimate area of enquiry, sexualities 'remain silenced'. She also refers to the 'seductive' nature of teaching and to the ways in which the sexual identities of teachers are 'neutralized in educational contexts' (*ibid.*, p. 9). Mitchell and Weber (1999, p. 125) refer to a 'culture of teaching that ignores the body or regards it with suspicion'. Power is an ever-present feature of classroom interaction, school organisation and school–community relations. Sexual desire, sexual objectification and sexual identity all impinge upon power dynamics. Popular culture can be particularly effective at revealing the detailed operation of sexual politics in educational environments.

There is a fevered anxiety in the UK about teachers, and other school employees, with regard to their potential to exploit young people sexually. The Sexual Offences (Amendment) Act (2000) made it a criminal offence for teachers and others in positions of trust to be sexually involved with young people, including students between sixteen and eighteen, even though they are over the age of consent. There have been a number of high profile court cases and the media enjoys featuring stories about teacher–student 'romances', sometimes salaciously emphasising the illicit nature of the liaison. The establishment of the Criminal Records Bureau (CRB) through the Police Act (1997) is indicative of the extent of public anxiety and government desire to be seen to address this issue. The CRB reports criminal convictions to employers, and everyone likely to have connection with young people, however slight or temporary, must be granted clearance by it. The system has been subject to repeated criticism regarding delays and inaccuracies. It seemed to fail with tragic consequences in the Soham murder case of 2003 in which a primary school caretaker who murdered two girls was subsequently found to have been the subject of a series of complaints relating to sexual offences against young girls prior to his appointment. In January 2006 there was extensive coverage in the British news media of cases of 'paedophile teachers' working in schools, causing then Secretary of State for Education Ruth Kelly to promise a review of screening procedures.

Advice is issued to teachers from their trade unions about avoiding allegations of abuse or inappropriate behaviour. Jones (2004, p. 53), in a study based on teachers in New Zealand primary schools, employs a Foucauldian analysis in her exploration of the ways in which 'social anxiety about touching children' has led to 'an intensification of self-surveillance by teachers'. She argues that 'The safe teacher must engage in pedagogical work to discipline children's desires for touch and for unrestrained physical affection, because expressions of sensual affection and pleasure between teacher and child have been recoded as unprofessional in the proper classroom' (*ibid.*, p. 59). This theme is further discussed by McWilliam and Jones (2005, p. 109), who argue that the 'regime of truth' being constructed around issues of child protection is one that 'produces new tyrannies for the teacher at the same time as it works to eliminate tyrannies for the child'. Popular culture both feeds and reflects this process of self-regulation and surveillance.

There is a sense in which the British tabloid press may be regarded as an aberrant product of popular culture. In February 2002, Amy Gehring, a twenty-six-year-old Canadian teacher of biology working in England, was acquitted by a British court on four charges of indecent assault on teenage male students below the age of consent. Gehring subsequently admitted to inappropriate behaviour on previous occasions, and the British press went into a feeding frenzy that was part moral panic and part salacious reportage. While the Gehring case was relatively rare in that the perpetrator was a female teacher preying on male students, cases of male teachers abusing girls and boys are by no means unknown in the UK. Despite appearing on 'List 99', the government's official list of teachers (DfES Circular 11/95) posing a danger to children, Gehring had still been employed by a teacher agency. Certainly cases of this type are reported very differently when the teacher is female and the student male than when the roles are reversed. The Canadian *National Post*, reporting on the case of schoolteacher Heather Ingram in April 2000, stated:

> Male teachers having sex with young female students is a shameful, shocking breach of a power relationship that earns opprobrium and disgust from all corners of society. Yet for many people . . . an attractive young female teacher having a sexual relationship with a willing, albeit much younger male student, is something else again.
>
> (Dube and Moore, 2000, p. 1)

The piece goes on to report other Canadian cases, revealing that 'A female teacher at a suburban high school in British Columbia is being investigated for allegations that she was sexually involved with as many as 15 male students . . . Police are finding it a tough slog, though. None of the boys are complaining' (*ibid.*, p. 2). The paper refers to psychiatric research indicating that studies of girls preyed upon by men show high levels of psychological disorder, then quotes a British psychiatrist who claims that boys 'seduced into vaginal intercourse' may, on the contrary, feel a sense of accomplishment. The US *Eagle-Tribune* newspaper carried a similar report in December 2001, citing numerous American cases of female teachers facing charges of sexual misconduct. There is US research indicating that about one-fifth of US cases involving sex between staff and students involved female employees (Perkins, 2001). More recently, the *Sunday Times* carried a large feature on the case of Mary Kay Letourneau, a Seattle teacher who, having spent seven years in jail for the rape of a twelve-year-old boy as a thirty-four-year-old in 1996, married her victim on 20 May 2005 (Allen-Mills, 2005).

Sikes (2006, p. 266) presents a discussion of consensual sexual relationships between female pupils and male teachers in secondary schools which is based on positive accounts from those involved and produces a counterweight to media, and other, representations where 'sexual intimacy between teachers and students is almost always stated, or taken, as being illegitimate, abusive and exploitative on the part of the teacher'. For Sikes, the prevailing discourse in relation to girls in secondary schools, as well as the nature of sex education in schools, 'victimises and also infantilises women' (*ibid.*, p. 278). She believes that the nature of pupil–teacher relationships is in need of deeper critical consideration.

Cultural representations of sexual relations in various educational contexts are not new in drama (whether theatre or film). They range from the serious treatment given by David Mamet's play *Oleanna* (1993; made into a film the following year) through to a diverse range of (s)exploitation productions, such as John McNaughton's *Wild Things* (1998). Tracing the evolution of Hollywood's treatment of teachers and teaching through the 1980s and 1990s, Bauer (1998, pp. 302–303), in a paper that focuses on teachers of English literature, discusses the way in which teaching is 'now represented as a sexual proposition', suggesting that 'When movies are *not* about actual sexual desire/harassment between professors and students, their desire is for discipline: instruction in how to control libido through channelling it into proper social norms.' In the 1980s, Bauer argues, films such as *Ferris Bueller's Day Off* (1986, directed by John Hughes), *Heathers* and *Dead Poets Society* represented 'disciplinary intimacy' – the teacher imposes his/her authority, even if, as is the case in *Dead Poets Society*, this is masked by an eccentric individualistic persona. In the 1990s, films developed a concern with what Bauer terms 'erotic intimacy', where the image of teachers was glamorised and where they had a transformative impact. Examples cited are *Dangerous Minds* and *Mr Holland's Opus*. Other films of the 1990s, such as *Oleanna* and *The Mirror Has Two Faces* (1996, directed by Barbra Streisand), foreground the sexuality of the teacher.

In literature, representations of teachers range from stories in popular fiction through various campus romances to such classic novels as Charlotte Brontë's 1847 novel *Jane Eyre* (2006) and Winifred Holtby's 1936 novel *South Riding* (2003). More recently, Zoe Heller's *Notes on a scandal* (2003) deals seriously with the issue of teacher–pupil relationships. It was a UK bestseller in 2004 and made into a film in 2006, directed by Richard Eyre. We do not intend in this study to consider the various categories of school/college-related 'erotic fiction' that cater to 'specialist tastes'. Examples of this kind of text include the 'gay lit.' of Chris Kent's *Boys of Swithins Hall* (1999) and *The real Tom Brown's school days: an English school boy parody* (2002). There are equivalent 'lesbian' titles, although Petra Waldron's *The adventures of a lesbian college school girl* (2003), an explicit graphic (that is, illustrated) novel, probably sells primarily to a male market. Ray Gordon's *School of corruption* (2002) is another example of this kind of school-based 'erotic literature'. In the context where school uniforms are a frequent theme of the murkier areas of pornography, as well as a staple of both risqué fancy-dress parties and of fetish-orientated clubs, the existence of a significant market for texts of this kind is deeply problematic. Instances of the sexualisation of school uniforms, however, continue to be manifest in relatively mainstream culture, too. The summer of 2002 saw the growth of a club phenomenon known as 'School Disco' throughout the United Kingdom. Promoted by www.schooldisco.com, country-wide dance events and CDs of 1980s music compilations became big business, riding a wave of school nostalgia, perhaps best exemplified by the success of the Friends Reunited web site. At School Disco events, the prescribed dress code is school uniform; most clubbers are in their twenties or thirties.

This chapter will consider some instances of the sexualisation of teachers. It begins with a discussion of popular romantic fiction, continues with a comparison of two films from different eras, and concludes by exploring some examples taken from popular music.

Romancing the teacher

As the teacher is so often presented as the object of sexual fantasy in popular culture generally, it might be expected that teachers would feature as heroes or heroines in contemporary popular romance. The popular romantic novel, epitomised by publications from Mills and Boon, Harlequin, Silhouette and their various imprints (Desire, Intrigue, Temptation and so on), changes rapidly to reflect changes in social mores and interests, particularly with respect to gender relations, love and marriage. Mills and Boon began trading in 1908 as a general publisher, but over time it increasingly concentrated on its phenomenally successful romantic novels (see Dixon, 1999). Their popularity is such that, as a series, they take their place alongside selected bestsellers in every supermarket. In many ways these novels can be seen as a barometer of shifting beliefs. The stereotypes that prevailed in the 1950s, 1960s and 1970s of virginal heroines occupying humble but respectable jobs, swept off their feet by arrogant super-heroes (secretary marries boss; nurse marries doctor; nanny marries landowner) have been joined by lead characters who are single parents or women successfully pursuing jobs previously the preserve of men, everything from fire-fighter to international financier. Many portray closer, more equal relationships between the sexes. The romances of the 1980s and early 1990s in particular, focused on the problems of the dual-career couple, resolving these in unconvincing ways that leave the real issues raised by this development unchallenged. At the same time, real differences persist in the way men's and women's work is portrayed and in the roles their professions play in the romantic plot that drives the narratives.

In some 300 Mills and Boon novels published in the mid-1990s, not one hero was a schoolteacher. A less intense but systematic assessment of these novels up to the present day similarly has not so far discovered a teacher as the hero. Doctors, entrepreneurs, novelists, rock stars, opera singers, cowboys, a policeman, a probation officer, a lumberjack, landowners, even a footballer all featured in the novels, but teachers were completely absent. The nearest was a Cambridge mathematics professor whose job was portrayed so unrealistically that he was able to spend months each summer taking a barge along the river, fooling the heroine into believing that this was his real job. A management training consultant developing teamwork for private companies returned to work as a psychology lecturer because this would allow him to spend more time with his family(!). No other male characters had any connection with teaching.

Heroines, on the other hand, are occasionally teachers, and an examination of their portrayal suggests that in spite of the many changes that have taken place in these novels, they appear to retain an inflexible core of beliefs about male and female characteristics. It also shows that the novels employ discourses about teaching that are relatively unflattering, perpetuating an image of this as a low-status, female profession.

Feminists have noted that Western society has come to analyse the world in terms of sets of dualisms which place in opposition to each other: emotion and reason; nature and culture (Ortner, 1982); object and subject (Kaplan, 1986); body and mind; and private and public (Cirksena and Cucklanz, 1992). Women are often associated with the former of each of the oppositional pairs listed above. Gatens (1992, pp. 121–122) comments:

> A feature common to most, if not all, dominant socio-political theories is a commitment to the dualisms central to Western thought: nature and culture, body and mind, passion and reason. In the realm of social and political theory, these dualisms often translate as distinctions between reproduction and production, the family and the state, the individual and the social. As many feminists have argued, the left-hand side of these dualisms is more intimately connected with women and femininity and the right-hand side with men and masculinity.

Moreover, the 'feminine' aspects of the dualisms are often valued less highly than their 'masculine' counterparts. Malson (1998, p. 119), writing about anorexia, notes, 'dualist discourse rearticulates these patriarchal dichotomies that equate woman with the body, with weakness, irrationality and lack of control and man with the mind, with rationality, strength and control', and this has been a continuing concern for feminist writers (see, for example, Greer, 1971; Mitchell, 1971; Wilson, 1980; Brown, 1981; Ortner, 1982; Oakley, 1990; Belsey, 1994). Dualisms are linked by French (1994, p. 29) to class subordination: 'all dualities are created to justify and bolster inequality. If mind is superior to and governs body it is right and proper that those possessed of greater mental power rule over those whose power is linked to the body.'

Although this section concentrates on the private/public division, the sets of dualisms listed above interconnect. For example, the private world of the home is associated with the emotions, with feelings and relationships, and, as the locus for pregnancy and child-rearing, with the body. Thus, the readings of romantic fiction here draw on the idea that beliefs about women are based in a number of dualistic perceptions of the world, not only in the opposition private/public. The association between women and the private sphere could be seen to be oppressive in that it creates restrictive expectations about women's lives, roles and natures.

Romantic texts encode struggles between the ideology of woman as private homemaker and guardian of family values and liberal-feminist discourses asserting women's right to a place in the paid and public labour force. Contradictions and tensions emerge when heroines enter the workforce or challenge their private roles. Mills and Boon novels from their UK 'sweet' romances often suggest that the successful woman who is the subject of her own life cannot be a true woman unless she is also the object of male desire. Nor can the successful woman who contributes to the cultural life of her society be a true woman unless she represents nature as well as culture. This is generally demonstrated as the desire to mother and nurture others, and it is noticeable in female teachers in Mills and Boon books.

It was possible, when looking at the 300 Mills and Boon romances mentioned above, to divide heroines' jobs into three categories. The first included jobs which relied on the public employment of traditionally private virtues and skills, such as childcare and service work, looking after the sick, undertaking routine tasks to save men the trouble. The second grew hugely from the 1980s: women undertaking jobs traditionally associated with men. These apparently mould-breaking heroines took on roles that required physical strength, courage or mechanical skill (fire-fighters, pilots) or had very high status and salaries, usually in international conglomerates. Finally, there were women in glamorous gender-neutral, creative jobs: advertising, illustration, photography and so on.

Teaching could fit into either of the last two categories but never did. It could be presented as a tough, macho job (working in an inner-city school, perhaps) or as a powerful job (running a large organisation which requires a high level of education, specialist skill or knowledge). It could even be shown as a very creative activity, emphasising the talent needed to design learning activities, plan for maximum differentiation, present an inspiring lesson. Heroines who taught, however, were always placed in the first of the three categories, publicly deploying their private virtues.

They were usually shown teaching young children. Although the novels often asserted that they were 'passionate' about their jobs, they had a remarkable amount of free time. An analysis of a typical example, *Trial by marriage* (Armstrong, 1994), shows how the role of teacher is used to support a set of beliefs about women and the private sphere. This, in turn, helps to explain why the profession continues to be seen as feminine and low status. The novel also exploits the idea that educated women are sexless and uses this to create a frisson of excitement as the heroine discovers her 'true womanly nature'. Teaching is thus shown to be a job for girls – and not very pretty ones at that. The novel is set on an Australian cattle station, creating the isolated, closed community typical of many romances. The hero is the owner of this and several other stations, so the teacher is his employee, educating children at the station school. During their very first encounter, an unlikely dialogue includes statements from him that confirm hackneyed views of the teacher: 'you even look like the kind of spinster that is born admirably to the vocation. You are I gather a confirmed spinster? . . . But you wouldn't be a bad-looking girl if you took some trouble you know. A bit thin, a bit intense maybe' (*ibid.*, p. 7). Already we know that he will soon be taking off her spectacles and loosening her hair.

Also very early in the novel (*ibid.*, pp. 15–16), we discover what a teacher is thought to be when the heroine is described as follows:

> she was passionate about teaching and knowledge . . . heavily into creative arts such as papier mache, rug-making, decoupage et cetera, she was a fine seamstress, a creative cook, she loved growing things and grew her own herbs and anything else she could get to grow in pots, and she was the one who always got landed with any sick or stray wildlife, such as orphaned baby kangaroos or koalas, and birds with broken wings.

She is, then, portrayed as the pinnacle of domestic feminine virtues. Certainly this woman looks as though her role in the community is about practising to be a wife. Her passion for knowledge is lightly worn. Occasionally we see her using or recognising a quotation, but there is no sign of any serious reading or engagement with knowledge. One of her older pupils, Darren, is brilliant at physics, so she persuades the boss to send him away to school, suggesting that academically challenging teaching would be beyond her capabilities.

The nurturing motif, conveyed by the mention of sick koalas, is particularly important. When one of her pupils runs away from home, she pursues him into the bush, injuring herself in the process. In effect, teaching is presented as a form of babysitting, rather than an academic or intellectual pursuit. Her pupils include itinerant children and adults from 'the mostly aboriginal pool of stockmen and rangers'. Mostly, however, she cares for the twelve regular pupils on the station. Her role in the community is defined: 'she was more than just the teacher; she was the confidante of their parents, often the baby-sitter, sometimes the relief nurse, the adviser who knew a bit about the big cities some of them had never seen and lots more' (*ibid.*, p. 16).

We also see her thrown into close proximity with the hero because she agrees to move in and look after his sick nephew and niece. This display of 'private' virtue – through domestic, wifely acts such as cooking, sewing, gardening, home-making and, above all, nurturing the sick and vulnerable – shows that she scores as a potential mother, rather than as a professional. This behaviour contrasts with her rival, the hero's ex-fiancée, who is sophisticated, worldly and, as a 'senior stewardess', has 'a really top job' – one of the reasons why she split up with the hero. Presumably she found the prospect of nursing sick koalas less appealing than jetting round the world.

Moody (1998) and Dixon (1999) both note that the city/country dichotomy is a prevalent theme in romantic fiction. In the novels studied, the country is allied with feminine virtues – even where the heroine is a city girl. In line with the tradition of pastoral literature, the country is presented as free from corruption, a good place for family, growth, nature and human relationships. Thus, the country school-mistress has a fixed place in this world: she is not so much pursuing a career as fulfilling an organic role in a deceptively timeless reality. (See the Miss Read 'Thrush Green' stories for comparisons: for example, *The school at Thrush Green* (1988)). Teaching is not about career but about character.

The unimportant nature of the job is underlined by the way in which the hero expresses his disappointment that the teacher continues to focus on the job after they are married. He decides (without asking her) to advertise for a new teacher because she is not spending enough time on her wifely duties: 'You're the perfect wife in most respects for this kind of life. But I had hoped by now you would see it as – well, a wider field' (Armstrong, 1994, p. 125). Teaching is so insignificant that even being a wife, and especially the wife of a wealthy man, offers wider horizons. Certainly, the way the profession is described in this novel reinforces that. Teaching itinerant workers and their children, often from different cultures, against a background of cultural invasion and racism could have been presented as deeply challenging morally, emotionally and intellectually. It should have connected with wide political issues. Instead, these are not even raised, so the novel perpetuates the belief that one white man, through his natural authority (he has everyone's respect, almost veneration), has created a little Eden, and the woman/teacher's role is to support this. A Freirean perspective on teaching in this community, for example, would indicate that the teacher should be engaged in raising the consciousness of variously oppressed groups to enable them to take charge of their own situations. Instead, the only person to progress beyond education in the service of the cattle station and its boss is Darren, who, by the grace and favour of the hero, goes to university.

The way the teacher is sexualised in the novel relies on the stereotypical image of the teacher just discussed. The fantasy is a common one in romances: the very fact that the heroine is apparently insignificant and dull makes it exciting that the hero chooses her. Beneath a seemingly demure exterior, we are led to believe, lurks a sexually powerful creature. The plot is essentially identical to Charlotte Brontë's *Jane Eyre*, another novel featuring a teacher (more precisely a governess) whose underlying passionate nature is perceived by her wealthy employer. Romantic fiction is aimed primarily at women. We therefore have to assume that this identifies a female sexual fantasy: however dull and worthy your life may be, the real (sexual) you will be seen by an alpha male and your virtue will be rewarded. Thus, in this type of fantasy, it is important that the teacher has an unimportant, rather mundane existence. The drearier the heroine, the more powerful her transformation and the better it is for the reader to identify with her salvation from tedium. As the hero of

Trial by marriage says (*ibid.*, pp. 110, 132): '"Men have a fatal fascination for women who don't advertise their sensuality to the world. There's a primitive urge in us, I think, to want our women to be very private about this" . . . "You look positively exotic, Mrs Wyatt." And he tucked a creamy camellia from a vase of flowers into her hair.'

These fantasies may be read in many subtle and different ways that cannot be fully explored here (see Modleski, 1990; Thurston, 1987; Owen, 1990; Cohn, 1988), and it would be a mistake to assume that their popularity implies women like to be subordinate. It is possible to argue, for example, that they are an expression of female resentment and anger at material and social inequalities between the sexes that manifests itself in fantasies about the subjection of extremely economically and socially powerful males to the dullest, poorest females, through love. For the purposes of this book, it is interesting that this particular fantasy is dependent on the sheer insignificance of the heroine in the public sphere, on the way her work skills are coded as private and feminine, and that both of these factors are signified by her role as a teacher.

Silhouette Desire and Mills and Boon Temptation novels claim to offer more realistic settings and greater sensuous detail than the 'sweet' romances. They are more likely to feature heroines seriously connected to the world, maintaining jobs and relationships generally. Rabine (1985) and Jones (1986) noted that during the 1980s it became common for romantic heroines to venture much more seriously into the world of work. One of the decade's Silhouette Desire series features a heroine with a very different kind of teaching job from that shown in *Trial by marriage*. In *Teacher's pet* (Berk, 1985) teaching is central to the life of the heroine, Cecily Adams, part of her core values: 'I have principles, Nick. One of those principles is that school matters, that it's important, that it's essential' (*ibid.*, p. 168). Moreover, she spends 'the better part of the weekend' (*ibid.*, p. 16) sorting out the papers she has to mark, and we do see her using her skills to control a challenging class and expending energy thinking about teaching methods.

Her relationship with Nick Faro, however, challenges her beliefs. He is a self-made man, but also a high school drop-out. The tensions between them are constructed explicitly in class terms. He argues that the world is divided into 'people and snobs'. The snobs live on the 'Heights', which is where she rents a flat. As an educated person, she is a member of a class which excluded him in the past; a representative of a system which sent poor boys like him to fight in Vietnam; a part of society he still resents and despises, in spite of the fact that he is now much wealthier than she is. The novel effectively pits a raw working-class masculinity against a set of values relating to education, leisure and culture, which are seen to be feminised. The protagonists clash over the future prospects of Nick's nephew, Bruce, who is Cecily's pupil. Nick is happy for Bruce to continue to work for him in his factory, whereas Cecily wants to push him to make adequate grades so that he might take up a football scholarship.

Teacher's pet is a much more explicitly erotic novel than *Trial by marriage*. As the title suggests, the fact that Cecily is a teacher is an important part of the fantasy. The title is illustrated by a lurid depiction of an embrace in a bedroom, where Nick is stripped to the waist, all bulging muscles and suntan, and Cecily wears a delicate pink blouse that is already slipping from her shoulders. Her eyes are closed in ecstasy. The idea that teachers are objects of fantasy is set out in the opening scenes, where the heroine has to cope with the excessive admiration of a teenage boy.

Cecily and Nick's sexual liaison symbolises the merging of their two worlds and a developing understanding each of the other. The novel shows the influence of feminism and changing social attitudes towards women by the seriousness with which Cecily's career is treated and by the sensitivity towards her and the respect for her sexual integrity shown by the hero. Nick, for instance, does not employ the sexual bullying tactics that can characterise the genre. Nevertheless, in the end, the concept 'teacher/success' is set against the concept 'woman' and is exemplified by this exchange: "'Nick, I really do have to grade papers." "Don't be such a teacher," he chided her. "I like you better when you're a woman"' (*ibid.*, p. 43).

The novel treats a woman's career seriously and specifically treats teaching seriously. Nevertheless, the process of sexualising the teacher has to be understood in terms of power and control as well as personal feelings. Many female teachers have been on the receiving end of sexual comments and advances from males that are less about finding the teacher attractive than they are about reducing her authority. In a highly gendered world in which sexual congress is still perceived as female submission, one way in which boys and men can attempt to reduce a female teacher's power is to respond to her not as a teacher, but as a woman. Thus, a situation in which a woman may appear to be socially and politically superior, because of class and education, can be reversed if the focus shifts towards sexual difference. In this respect, the novel undermines the female teacher and the civic values associated with education, once she places her feelings for the hero above her beliefs about education, renouncing the value she had once placed on qualifications and their capacity to offer social mobility: 'Loving you is more important than any piece of paper in the world' (*ibid.*, p. 187).

In *Trial by marriage*, then, the sexualising of the teacher is indicative of the low status attributed to teaching, especially the teaching of young children. It is seen as good training for wifeliness, rather than a career in its own right. Insisting on this, and on the primacy of the wifely role, ensures that this predominantly female career cannot confer real independence or status on women. In *Teacher's pet*, the relative statuses of the protagonists are initially reversed. We see how, from the perspective of the less well-educated, blue-collar working class, the teacher is representative of values and structures that exclude and belittle them. Part of the pleasure, of the fantasy of seducing the teacher, is the dream of subduing the class enemy. Yet, as is usually the case with popular romance, the story is told from the heroine's perspective. This raises the question of where the pleasure lies for the female reader. It seems to operate by exploiting the frisson of engaging with, and ultimately subduing through 'love', the 'otherness' of the working-class male, representative of the resistant males who 'think they've got nothing to aspire to, nothing to hope for but a life on the assembly line' (Berk, 1985, p. 125) and therefore make the teacher's life difficult. By displacing this fantasy on to a relationship with an adult who was a school drop-out, the teacher avoids the charge of sexual exploitation.

Teacher–student relationships in film

Among the films that have dealt with the 'difficult' theme of relationships, or accusations of relationships/sexual conduct, between students and teachers are: *Girl's Dormitory* (1936, directed by Irving Cummings), *Oleana* (1994, directed by David Mamet), *Art for Teachers of Children* (1995, directed by Jennifer Montgomery), *Wild Things* (1998, directed by John McNaughton) and *Amy and Isabelle* (2001, directed by Lloyd Kramer). The discussion below will focus on the way in which the subject has been represented in two contrasting productions: the 1962 UK film *Term of Trial* (directed by Peter Glanville) and the 1996 US film *Indecent Seduction* (directed by Alan Metzger; alternatively titled *For My Daughter's Honor*).

Term of Trial

Term of Trial followed 1961's *Spare the Rod* (directed by Leslie Norman) as a British film set in the context of a secondary modern school, as opposed to the more usual contemporary setting of a public school. It stars Laurence Olivier as teacher Graham Weir. Despite holding a 'good degree', Weir is condemned to teach in the undesirable secondary modern school because of the 'moral defect' that hangs over his character following his conscientious objection during wartime. His disgruntled French wife, Anna, frustrated by their domestic circumstances, social status and the hours he devotes to the job, as well as his drinking, also has doubts about his character, at one point asserting that his conscientious objection was really cowardice.

Term of Trial was closely related in atmosphere and look to the series of British 'kitchen-sink' dramas that strove for an element of social realism and addressed issues of social class in a new and daring way. The film, however, was far from radical in its outlook. Weir is portrayed as a committed and idealistic teacher who bravely attempts to teach classes that are constantly disrupted by working-class children presented as ungrateful, loutish youths. It is implied that his inability to deal effectively with their uncouth behaviour is partly the result of his dignified unworldliness and partly due to self-doubt. When fifteen-year-old Shirley Taylor (played by Sarah Miles) shows an interest in furthering her education so that she can 'become a secretary', Weir offers her free extra tuition in English. On visiting the girl's parents to gain their permission, he is confronted by bleak tenement blocks with landings frequented by prostitutes. The 'lower orders' in the film are generally presented as materially and sexually obsessed, as well as violent. Shirley quickly becomes infatuated by Weir. On the return journey from a school trip to Paris, she enters his London hotel room at night and, undressing, declares her love for him. Weir unambiguously rejects her, explaining that she would have regrets, that he is more than twice her age, and that he is married and loves his wife. The rejected and distraught girl leaves the room chillingly telling her teacher that she hates him.

Weir's 'reward' for his efforts to help the girl and for not taking advantage of her is that she makes a complaint of indecent assault. In preparing for his appearance in court, Weir wanders through streets filled with 'decadent' jukebox cafés, sex shops and sleazy cinema hoardings viewed by vacant-eyed youths. What he witnesses is presented as a nightmare of culture in the process of destruction by modernist decadence. Each youth, just like those he teaches, is the kind evoked by Richard Hoggart (1957, p. 250) when he warned: 'The hedonistic but passive barbarian who rides in a fifty-horse-power bus for threepence, to see a five-million-dollar film for one-and-eightpence, is not simply a social oddity; he is a portent.' On seeing a gun shop, Weir even contemplates suicide. In the subsequent trial, Shirley continues her lie. On hearing the verdict of guilty, and receiving a 'light' sentence of twelve months' conditional discharge, an emotional Weir tells the court that *he* is the victim of a society that is corrupt and obsessed with titillation, and that his love for the girl was inspired by innocence, not sex. It is only after hearing Weir's impassioned speech that the girl finally breaks down and tells the truth, leading to the verdict being commuted to a free pardon.

The irony is that post-trial, Weir can win the respect of his wife only by pretending that he lied to the court and had indeed assaulted the girl. In that sense, Weir appears as the victim not only of a society losing moral propriety but of venal women: first his ungrateful student; then his selfish, unappreciative, shallow wife. The film shows an educated and morally courageous man who is not understood by a society that has lost its higher ideals along with any sense of order. A good man is accused of bad things by an aspirational working-class girl he foolishly tried to help. The film appears to vindicate the discrimination against girls and the work-ing classes that characterised the UK education system of the time. It suggests that working-class children cannot take advantage of the opportunity of a good education and are too debased to be able to benefit. It also presents the central female character primarily as a sexual being. Moreover, it indicates that female sexuality is dangerous and threatening to men. This is a very insidious message, akin to that used for many years to prevent the progress of women in many professions. By refusing to see them as anything other than a disruptive sexual force, the film implies that removing them from their allotted and subordinate place can only be destructive to society and to individuals.

Indecent Seduction

The film *Indecent Seduction* provides an interesting counterpoint to *Term of Trial*. Made in the US some thirty-four years later, and based on a true story, it essentially deals with similar territory in that a teacher appears in court accused of having had a sexual relationship with a student. A key difference is that this time the charge is true. Fourteen-year-old Amy Dustin begins an 'innocent flirtation' with her teacher, Pete Nash, who is also the school's football coach, in a small American town. Coach Nash, however, quickly becomes manipulative and, offering declarations of love, effectively coerces the reluctant Amy into a sexual relationship. He becomes jealous and sexually demanding, and after he sees Amy dancing with a boy her own age he publicly makes a scene. He then drives her to the woods late at night and apologises for the incident, proclaiming his love for her, and again has sex with a reluctant but passively acquiescent Amy.

Ultimately, following pressure from her parents, who are concerned about her apparent moodiness and find a suggestive note that Nash has written to her on the back of a photograph, Amy admits what has been going on. It emerges that Nash has a record of such behaviour, though the school has not taken the previous accusations seriously. Following a trial, he is imprisoned, and the previously all-conquering football team begins to lose. The community turns against Amy and her family, and their home is vandalised, so again she becomes the victim. Other students, apart from one girl who understands because she was another of Nash's victims, call her a slut as she passes in the corridors.

Indecent Seduction is essentially a film about abuse of power. The bureaucracy of the school, and the attitudes of society, effectively protect a teacher who has corrupted the innocence of a young girl from justice until such time as a brave family is prepared to take a stand. Even then, paradoxically, they lose their status in society for doing so. *Term of Trial*, on the other hand, portrays the teacher as powerless in the face of a corrupted society that no longer respects hierarchies. *Indecent Seduction* shows the hypocrisy of a society that vilifies female victims of abuse. Nevertheless, it still associates female student sexuality with danger: to girls themselves, to teachers and to society.

This kind of danger is rarely associated with male student sexuality. The *American Pie* series, for example, presents male students' sexual obsessions as humorous, even endearing, if a little pathetic. It is also fair to add that the stereotypes of the sexually aware and exploitative female student and the hapless male teacher persist to the present day. In the 1999 film *Election*, directed by Alexander Payne, for example, Reese Witherspoon's character callously seduces her teacher, ruining his career.

Sex and teachers in popular music

> In high school I'd swapped notes with my best friend speculating as to the sexual intrigues amongst the staff. Oh, the orgiastic world of adults: at the center of our fantasy was the ruddy sports teacher, who delighted in confiscating mis-colored ribbons or stray jewelry. We found the harshest disciplinarians to be the most libidinous . . . Understanding our teachers' frustrations helped my friend and I, both still virgins, feel more kindly towards these people trading in petty humiliations.
>
> (Hooper, 2002, p. 45)

Britney Spears was seventeen when the video for her song '**Baby One More Time**' was a career-launching success. In it she appears as a sexually provocative schoolgirl while singing a lyric that speaks of the surrender of the self in an adult relationship.

A seemingly frothy pop song is therefore given a dark centre. The song itself does not refer to school; the association comes only through the video. However, the video presentations that now accompany popular music contribute significantly to the construction of the meaning of the song as a whole.

'Baby One More Time' encapsulates a recurrent contradiction in the portrayal of the schoolgirl. Her image is constructed so that she is both innocent and provocative, with the latter dependent on the former. Popular music mirrors in its own way the paradox of innocence and seduction that has already been discussed in the analysis of film. This is intensified by the way the artists are conflated with the images in the video. Thus, Britney herself, in her early incarnations, was presented as an innocent, virginal 'creature', yet also deliberately in a sexualised manner. In this way her unavailability as a sexual being intensifies the desire the sexual images provoke. This is not unusual. We do not know in detail how girls respond to these presentations of their sexual identities, but it might be reasonable to speculate that this is problematic. In order to please, they are expected to be childlike and simultaneously sexual; available and unavailable; untouchable and an object of fantasy.

Problems resulting from the way in which pop has exploited images of young women performers have been specifically addressed by Sheila Whiteley (2004). Popular music has essentially been a young person's form of expression, and a young person's commodity, though the consumer (and performer) demographic has changed as the history of popular music has developed. Often artists and fans have 'grown old' together. The school and the college, and the powerful emotional relations that they house, are natural sources of inspiration for pop music. So are love and sex. Popular music lyrics are not usually intended to stand alone like poetry, so when separated from the music and the tone and intonation of vocalisation they may lose important elements of their signification. But they are often both clever and profound, and they are certainly worthy of serious attention. There are frequently complex codes at work (where, for example, 'bad' may mean 'good'); 'shocking stances' may be adopted in order to critique rather than support what appears to be the overt message. On occasion, however, the writer's imperative may be something as simple as a cheap rhyme. Caution is therefore necessary.

Songs that purport to represent the schoolgirl's perspective generally have something of the superficial innocence of Britney's song. Lulu's **'To Sir with Love'** (1967) was the title track for the British secondary school-based film of the same title. In that drama (discussed more fully in Chapter 2) a black male teacher in a 'rough/tough' London school ultimately earns the respect of his students by treating them as adults. He also deals with the problem of a 'schoolgirl crush'. The title song is a romantic, but not sexualised, paean to a teacher which captures the way in which teaching can be seen as an initiation into adulthood. Although the lyrics make it clear that the girl appreciates the teacher's professional and moral qualities, it is significant that she feels she can show this appreciation only by giving him her heart, reinforcing her limited range of identities. While a schoolboy could presumably 'reward' his teacher by achieving success in later life, the schoolgirl is defined solely in terms of her romantic relationships.

There are, however, many songs written from the schoolgirl's perspective that are more suggestive, without ever becoming explicit. Jo Stafford's US hit '**Teach Me Tonight**' (1953) is an early example. Brehony (1998, p. 128) feels Doris Day's '**Teacher's Pet**' (1958) is a song where 'the narrator . . . comes across as a firm supporter of family values . . . [However,] there is a darker edge that derives from a literal reading of the lyric that this is indeed a schoolgirl singing of her male teacher.' This song has another common characteristic: an interest in how the relationship will be perceived by others. Here we see the schoolgirl wanting to be publicly displayed by the teacher who is the object of her affections and hoping that she will be able to show those at home that he loves her. This also clearly preoccupies the student in Abba's '**When I Kissed the Teacher**' (1976), which goes from a female student longing for her teacher to her taking direct action by kissing him as he leans over her in class. The first line of the song describes the euphoric reaction of the class to this action. Teenage girls in these lyrics are intrigued by the way their romantic and sexual behaviour is perceived by others.

The Bing Crosby/Connee Boswell duet '**An Apple for the Teacher**' (1939) has the female protagonist proclaiming both her desire for her teacher and her wish to be kept in detention after school. The male teacher's response is encouraging, and the song features sexual innuendo throughout. The schoolgirl is given a provocative persona, as a wayward pupil who is prepared to be compliant in a sexual context. The lyrics suggest she deliberately exploits her allure to gain favours from the teacher when she is academically lacking. The apple, with its connotations of sexual sin, easily takes on a double meaning, especially when the rest of the fruit metaphor in the song is considered: he must think she is a peach, a term that implies the girl is something luscious for consumption, rather than a lemon, a stupid individual.

The Police's 1980 hit '**Don't Stand So Close to Me**' is, to our knowledge, the only song of this nature that both takes the perspective of a male teacher and makes the issue of his sexual desire explicit and problematic. Brehony (1998, p. 129) thought it 'perhaps the most explicit treatment of teacher–pupil sexual relations to date in any pop song'. As well as acknowledging the male teacher's sexual temptation, the song recognises more directly the schoolgirl's sexual desire. It indicates that their liaison is resented by her classmates and condemned by his colleagues. Through a reference to Nabokov's *Lolita* (1998; first published in 1955), it also shows his awareness of how the relationship would be viewed by wider society. It includes little, however, to suggest that the relationship is based on the kind of exploitative fantasies heard in many other lyrics. The song largely ignores the problems of power and gender that shape such relationships, presenting instead a naïve view of social disapproval of a natural attraction.

Songs from a male student perspective are more common and offer a different set of values. Heavy metal, 'sleaze glam' band Hanoi Rocks' song '**High School**' (1984) outlines a male student's fantasy of becoming a teacher. The context is one in which school is a location for abuse generally, where he has experienced suffering and been labelled a parasite. The language and music convey an intense hatred of the institution. The motivation for becoming a teacher is to gain revenge by in turn brutalising those he teaches. This includes ensuring that academically bright girls are detained after school for practical biology classes. In this context, the sexual relationship with the girl is very different from that suggested by the lyric in 'Don't Stand So Close to Me'. There is no suggestion that the 'teacher' is conflicted: sex is merely an act of revenge or even hatred. In a similar but more crude vein are '**Sex Education**' by Mia X (1998) and LL Cool J featuring La Shawn's '**Imagine That**' (2001). By contrast, '**Mary of the Fourth Form**' by the Boomtown Rats (1977) describes a young femme fatale who has all the boys in the class in thrall to her, as well as the male teacher, whom she sexually titillates, and who cannot resist her 'because he is a man'. This portrayal shows the female student's actions to be deliberate and teasing.

In Chloe Hooper's novel *A child's book of true crime*, a young female school-teacher reflects on her lover, the father of one of the children in her class: 'I walked out of the gates, and felt a wave of disapproval rising within me: *Imagine fucking your own child's teacher!* How could he do that?' (Hooper, 2002, p. 179). Teachers have, in post-war society, stereotypically been depicted as female and, to a large extent, as asexual beings. This may, as the above quotation suggests, be a kind of taboo arising from their association with children. Modern popular music also generally sees a teacher as female, but here she is also often an object of sexual desire. There are, to the best of our knowledge, no songs that address desire for a student directly from the perspective of a female teacher. There are a great many songs, however, that are written from the perspective of a male student who has sexual designs on his female teacher. A relatively early example was Johnny Mathis' hit '**Teacher, Teacher**' (1958); another is Elton John's '**Teacher I Need You**' (1973).

The heavy metal genre, much beloved of testosterone-fuelled young men, has often been criticised on the basis of a perceived lack of subtlety. Van Halen's '**Hot for Teacher**' (1984) is effectively a series of exclamations of sexual arousal accompanied by frenzied guitar. It was released with a promotional video of a scantily clad teacher 'controlling' a class. The male student uses his sexual fantasy to shift the grounds of his relationship with the teacher and with the school. Before he meets her, she is objectified: he wonders what the teacher is going to look like; not what she will *be* like. He sexualises her in a context in which success at school is associated with social class betrayal. He rejects additional work because he does not want to look like a middle-class 'swot'. He implies that the teacher is having an affair with him by saying she is assertive, does not know the rules, and offers a different kind of homework. By diminishing her social class superiority, he turns her into a mere sexual being. Extreme's '**Teacher's Pet**' (1989) is less obviously social class-based, but it also has as the central persona a male student who resists academic work. The song's appeal relies on the witty appropriation of academic terms for sexual purposes, thereby using the lyrics to subordinate academic achievement. **Venom**'s song of the same title has a narrative in which a male student is held in detention by his female teacher, who has caught him masturbating. The song is highly explicit, focusing on the idea that the teacher punishes the pupil for his behaviour by engaging him in further sexual activities. The lyrics appear to be grounded in a stereotypical male fantasy about sex with women in authority, such as policewomen and nurses as well as teachers, who can dole out punishment.

Whether these songs, however offensive, entertaining or amusing they may be perceived to be, are in any way harmful is a difficult point to argue. We are aware of no empirical research that addresses this question. There is, though, a recorded US case whereby a fourteen-year-old boy recorded a song about his female teacher and uploaded it to the Napster website. Titled the 'Mrs Dunn Song', its lines included:

> I'll be the pimp, you be the whore
> . . . When I see you I fall in rage
> I don't really care if you're double my age
> . . . I'm not a stalker, I just like to peep.

The song was brought to the attention of the teacher, who accused the student of harassment. He was subsequently suspended for breaching the Cumberland High School's sexual harassment code before being readmitted when the American Civil Liberties Union intervened, claiming that the student was protected by the US First Amendment (ACLU, 2003). The summer of 2003 saw young British pop 'boy band' Busted, whose fan base comprised mainly teenage girls, enjoy a huge chart hit with **'What I Go to School for'**. The teenager here has struggled to sneak forbidden glimpses of the teacher yet believes that she desires him and is giving him good marks for that reason. The lyrics veer between a mildly lascivious view of the teacher through to a revealing glimpse into the desperate voyeurism of the lust-crazed teenager looking into her room. It ends with a perspective that again shows how important the peer group is in the construction of sexual fantasy: not only does the fantasy include the idea that this woman is besotted with him; it is essential that she makes her feelings public. Initially, his friends all laughed at him because of his infatuation, but then he proves his manhood when they see him passing by the school in a car with the teacher. Clearly, scoring with the teacher would not be half as satisfying if his mates did not know about it.

Armstrong (2001, p. 103) points out that 'every variety of Western music, including classical symphonies and opera, is an almost exclusively male domain'. Furthermore, all varieties of popular music, including the more politically radical (such as punk), have been and remain overwhelmingly patriarchal. This is reflected in the lyrics that appear in this and other chapters of this book. The discourse of pop, its 'performative utterances', can, where oppressive, be read as a form of symbolic violence. They can also be an expression of real tensions that are at play in society generally, and specifically in schools, and which have implications for pedagogy. Bauer (1998, pp. 315–316) confronts the difficult question of what teachers can do about the eroticised classroom:

> Good teaching turns the primary desire to be liked, or loved, into the recognition of social needs within the classroom: the value of communal work, discipline, even a 'calling' or commitment to change . . . It also means relinquishing the personal for the political, since the equation of the personal and the political has unfortunately been translated onto the screen as erotic or disciplinary intimacy.

Summary

The representation of teachers as sexual beings, and as sexual objects, in the texts we have studied suggests that there is still a powerful discourse that constructs the profession as feminised. Male teachers are often presented as objects of schoolgirl fantasy, but rarely, if ever, as full-blown romantic heroes, worthy partners for some feisty female heroine. The profession does not appear to have the cachet, the status that confers the sexual glamour pertaining to a romantic hero. Instead, they can be objects of schoolgirl crushes, almost as though they are pretend adult males, people on whom girls can practise harmlessly until a real hero comes along. Popular songs and situation comedies highlight these gentle crushes, presenting them as a wholesome, if occasionally embarrassing, part of female adolescence, as long as they are not reciprocated. Representations of two-way relationships between male teachers and schoolgirls are much darker. They are not usually shown, for example, as instances of forbidden but nevertheless genuine love, in which two people struggle against social restrictions. Instead, the discourse is one of danger, betrayal and exploitation on both sides, indicating the depth and universality of this taboo in our society. In such tales adolescent female sexuality often acquires an almost terrifying power, threatening any male teacher who steps out of the strictly de-sexualised role he must maintain.

Female teachers, on the other hand, appear as objects of fantasy both for schoolboys and for a wider male audience. They can represent an amalgam of idealised female virtues, making them desirable as conventional wives and mothers. In these instances, teaching is presented as something that is 'natural' for women, through which they serve and nurture rather than control. Therefore, it is not threatening to men. Alternatively, though, they are presented as highly sexualised beings in a series of texts in which male fantasy focuses on the subjugation of female authority. The aggression which fuels these texts may be overlaid with apparent respect for the teaching role and present the relationship as challenging or complex, but they rely, nevertheless, on the need for the male to control the female teacher. They are open to interpretation as revenge stories in which males exert sexual control over teachers, who have in the past offended male dignity by having control over them. In some instances, this revenge is extremely raw, taking on an edge of violence or hatred, especially in the lyrics of popular songs.

Ultimately, then, sexual fantasies about teachers seem to confirm a generalised discomfort with female authority, and with men in roles that involve nurturing the young. This power dynamic is often intensified by the way in which the female teacher is seen to be representative of a kind of social gentility, so subduing her to one's sexual whim strikes a blow for the class war at the same time. The element of power in these fantasies that take the student perspective is also indicated by the recurrence of the wish for a public display that will enable the student to parade his or her conquest.

6 Don't pick on me

In previous chapters, we have explored the complexity of schools and colleges as social and cultural environments. We have examined the relationships between teachers and students in different ways, analysing, for example, how power is exercised and experienced. It has emerged that teachers, even the most benign and vulnerable of them, have institutional power, while students, even the most influential and aggressive of them, are susceptible to authority. The latter may resist or rebel, and, in extremity, teachers may call upon external agencies or even risk their lives to restore the traditional hierarchy in which staff have at least notional power over students. However, the relationship between teachers and students is not the only structure operational in education. If we step back and move away from the staff room, we enter a complex and confused environment where young people establish and maintain, experience and endure their own social and cultural networks. In the closed world of young people, meaning, knowledge, control and authority are not mediated through prescribed formulae, although, routinely, such factors as affluence, age, appearance, attractiveness, articulacy, class, gender, height, intelligence, race, size and even musical preference may all be significant.

Within schools and colleges, students might function as individuals, but often their identity is circumscribed by their position in or exclusion from the various groups, gangs, cliques, clans and tribes that exist in each institution. Social hierarchies are fluid and flexible, perpetually shifting and changing in this volatile student world. People come and go; they gain influence or lose power; they grow older, bigger and possibly even wiser. School is a physical and cultural environment and a site of social interaction where physique, proximity, language and looks are all part of the communicative and intimidatory arsenal. In classrooms, corridors and playgrounds, during journeys to and from school, those with power walk the talk and name names. These are the queen bees and the main men; those with voices that can be heard; those with power and popularity. On the margins are the socially excluded, identified by Busted in their song '**Loser Kid**' (2002) as the last to be selected for sports teams. They are largely silent and easily ignored. Billy Casper in *Kes* (1969, directed by Ken Loach) epitomised them, standing alone in his baggy, borrowed shorts as, one by one, others were picked in preference for the class football teams. These are the unpopular kids whose very existence seems to invite abuse. Lisa Simpson explains the phenomenon in 'Bye, Bye Nerdy' (*The Simpsons*, 2001) when she reveals to the Twelfth Annual Big Science Thing that nerdy kids give off pheromones which attract bullies. Billy Casper is pathetic rather than nerdy, but the result is the same; even his family intimidates him. In the book that inspired the film, Mr Farthing, the English teacher, interrupting a fight between Billy and MacDowall, castigates the latter: 'You're nothing but a bully boy. The classic example of a bully! If it isn't Casper, then it's someone like him' (Hines, 1968, p. 97).

At worst, these young people are victims not just of their peers but of a system which cannot protect them. For some, this leaves what might seem like the only option of violence, such as that imagined by the protagonist in the Donnas' **'I Wanna Be a Unabomber'** (1997), who describes how he wants to slice up the 'cool' kids at school. Such a stance can be a factor in reality. A video sent to NBC suggests it was instrumental in the deaths of thirty-two people killed at Virginia Polytechnic and State University by a lone gunman in April 2007. The twenty-three-year-old perpetrator, student Cho Seung-Hui, who had been referred for counselling and therapy several times, blamed others for his actions and clearly believed that *he* was the victim:

> You had a hundred billion chances and ways to have avoided today. Your Mercedes wasn't enough, you brats. Your golden necklaces weren't enough, you snobs. Your trust fund wasn't enough. Your vodka and cognac weren't enough. All your debaucheries weren't enough. Those weren't enough to fulfil your hedonistic needs. You had everything.

We shall identify a similar sense of anger and alienation when considering the behaviour and bullying in films such as *Elephant* later in this chapter.

Before the 1980s, the concept of bullying between schoolchildren was largely unacknowledged in educational debate and under-researched in academic study or professional practice. Teachers dealt with bullies and attempted to counteract bullying, but public admissions were avoided in case they were construed as an institutional lack of discipline. Despite this, however, bullying was prevalent in popular culture, especially in children's literature, starting with the nineteenth-century novel *Tom Brown's school days*:

> Tom and East slept in the farther corner of the room, and were not seen at first. 'Gone to ground, eh?' roared Flashman.
>
> 'Push 'em out then, boys; look under the beds.' And he pulled up the little white curtain of the one nearest him. 'Wh-o-op!' he roared, pulling away at the leg of a small boy, who held on tight to the leg of the bed, and sang out lustily for mercy.
>
> 'Here lend a hand, one of you, and help me pull out this young howling brute. Hold your tongue, sir, or I'll kill you!'
>
> 'Oh please, Flashman, please, Walker, don't toss me! I'll fag for you – I'll do anything – only don't toss me.'

'You be hanged,' said Flashman, lugging the wretched boy along; ''twon't hurt you – you! – Come along boys; here he is.'

(Hughes, 1857, ch. 6)

School stories, including the more recent *Harry Potter* novels by J. K. Rowling (published between 1997 and 2007), often appear in series that chart the progress of the central character through adolescence, allowing him/her to grow in stature and confidence. Following each edition, dedicated readers can be comforted that, if bullies did not get their come-uppance by the end, then scores will be settled in a subsequent book. In the early twentieth century, the young heroes were usually schoolboys: for example, Penrod in the US books of the same name by Booth Tarkington, first published in 1914; and William Brown in the *Just William* series by Richmal Crompton, first published in 1924. From 1940, however, Enid Blyton readdressed the gender balance of the school novel, publishing the *Naughtiest Girl*, *St Clare's* and *Malory Towers* series. Bullies emerge in each: even Elizabeth Allen, the 'naughtiest girl' herself, is not immune to being bullied, just like the children half a century later in Jacqueline Wilson's *Bad girls* (1997). Finally, John Christopher Timothy Jennings, the rascal who first appeared in a 1948 radio play and subsequently was the eponymous hero of a series of novels by Anthony Buckeridge, knew bullies, but, despite his many misdemeanours, he could never be accused of being one himself.

So what or who is a bully? Valerie Besag (1989, p. 3), examining various definitions, asserts:

> Most definitions agree that three factors are implicit in any bullying activity: it must occur over a prolonged period of time rather than being a single aggressive act; it must involve an imbalance of power, the powerful attacking the powerless; it can be verbal, physical or psychological in nature.

An 'imbalance of power' in this context is complex, however, especially when one examines both direct and indirect bullying. Information, for example, can be power, and words wound. Foucault (1980, p. 39), whose discussions of power have been referred to previously, emphasises how power can affect individuals at a very personal level:

> In thinking of the mechanisms of power, I am thinking rather of its capillary form of existence, the point where power reaches into the very grain of individuals, touches their bodies and inserts itself into their action and attitudes, their discourses, their learning processes and everyday lives.

Power, for Foucault, is not simply an expression of domination where the apparently strong oppress the notionally weak, but rather it can be constructed in alternate and unique ways. Although not all definitions place the same emphasis as Besag does on an imbalance of power, others, like that of the UK Department for Education (DFE, 1994, p. 7), also identify three facets to bullying:

- deliberately hurtful behaviour;
- often repeated over a period of time;
- difficult for those who are bullied to defend themselves.

This definition is echoed by the UK Office for Standards in Education (Ofsted, 2003, p. 1): 'Bullying is aggressive or insulting behaviour by an individual or group, often repeated over a period of time that intentionally hurts or harms.' Consistent to all definitions is that bullying is of a sustained nature. Smith and Sharp (1994, p. 2) also emphasise this but acknowledge a further difficulty in explaining what is meant by 'hurt' or 'abuse': 'Bullying can be described as a systematic abuse of power . . . the exact definition of what constitutes *abuse* will depend on social and cultural context.' Commenting on the paucity of research prior to the 1980s, Besag (1989) highlights the way in which 'seemingly innocuous acts' can be classified as bullying because experience and interpretation are as important in an analysis of the phenomenon as intention and initiation. Similarly, an Ofsted study (2003, p. 5) notes that individuals accused of bullying will often underestimate its significance and severity: '"We were only having a laugh"; "I was only teasing"; "We didn't hurt him"'. While some victims 'choose to remain silent. Disclosing what is happening runs counter to a culture of not telling tales and it can also risk making things worse.'

In schools, Besag (1989, p. 4) suggests, bullying exists largely as a 'covert activity, occurring without adult witness', and 'the bully, victim and any observers remain silent'. This clandestine aspect makes bullying even more dramatic and well suited to cinematic or televisual representation. Relationships between the bully and the bullied provide grounds for narrative tension through apprehension, intimidation and dread. Furthermore, it is rare for bullying to involve only a perpetrator and victim since, inevitably, there are bystanders who witness or are aware of the activity. Their compliance is not insignificant because observers, by definition, collaborate and condone the activity. For an audience, recalling their own school days, this can raise issues of identification, acknowledgement and guilt. Almost without exception, everyone at some point will have been a bully, a victim or a bystander.

Child developmental theory (Rigby, 2003) suggests that early in childhood, individuals are inclined to assert themselves physically, but with time they discriminate more socially acceptable behaviour, and physical bullying becomes less common than verbal abuse. Analyses of bullying have studied its pathogenesis in individual, social and cultural terms. Rigby (*ibid.*, p. 4) in his examination of bullying in Australia, classifies the following groups, recognisable from films such as *Dangerous Minds*, *The Craft*, *187*, *Cruel Intentions* and *Elephant*:

> Children who repeatedly bully others at school tend to be low in emphatic regard for others and inclined towards psychoticism (Rigby and Slee, 1993). Children who are frequently targeted as victims at school are inclined to be psychologically introverted, to have low self esteem and lack social skills, especially in the area of assertiveness.

An examination of bullying as a socio-cultural phenomenon might focus on class, race, gender, sexual orientation and so on. For example, Jack Read in *The Guinea Pig* accepted that, as a scholarship boy in a private school, he would be bullied until he adopted the upper-middle-class values inherent within the institution.

Gender forms a significant element in representations of bullying in popular culture, and, while both same-sex and cross-gender bullying occurs, the latter is often manifest through the use of pejorative and sexist language and through sexual harassment. *Cruel Intentions* (1999, directed by Roger Kumble), for example, explores through sexual exploitation of the vulnerable by the more powerful the ways in which heterosexual relations and sexual politics are constructed within society. Mac an Ghaill (1994, p. 9), who has written extensively about gender identity, especially developing masculinities and schooling, refers to:

> The constitutive cultural elements of dominant modes of heterosexual subjectivity that informed male students learning to act like men within the school arena. These elements consisted of contradictory forms of compulsory heterosexuality, misogyny and homophobia, and were marked by contextual contingency and ambivalence.

The following sections draw on Mac an Ghaill's work to examine how these elements could lead to tensions within school and college that might result in aggression and generate the sort of oppressive practices that create victims.

Binary oppositions, such as acceptance and rejection, victim and aggressor, are fundamental to Foucault's discourse paradigm in *The archaeology of knowledge* (1972). A concept such as that of a bully, for example, by definition constructs the notion of victimisation, since the relationship of bully and victim is both contradictory and symbiotic:

> Discourse is the path from one contradiction to another: if it gives rise to those that can be seen, it is because it obeys that which it hides. To analyse discourse is to hide and reveal contradictions; it is to show the play that they set up within it; it is to manifest how it can express them, embody them.
>
> (*ibid.*, p. 151)

As was suggested earlier, for Foucault, power is productive: it is about creation as well as oppression, and, as a result, produces social and cultural practice which is both revelatory and oppositional. Power is also constantly shifting, giving rise to transpositional discourses in which a victim may, in his or her turn, become a bully or abuser, as in *The Craft*, when Rochelle turns on Laura Lizzie, who had persistently criticised her (Rochelle's) appearance, or *Elephant*, when Eric and Alex eliminate not just their tormentors but anyone else with whom they come into contact.

Achievement and acceptance

Bullying is an experience and it is an aggressive and manipulative act. A victim can be hurt physically, emotionally or psychologically, but, inevitably, all bullying will have an emotional or psychological dimension. Mac an Ghaill (1994, p. 60) categorises different groups of young men within an English comprehensive school, drawing attention to the laddish, anti-academic culture that was and is prevalent among some teenage boys and which can lead to vilification, especially against those who study arts-based subjects: 'We were in the school band and they would really take the piss, saying we were girls because we carried violins and that. And then we got into drama, the macho mob were really bad, every day threatening and punishing us.'

Research into underachievement – for example, Epstein *et al.* (1998), QCA (1998), Francis (2000), Noble and Bradford (2000) and Marks (2001) – stresses the significance of social and cultural factors in boys' performance. High achievement is rarely linked to popularity in school unless, like Zack Siler in *She's All That*, it is associated with sporting prowess. In *Mean Girls*, Cady Heron, a very able mathematician, deliberately hides her academic ability in order to become socially acceptable. Willow Rosenberg, the academic witch in *Buffy the Vampire Slayer*, is part of a close-knit group of friends but not popular outside that group. In contrast, the apparently vacuous Cordelia is admired and surrounded by acolytes. Usually in popular culture, academic success is associated with nerds, geeks, dweebs or dorks: people who dedicate their lives to dull and boring study because they are not able to achieve in any other way. This, by definition, makes them subject to abuse, like Casey Connor in *The Faculty*, dismissed as 'that Stephen King kid', or Eric in *Elephant* (2003, directed by Gus Van Sant). Eric is bombarded by bits of paper as he works during a physics lesson. He then goes home to play Beethoven's 'Für Elise' on the piano. Eric is reminiscent of **Jeremy** in the 1991 Pearl Jam song of the same name who initially seems harmless, but then reveals a brutal streak.

In *Elephant*, the persecution of Eric and his friend Alex is terminated by their killing spree. Their motivation, like that of the perpetrators of the 1999 Columbine High School massacre (on which the film is based), is not easy to isolate. However, evidence from the killers at Columbine, Eric Harris and Dylan Klebold, does apportion blame. Harris' diary, for example, highlights his alienation: 'I hate you people for leaving me out of so many fun things. And, no, fucking don't say, well that's your fault, because it isn't. You people had my phone number, and I asked and all, but, no, don't let the weird Eric kid come along. Oh, fucking no.' And in a home video Klebold crows: 'You've given us shit for years. You're fucking going to pay for all the shit.' Eric and Alex in *Elephant* are misfits, too: they are bullied; they have a homosexual encounter; they watch programmes about Nazis. But all the kids at school have issues, and the quiet, intense narrative of *Elephant* ensures that, despite the relative absence of dialogue, these problems are apparent: whether it is John's alcoholic father; Carrie's possible pregnancy; Brittany, Jordan and Nicole's bulimia; or Michelle's bodily inhibitions. One by one, however, they die, except for John, who is told: 'Get the fuck out of here and don't come back. Shit's going down.' Exhilarated, Eric exhorts Alex to 'Pick off the kids . . . Pick them off one by one . . . We've enough explosives to last us half a day. Most importantly, have fun, man.' This casual acceptance of murder echoes the amorality of the Shadow Man song **'Day at School'** (2000), which tells how a student, having been picked on, joins a gang and goes on a gun rampage.

Stam and Shohat (1994, p. 319), exploring the wider social and educational implications of violence in schools, highlight the need for a structured response:

> Educators need pedagogical strategies that move between dominant and oppositional appropriations of violence. These will enable them to develop alternative understandings of how violence is produced, framed aesthetically, circulated and ruptured. Violence may then be connected with broader considerations of critique, public discourse and social engagement.

Many academic achievers, if they do not burn out, do survive, however, and acquire the kind of material success which leads to social and professional well-being. They come back ten years later to school reunions to show how successful they are. In *Romy and Michele's High School Reunion* (1997, directed by David Mirkin), the former class nerd and butt of teenage jokes takes great pleasure in revealing he is the new Bill Gates. While Romy, who was overweight, and Michele, who wore a back brace, manufacture their success as the inventors of Post-its. The rich social and cultural mix that comprises the average high school inevitably results in cliques and gangs, and this is replicated in teen films and accounts of schooling because it quickly ascribes interests and allegiances. Michael Eckman tells Cameron James at the beginning of *Ten Things I Hate About You* (1999, directed by Gil Junger), a film loosely based on Shakespeare's *The Taming of the Shrew*, about the lines of demarcation in Padua High School, which are based on student appearance, consumption, politics and educational and economic aspiration.

Schools and colleges bring disparate people together in large, complex organisations where jealousy and frustration inevitably result in confrontation, estrangement and aggression. The lyrics of Insane Clown Posse's **'Never Had It Made'** (1992) provide a narrative where hope and aspiration are juxtaposed with violence from the very first day at school, when the speaker is stabbed in the head with a pencil. In **'Willy Bubba'** (1998), Insane Clown Posse offer an even more graphic description that combines nationalism, class, gender and racial antipathy alongside a debunking of academic achievement, the denunciation of teachers and an affirmation of gun culture. Mac an Ghaill (1994), in his study of male student society, identifies, in addition to 'academic achievers' and 'new enterprisers', 'macho lads' and 'real Englishmen'. Within certain school and college microcultures, race is, inevitably, a sensitive and provocative issue. Sewell (1995, p. 34), in his study of black masculinity and schooling, draws attention to how one student positions himself in a way that undermines education, gender and sexual politics:

> Mike, like some African-Caribbean boys in Township, perceived being pro-school as unmanly. Jeff Taylor is not a real man because he does not get into

trouble with the teachers. It is in a sexual framework that Mike describes his position and how he has been positioned. He dismisses conformist pupils as 'pusses', compared to his confrontational approach.

Mac an Ghaill (1994, p. 85) also reveals that 'real Englishmen' resent the demise of 'English culture' and white 'macho lads' feel the need to 'defend our territory'. Yet, beyond this, tensions within inter-ethnic relations lead not only to bullying but to community conflict: 'The black macho lads were particularly vindictive to African Caribbean academic students, who overtly distanced themselves from their anti-school strategies. In response, the black macho lads labelled them "botty men" (a homophobic comment)' (*ibid.*, p. 87). Such tensions are apparent in films like *Dangerous Minds, 187* and *Freedom Writers*, where we see teachers working with 'difficult', usually black, Latino or Asian, students.

Race and gender

> Media culture is the central terrain on which the new racism has emerged.
> (Giroux, 2002, p. 198)

In *Dangerous Minds* (explored in Chapter 2), new teacher LouAnne Johnson is given an especially challenging class comprising mainly disaffected African-American and Chicano/Latino students. Although the film focuses on the teacher, there is evidence of the pressure on individuals to conform to peer and social expectations. Emilio, for example, is drawn into a web of violence from which he can't escape and which ultimately kills him. Connell (1987, p. 282), commenting on young men in similar situations, explains the implausibility of the notion that academia could present an escape route for such individuals:

> The differentiation of masculinities occurs in relation to a school curriculum which organises knowledge hierarchically and sorts students into an academic hierarchy. By institutionalising academic failure via competitive grading and streaming, the school forces differentiation on the boys. But masculinity is organised on the macro scale – around social power. Social power in terms of access to higher education, entry to professions, command of communication, is being delivered to boys who are academic 'successes'. The reaction of the 'failed' is likely to be a claim to other sources of power, even other definitions of masculinity. Sporting prowess, physical aggression, sexual conquest may do.

Giroux (2002, p. 148) argues that *Dangerous Minds* positions whiteness at the forefront of what is acceptable and desirable, and that the intimidation and aggression within the film are symptomatic of this racial paradigm: 'The film attempts to represent "whiteness" as the archetypal of rationality, "tough" authority, cultural literacy, and high academic standards in the midst of the changing racial demographics of urban space.' He also comments (*ibid.*, p. 149) on the film's musical score, reinforcing how seductive to certain sectors of the white audience is the 'Right wing assumption that rap music signifies black culture as one of crime and violence.' The more recent *Freedom Writers* (discussed in Chapter 2) does little to dispel this notion, although it does posit a greater sense of ethnic groups articulating hopes and aspirations through their own music and writing. Rap and hip hop challenge white middle-class concerns, but Gates (1990, p. 236) argues for a positive slant on black masculinities and music, emphasising that they should be analysed and interpreted within the context of black youth culture, where a shared physical and social reality exist between audience and performer: 'Just as Blacks have "imitated" white western languages, literatures, religions, music, dance, dress and family life, but with a critical "signifying" difference, so shall Afro American literary criticism steal the meat out the sandwich but leave the white bread untouched.'

187 is another movie where the teacher takes centre stage against a backdrop of urban degeneration and violence in which the students intimidate, bully and oppress not only him but one another. Rita, who is mixed race, lives in a brutal and misogynistic world where women are commodified. She is simply used and abused physically and emotionally by the young men at school and by the white teacher, Dave Childress. This exploitation of girls and women is not unique, of course, to Rita's community. In *Cruel Intentions*, Sebastian Valmont callously exploits the young women he dates. Rachel Greenbaum, for example, is victimised simply because she is Sebastian's psychotherapist's daughter. When Sebastian realises Dr Greenbaum is unimpressed by accounts of his sexual prowess, he is aggrieved. Later, confessing to her mother about nude pictures of her that have appeared on the web, Rachel explains how she was seduced by the photographer's charm, using language which makes it clear who has exploited her and her 'killer legs'. Dr Greenbaum had tried to involve Sebastian's parents in her attempts to regulate his behaviour, but, as Morrissey indicates in his song **'The Teachers Are Afraid of the Pupils'** (1995), parents are often part of the problem. Sometimes, they cause or are victims of the situation. In *Heathers* (discussed more fully later), Jason Dean's father is more childlike than his son, and he would be incapable of moderating his offspring's behaviour, even if he were aware of it. Similarly, in *Mean Girls*, Regina George's mother is woefully inadequate and self-absorbed, her main interest in her daughter being to ally herself with youth in a vain attempt to resist middle age. Finally, in *187*, Cesar's mother is as much one of his victims as the other people he terrorises: 'God forgive me,' she bemoans. 'Sometimes, I just wish Jesus would take him.'

The preceding section has looked at bullying in the context of violence, race and gender, in order to position it institutionally within school and society. In so doing, the aim has been to highlight the way in which bullying thrives in a culture where intimidation is tolerated; where abuse is absolved; and where knives and guns are legitimised as manifestations of manhood and/or as weapons of defence. This is a culture that corrupts bystanders as well as perpetrators. An eradication of bullying is not merely a process of identifying or excluding individuals. It should not simply seek to problematise race or class, nor to marginalise the serious issues which confront young people on a daily basis. The eradication of bullying requires the generation of a social and educational environment in which bullying and aggression have no place and where individuals have sufficient hope and compassion to be able to respect themselves and each other.

This may well be easier said than done, but many anti-bullying policies seek a reciprocity that leads people to explore their own feelings and motivations and to acknowledge the perspectives and sensitivities of others. The 'circle of friends' is one such strategy aimed at encouraging students to be inclusive and listen to alternative points of view:

> The effect of the 'circle of friends' on the victims of bullying was significant. They felt less isolated and knew their peers would not remain passive if anyone intimidated or troubled them. The friendship group broke down the isolation of the victims and helped them to belong. A strength of the system is that it can not only support victims, but also those who bully.
>
> (Ofsted, 2003, p. 16)

In *Mean Girls*, Ms Horbury gets all the girls together in the gym in order to express their feelings about one another. She seeks an atmosphere of openness and trust in order to calm aggression. Although *Mean Girls* explores this as an anti-bullying initiative, popular culture, and film in particular, is drawn to the dramatic conflict that results from confrontation, and, therefore, in its representations of schooling, bullying almost invariably has a place.

A wide range of behaviour – name-calling, extortion, physical violence, slander, exclusion from a group, damage to property, physical and verbal intimidation (Smith and Sharp, 1994) – may all be classed as forms of bullying, and these have recently been joined by cyber-bullying. We shall now look at such behaviour with specific reference to girls, focusing particularly on a comparison between two films: *Heathers* and *Mean Girls*. It has been noted that bullying received relatively little academic attention before the 1980s, but even when it became the subject of research and professional concern, the focus was on bullying perpetrated by boys. Young males were constructed as testosterone-fuelled menaces who found it difficult to manage their anger or moderate their behaviour with the result that youthful and confused masculinities found expression in belligerence and intimidation. The conceptualisation of this form of bullying is direct, explicit and often public, so it cannot easily be ignored by the authorities.

Simmons (2002) sought to shift the emphasis somewhat, by exploring girls' bullying, arguing that it had received relatively little attention because relationships between girls, even oppressive ones, are likely to be more subtle, less obviously aggressive and more socially restrained than those typically occurring between boys. As a consequence, she started her study by exploring the silence familiar to much feminist research, and identified by Cameron (1985, p. 5) as 'a constant theme of feminist writing'. Coates (1993, p. 35) describes how, politically and historically, silence in a patriarchal society is equated with conformity, acquiescence and

obedience: 'The model of the silent woman is still presented to girls in the second half of the twentieth century: research in English schools suggests that quiet behaviour is very much encouraged by teachers, particularly in girls.' French feminist Luce Irigaray (1977, p. 187) also charts the inhibition and uncertainty complicit in silencing women:

> If you/I hesitate to speak, isn't it because we are afraid of not speaking well? But what is 'well' or 'badly'? With what are we conforming if we speak 'well'? What hierarchy, what subordination lurks there, waiting to break our resistance? What claim to raise ourselves to a worthier discourse?

So Simmons (2002, p. 3) probes the silence that is traditionally part of the more secretive aspects of female experience:

> Silence is deeply woven into the fabric of female experience . . . Now is the time to end another silence. There is a hidden culture of girls' aggression in which bullying is epidemic, distinctive and destructive. It is not marked by the direct physical and verbal behaviour that is primarily the province of boys. Our culture refuses girls access to open conflict, and it forces their aggression into non-physical, indirect and covert forms.

Although we will return to Simmons' argument, it is worth noting briefly that recent studies have provided increasing evidence of aggressive physical contact between girls' gangs in socially deprived urban communities, and hard-core gang alliances seem to provide a refuge for some desperate, underprivileged young women. Chesney-Lind and Hagedorn (1999, p. 9) observe: 'Factors such as early motherhood, domestic violence, gang rape and boredom shape the unique world that girls inhabit in these communities and the choice of gang membership is a way that girls who find themselves in this world survive.' For those interested in how these female gangs are represented in popular culture, Bev Zalcock (1999) analyses a range of films in which girl gangs and female violence are explored.

Simmons (2002, p. 3), however, seeks to illuminate the less explicit, more indirect aspects of bullying between girls: 'Within the hidden culture of aggression, girls fight with body language and relationships instead of fists and knives. In this world friendship is a weapon, and the sting of a shout pales in comparison to a day of someone's silence.' This activity is so abstruse that it might be difficult for the victim even to describe what has happened in a way which will persuade others to take her seriously. For many girls, fear of being isolated and friendless is over-whelming, and the fact that ostracism might be seen by adults as transitory provides no consolation or comfort to sufferers. Simmons (*ibid.*, p. 43) refers to this as 'relational aggression' (drawing from Crick and Bigbee, 1998), pointing out that, since it involves a relationship, it could include all manner of indirect intimidation, such as segregation, silence, whispering, staring or even spreading rumours about the victim: 'Where relationships are weapons, friendship itself can be a tool of anger.' The people with whom you have or have had a relationship are invariably the ones who know you best, and therefore also know how to hurt you most effectively.

Frenemies

Heathers

Heathers (1989, directed by Michael Lehmann) focuses on popularity and its potential for corruption and bullying. Popularity in the context of schooling can be a difficult concept. It is not necessarily about having lots of friends and more about having status and being admired rather than being liked. Other kids want to be with popular people in order to gain cachet by association. Simmons (2002, p. 156) explains just how much girls are prepared to forfeit for popularity:

> But here is the truth about girls and popularity. It is a cutthroat contest into which girls pour boundless energy and anxiety. It is an addiction, a siren call, a prize for which some would pay any price. Popularity changes girls, causes a great many of them to lie and cheat and steal. They lie to be accepted, cheat their friends by using them, steal people's secrets to resell at a higher social price.

Heathers focuses on a student clique comprising Heather Chandler, Heather Duke, Heather McNamara and, on its fringe, Veronica Sawyer, played by Winona Ryder. Veronica is in training to become a fully fledged Heather, which means being relentlessly superior, uncompromising and domineering. Occasionally, she shows some independence and resistance to the remorseless creed, but the clique's leader, Heather Chandler, is resolute: 'Do I look like Mother Teresa?'

Simmons (*ibid.*, p. 157) emphasises how, 'With scientific precision, girls track their bearings on the relational landscape.' Wiseman (2002, p. 10) agrees:

> Girls have strict social hierarchies based on what our culture tells us about what constitutes ideal femininity . . . but who is the prime enforcer of these standards? The movies? Teen magazines? Nope, it's the girls themselves. They police each other, conducting surveillance on who's breaking the laws of appearance, clothes, interest in boys and personality.

A clique is built on compliance and complicity, and bullying is a vehicle for this. Veronica is told to forge a note to the overweight Martha Dunstock, suggesting that one of the boys is interested in her. When Veronica resists on the basis that it is pointless and hurtful, Heather Chandler abuses her instead.

Bullies need victims, but they also need acquiescence and acceptance within their own social circle and a secure footing in a group or gang in order to define themselves. To stay in a clique (or to gain access to one), individuals are persuaded to behave in ways that, in normal circumstances, they would deplore. Relationships drive the Heathers network, but they are fragile. When Veronica is sick at a university party to which Heather Chandler has taken her, the latter, having groomed Veronica, is caustic in her condemnation. Veronica, to her credit, defends herself, replying 'Lick it up, baby,' in the face of Heather's tirade. It is perhaps this streak of independence which draws her away from the Heathers into what is, ironically, the darker and more sinister world of Jason Dean, played by Christian Slater. Jason (whose name, of course, echoes that of James Dean, the original 'rebel without a cause') intrigues Veronica because, unlike most kids, he is careless of others' opinions. He, in turn, admires Veronica and mistakenly assumes she is a soul-mate who might be willing to share his perverse and solitary existence. He seduces her with thoughts of revenge, but she is horrified when Heather Chandler's death results, realising that she has killed both her best friend and her worst enemy. When Jason and Veronica then collaborate to write Heather's putative suicide note, they reveal another teenage paradox – that of popularity – by exposing the isolation and insecurity endured by the beautiful and popular. The note and her apparent suicide make Heather Chandler genuinely, widely popular because they give her credibility and a depth that she never enjoyed in life. Students who had dismissed her as an airhead now aggrandise her as a real and suffering human being.

Adolescence can be a disconcerting and difficult time. Achieving acceptance and popularity is hard; sustaining them is even more demanding. Simmons (2002, p. 173) explains: 'It may come as a surprise, but once a girl gets her coveted status, popularity is no walk in the park. Competition and insecurity are rampant. When popular girls talk about their social lives, many of them talk about losing themselves.'

In *The Craft* (1996, directed by Andrew Fleming), new girl Sarah Bailey's suicide attempt initially gives her status. However, Nancy Downs uses this and the unfortunate deaths of another student and Sarah's mother against her one-time friend to try to entice the vulnerable Sarah into another attempt on her own life. Self-harm, at its darkest, is a way of asserting control over one's existence, so suicide can seem a seductive option for young people who feel powerless in an insensitive world, especially for those who are victims of relentless bullying. An increasing number of contemporary reports catalogue tragic accounts of young people who have committed suicide presumably in the belief that they had no other option. In *Heathers*, Jason gains a sense of control and satisfaction from murder, seeing death as a validation of existence. Enjoying the thrill and power it gives him, he assumes the role of avenger, moving on to the sexist jocks, Kurt and Ram, whom he considers have nothing to offer the school community other than crude jokes and date rape.

Jason is not the only one, however, to see benefit in death. Heather Duke sees a vacancy for the top Heather spot and seizes it eagerly. In doing so, she demonstrates her credentials to Veronica by using an argument which, mixing explicit phallic language with fairy tale and baby talk, highlights the dialectic of growing up, with its conflicts between knowledge and naïvety, and between power and vulnerability, that is at the heart of *Heathers*. As an audience, we support and like Veronica, despite everything, and instead blame the sociopathic Jason, while simultaneously censuring a social and cultural environment which equates popularity with dominance. The final scene of the film resolves the dilemma, however, by abandoning social satire and instead opting for the fairy-tale ending familiar to much popular culture. Veronica, having defeated Jason and marginalised Heather Duke, announces she is the new sheriff in town and invites Martha Dunstock home for videos and popcorn.

Mean Girls

If Heather Chandler is the queen bee (Wiseman, 2002) in *Heathers*, in *Mean Girls* (2004, directed by Mark Waters), it is Regina George. Both meet the criteria for an ideal girl:

> The ideal girl was *physically* perfect, a Caucasian Barbie doll: bone thin, tall, pretty, blonde, blue eyes, big boobs, good teeth, good skin – in other words, what you'd expect. These girls also find perfect not just a flawless body, but also an indirect, middle of the road character. For them, the ideal girl's true perfection was her ability to hold herself back from the world, expressing herself through manipulation.
>
> (Simmons, 2002, pp. 125–126)

In *Mean Girls*, sixteen-year-old Cady Heron, played by Lindsay Lohan, comes to North Shore High School after living all her life in Africa with her zoologist parents. Home tutored, she is a novice in student society and largely ignorant of school organisation and culture. Tina Fey, who wrote the screenplay for *Mean Girls* and plays Ms Horbury in the film, acknowledges she did so after reading Rosalind Wiseman's (2002) book *Queen bees and wannabes*, which examines the complex social and cultural environments of 'girl world'. Wiseman explores the phenomenon of bullying from the standpoint of the bully as well as that of the victim. As Mark Waters (quoted in Hoggard, 2004) comments: 'In a way, that's more horrifying. Having your child being victimised is painful, but it allows you to adopt a righteous attitude. But if your daughter's the bully, you're like, "Oh my God, what have I done wrong, I've created a monster!"'

As a child, Cady had been trusted and secure, but she quickly realises that, in school, she needs to be wily and adaptable. Her classmates indicate the barbarism when they observe, 'New meat coming through'; later, Cady speculates on the feral nature of what she sees in school. Simmons (2002, p. 135) charts the particular difficulties of new or excluded girls, documenting just how distraught they can feel:

> Solitude, after all, undermines the essence of girl identity. Girls know we expect them to be sociable creatures, to be in nurturing relationships, especially with other girls. The constant sense that isolation is imminent and the ground unsettled can make girls feel desperate. Without the luxury of social security, a girl will do anything to survive at school – whatever will get her through the homework, the lunch hour, the hallway. Acts of exclusion in these instances

assure a girl that she is acting as part of a group and won't be the one left behind.

Initially, Cady is adopted by two students who for various reasons are themselves outsiders. Acerbic Goth Janis Ian and Damian, who is 'too gay to function', explain the demography of the cafeteria to Cady by identifying tables of nerds, cool kids, jocks, girls who eat their feelings and girls who don't eat anything. Then there are 'the Plastics', three girls reminiscent of the Heathers – Regina, Gretchen and Karen – who are 'popular' and have a strict regime: for example, pink on Wednesdays; pony tails on Fridays. Regina George, queen bee of the Plastics, has, in addition to her immediate clique, a number of adoring acolytes, keen for even minimal contact or the slightest acknowledgement. One girl reverentially tells Cady how awesome it was to be punched in the face by Regina.

Wiseman (2002, pp. 25–35) classifies a number of different individuals within the girls' hierarchy, several of whom can be identified in *Mean Girls*. The groups she lists are as follows:

- *The Queen Bee*: a combination of charisma, force, money, looks, strong will and manipulation . . .
- *The Sidekick*: the lieutenant or second-in-command . . .
- *The Banker*: information about each other is currency . . .
- *The Floater*: has friends in different groups and can move freely among them . . .
- *The Torn Bystander*: constantly conflicted between doing the right thing and her allegiance to the clique . . .
- *The Pleaser/Wannabe/Messenger*: almost all girls are pleasers and wannabes; some are just more obvious than others . . .
- *The Target*: the victim, set up by the other girls to be humiliated, made fun of, excluded.

Regina is interested in Cady as a potential target, while Janis, who has a history with Regina, is keen to persuade Cady to join the Plastics in order to undermine them. Intrigued by the challenge, Cady notes naïvely that Regina is like the Barbie doll she never had. However, this is a Barbie with barbs. Regina even dominates her parents, especially her attenuated and attention-seeking mother, demanding such privileges as the best bedroom in the house.

As was mentioned earlier, Cady is a bright student and particularly able at mathematics, but she soon learns to use her intelligence (not, as also noted previously, a popular quality) to disguise her abilities, especially when she becomes interested in Aaron Samuels. (This is a world where a girl would not wish to appear intellectually superior to a boy to whom she is attracted.) Although *Mean Girls* is inherently less dark than *Heathers* (nobody dies), Cady is still seduced by the lure of the Plastics. One of the most revealing aspects of the film is to juxtapose, using a split screen, girls' conversations: telling tales, revealing secrets, criticising and condemning each other. Cady becomes a mean girl, and one with increasing power and influence. She convinces Regina to eat a health bar to assist weight loss when, in fact, it encourages weight gain. Since the ideal girl has to be 'bone thin' (Simmons, 2002, p. 125), Regina's increasing weight (which is not that obvious) inevitably leads to diminishing popularity, leaving Cady, since Gretchen and Karen require leadership, as the new queen bee. Regina's cry, 'I, like, invented her' is dismissed, and her subsequent accident merely gives further kudos to Cady, since everyone thinks the latter is somehow responsible.

Heather Chandler comes back only briefly to haunt Veronica in *Heathers*, but Regina George remains alive, kicking and vengeful once she has been usurped. Her masterstroke is to devise a retaliatory gesture that not only adversely affects Cady but indiscriminately hurts virtually every female in the school, including the women teachers. The revelation of the *Burn Book*, which divulges all those insults that people would never normally make public, is bullying on a grand scale. In order to deflect suspicion, Regina writes a particularly vitriolic entry about herself and adds it to the book. Then, when all is revealed, the result is a kind of feral behaviour among the girls with which Principal Duvall feels ill-equipped to deal. In *Heathers*, the teachers are caricatures: for example, when ex-hippy Ms Fleming insists on inappropriately circulating Heather Chandler's putative suicide note, her own superficiality is demonstrated by the tasteless and inconsequential eulogy she offers in its praise. In *Mean Girls*, however, the adults and the system do have something to offer, and in this way it is a less anarchic film than *Heathers*. Ms Horbury, rising above the lies written about her by Cady, implements an anti-bullying strategy in which people reveal their true feelings and inadequacies, thereby, hopefully, neutralising the poison which has surfaced. The aim is to rebuild confidence and loyalties through a series of trust exercises. As each girl admits how she feels, the group, in theory, learns to accept one another and to behave in a more humanitarian and compassionate way. The inference is that the girls need to be more honest with themselves and with one another, devoting their time to what they really want to do. Cady, as a result, helps the 'mathathletes' to win the state championship, while Regina channels all her energy and rage into sport.

The next section will look at how bullying has been represented on television by examining *Grange Hill* from the UK and *Buffy the Vampire Slayer* from the USA.

Bully for television

Grange Hill

Grange Hill is a BBC television series which commenced in 1978 and has continued ever since. In its early years, it was considered ground-breaking drama since it moved away from a conservative model of children's television to present life in an inner-city comprehensive from a student perspective. The series deliberately aimed to confront contemporary and controversial social and educational issues, such as drugs, teenage pregnancy, truancy and racism. Furthermore, rather than delivering simple moral messages about these topics, it endeavoured to explore young people's experiences, dilemmas and traumas. Throughout successive series, several young characters have been given opportunities to develop, learn and, ultimately, grow up and move on (often to adult British soaps). Across the decades, a number of bullies have inevitably emerged to challenge the system, and terrorise their peers.

Grange Hill is a series with both a social conscience and a moral message. As Jones and Davies (2002) suggest, there is an element of British children's broadcasting whereby this can seem something of a 'burden' (in the rectitude required in children's TV presenters, for example). However, *Grange Hill* survives and has sustained its popularity not because of its social and moral import, nor because its adult characters offer sympathetic and sensible advice, but because it provides enjoyable and plausible drama for the children who watch it. Between 1981 and 1985, the notorious bully Norman 'Gripper' Stebson appeared in the programme. He had few redeeming features, and the extent and nature of his bullying escalated with each successive series. Although *Grange Hill* tends to have little plot or character development outside the school situation, enough was known about Gripper to suggest that his bullying may have been triggered by some of the risk factors outlined by Smith and Sharp (1994, p. 8):

> Some are individual characteristics such as temperament; Olweus (1980) describes bullying children as having impulsive and aggressive temperament . . . Another important set of factors relate to parents and the home environment . . . [H]ome factors that predispose to high aggression are: lack of warmth between parents or the family; use of physical violence within the family; lack of clear guidelines for behaviour and monitoring of children's activities.

Gripper liked to dominate. When he first appeared as a pre-teen in series 4, he was already involved in petty crime and exacted silence from witnesses through intimidation. By the next series, he had acquired two confederates. This is not uncommon: bullies often like to have partners (unlike the isolation preferred for victims), and a gang of three is typical. The Heathers and the Plastics are initially threesomes. Draco Malfoy in the *Harry Potter* series rarely provokes a situation unless he is backed up by his henchmen, Crabbe and Goyle. Gripper liked to be similarly supported when targeting the vulnerable.

Smith and Sharp (*ibid.*) also outline the factors that might make one susceptible to bullying:

> Children who get bullied may lack assertiveness skills . . . Generally being different in some way (for example, ethnic group) or being vulnerable are risk factors for being bullied . . . Children with special educational needs, often with a physical disability or mild/moderate learning difficulties, are especially at risk of being bullied.

Gripper especially intimidates Roland Browning, who is seeing an educational psychologist. Later, he manifests his most malicious persona as a racist thug, making whites swear allegiance to Britain while bullying *Grange Hill*'s Afro-Caribbean and

Asian students. He makes life particularly miserable for Randir Singh, and for Claire Scott, who defends him. When the worms turn, however, and Gripper is cornered, the teachers rescue him. Mr Baxter, asserting order, expels Gripper, explaining to the crowd that, despite their righteous anger, vigilantism can never be condoned. It is notable, however, that the students rather than the authorities trigger Gripper's departure.

Buffy the Vampire Slayer

The American television series *Buffy the Vampire Slayer* is different from *Grange Hill* in several ways. First, *BtVS* addresses a more sophisticated audience than *Grange Hill*; second, it was not developed as children's television; third, while set initially in the everyday world of school and teenage angst, it has an additional supernatural apocalyptic dimension, so any episode could see the end of existence. Yet, there is still bullying in Sunnydale High School. Verbal abuse is endemic, and physical violence is not confined to encounters with vampires. A dominant reading of *BtVS* would suggest it condemns bullying: Buffy befriends outsiders; the arrogant and beautiful circle around the popular Cordelia is presented as universally shallow and silly; bullying and thuggish boys are generally shown to be stupid and cowardly. This message is somewhat undercut, however, by the fact that all of the main characters in *BtVS* are also attractive, slim, bright and witty.

Buffy herself is clever, if not academically gifted, and certainly not the airhead she sometimes purports to be. Even Xander, perhaps the least talented of the group, is amusing, stands up for himself and for a time even goes out with Cordelia. In the original synopsis for the show, Willow was overweight, but instead the producers cast the svelte Alyson Hannigan, who in later seasons attracts a cool musician and a beautiful fellow witch. The short and geeky Jonathan Levenson is never taken seriously as a potential Scooby, while the beautiful, if somewhat artless, vengeance demon Anya is. In 'Superstar' (1999, 4.17), when Jonathan is presented as the cool, sophisticated idol of Sunnydale, it is immediately apparent that he could become so universally admired only through powerful magic.

Two episodes from the first series of *BtVS* are especially relevant to a chapter on bullying. They are 'The Pack' (1997, 1.6, written by Matt Kiene and Joe Reinkemeyer, directed by Bruce Seth Green) and 'Out of Mind, Out of Sight' (1997, 1.11, written by Joss Whedon, directed by Reza Badiyi). 'The Pack' begins with a barrage of verbal taunts that would be intimidating if directed towards someone who did not happen to be the Slayer. Buffy ignores them, but another student, Lance, is more easily cowed and has his sketchbook grabbed. Lance's fear of repercussions and his reluctance to tell tales (a typical victim response) ensure, however, that Principal Flutie is not told what has happened. This opening sets the scene for an episode in which Kyle's gang, plus Xander, experience a magical transpossession that gives them the aggressive and bloodthirsty qualities of a pack of hyenas. Before the supernatural reason for the gang's excesses is revealed, however, Giles, Buffy's Watcher and the school librarian, offers what he considers to be a plausible explanation for the way in which Xander, in particular, is behaving:

GILES: Xander's taken to teasing the less fortunate?

BUFFY: Yes.

GILES: And there's been a noticeable change in both clothing and demeanour?

BUFFY: Yes.

GILES: And, well, otherwise all his spare time is spent lounging about with imbeciles.

BUFFY: It's bad, isn't it?

GILES: It's devastating. He's turned into a sixteen-year-old boy. Course, you'll have to kill him.

BUFFY: Giles, I'm serious.

GILES: So am I. Except for the part about killing him. Testosterone is a great equaliser. It turns all men into morons. He will, however, get over it . . . Buffy, boys can be cruel. They tease. They prey on the weak. It's natural teen behaviour pattern.

Giles does not wholly justify the offensive conduct, but, as a middle-aged man explaining a boy's behaviour, it is difficult to construe his comments otherwise. Once the pack has consumed Principal Flutie, however, there can be no excuses for their conduct. Xander, fortunately, was not with them during that incident because he was preoccupied sexually harassing Buffy. From an atypical Xander perspective, she is a woman who says no, but really means yes, and encourages sexual advances through the way she dresses. This behaviour is predicated on the notion that a rapacious male cannot control himself and that females are in some measure responsible for what they are forced to endure as a result. Buffy, of course, is not a victim, and inverts female stereotypes because while she is a small, slight, blonde girl who is inclined to wear sexy or revealing clothes, she is not weak either physically or psychologically. Other girls in similar situations, however, can feel 'powerless':

> I now know that even highly articulate girls become voiceless when faced with the threat of sexual harassment or violence. These are the girls who won't tell someone to leave them alone because they're afraid they'll be labelled as uptight, a bitch, or because they don't want to hurt anyone's feelings.
>
> (Wiseman, 2002, p. 12)

Those hurt feelings do not, of course, include their own suffering, since self-effacement is fundamental to this response.

The idea of effacement is a key element in the second *BtVS* episode, 'Out of Mind, Out of Sight' (note the word order) in which student Marcie Ross is ignored so comprehensively by both teachers and her fellow students that she literally becomes invisible. The episode contains a number of flashbacks to when Marcie was still discernible, and it is apparent that people simply do not see, listen or respond to her. Her identity and then her tangible existence are therefore systematically erased by others' disregard. So her message to everyone is: 'Look, listen, learn'. Even the normally insightful Willow and the amiable Xander confidently assert that they never met her, only to find that they took classes together the previous year. Giles, reflecting on what might have happened, explains that reality is shaped by perception, and Marcie's invisibility is a direct result of being ignored by everyone around her. This anonymity is similar to that experienced by Jonathan in 'Earshot' (1998, 3.18, written by Jane Espenson, directed by Regis Kimble). When he berates Buffy about her attitude towards him, she bluntly tells him that she doesn't think he's an idiot because she doesn't think of him at all.

Marcie's disappearance is a gradual process that starts with the fading hand which is so persistently ignored when she raises it in class. As Buffy reminds us, this was not something over which Marcie had any control; it was done to her by those around her. Marcie blames her anonymity particularly on the popular Cordelia, although in this instance the latter proves surprisingly sympathetic. Worn down by the pursuit of popularity and using words that echo Heather Chandler's suicide note, Cordelia explains to Buffy that she understands isolation and vulnerability:

CORDELIA: Bummer for her. It's awful feeling that lonely.
BUFFY: So you've read something about the feeling.
CORDELIA: Hey. You think I'm never lonely because I'm so cute and popular? I can be surrounded by people and be completely alone. It's not like any of them really know me. I don't even know if they like me half the time. People just want to be in a popular zone. Sometimes, when I talk, everyone's so busy agreeing with me, they don't hear a word I say.
BUFFY: Well, if you feel so alone, then why do you work so hard at being popular?
CORDELIA: Well, it beats being alone all by yourself.

Later, Marcie is dismissive of this speech, but in many ways it and Cordelia's subsequent expression of thanks to Buffy mark a turning point in the popular girl's relationship with the Scoobies. At the end of 'Out of Mind, Out of Sight', however, two FBI agents exemplify the cynicism and moral bankruptcy with which the establishment treats individuals. They take Marcie to a place where she will 'learn' to be a useful member of society, despite being invisible, which in practice means that she will be exploited rather than rehabilitated because she can be useful to the government in the areas of 'assassination and infiltration'.

Summary

Bullying is represented in popular culture in many imaginative and disturbing ways. It is not a simple concept, as our definitions and discussion earlier in this chapter have indicated, but rather a complex phenomenon open to alternative explanations and interpretations. A wide range of behaviour can be construed as bullying – anything from silence to physical assault. Recently, technology has given the concept new dimensions through abusive and offensive text messages or cyber-bullying within social networks and/or the publication of offensive photographs on the web, like those of Rachel Greenbaum in the film *Cruel Intentions* or Mika Grainger in the BBC1 series *Waterloo Road* (2007). Whatever is published or received, it is intended to humiliate or oppress its subjects or recipients. The audience, listeners or readers are influenced by their sympathy for victims, their anger towards bullies, and/or their frustration at social or educational environments which blatantly ignore, tacitly condone or simply do nothing effective against bullying behaviour.

The position of popular culture in relation to bullying inevitably creates contradictions and produces paradoxes that serve to confound our repudiation of it as a wholly unacceptable practice. We all condemn bullying; yet, apparently, as a society we are unable to accept the overweight, geeky and unattractive as our heroes and heroines. Society, the media and popular culture constantly reinforce the kinds of arbitrary and unfair judgements that lead to bullying, while repeatedly telling children it is a bad thing to do. Beautiful people receive preferential treatment; the less attractive are disregarded or ridiculed.

One dubious but traditional perspective on bullying is that the experience can be character forming and morally fortifying. This implies that it is a rite of passage and, to an extent, predictable. It even serves to rationalise childhood misery. In the *BtVS* episode 'Earshot', Buffy, while not validating bullying or absolving trauma, nevertheless tells Jonathan that his pain is nothing special. All the students in school are suffering, even the popular, the beautiful and the strong. While this may be true, it could easily appear to negate the feelings of the lonely, victimised and bullied; to trivialise their experience and oppression by making it commonplace. The implication that what is experienced is merely typical teenage misery provides an excuse for not dealing with it. In the film *Elephant*, it is obvious that all the kids have problems. We witness their routine anxieties. What triggers a violent response like Alex and Eric's is difficult to explain, especially if we look only at partial aspects of the situation and at fragmentary events. The elephant may be there, but we cannot conceive of its size from an examination of its tail.

In *Dangerous Minds* and *Freedom Writers*, education purports to offer salvation, but it can do little to ameliorate the crushing social and domestic circumstances in which these young people live or, in some cases, die. Bullying here can be about self-worth, about not being the lowest of the low and about, despite everything, still having someone below yourself. Implying that Cesar in *187* really has choices merely serves to construct failure as a black problem, and absolve the dominant white community from responsibility for prevalent social conditions. As Henry Giroux (2002, p. 199) explains:

> Racially coded violence works to exclude dominant white society from any responsibility or complicity with the larger culture of violence while simultaneously shifting the burden of crime and social decay to people of colour, working class whites and other subordinate groups.

In reality, it is a no-win situation for Cesar.

Heathers and *Mean Girls* allow us to focus on the gender issue and the pressures of being popular. The latter film, in particular, suggests an institutional culture can resist bullying through the way in which it encourages and promotes student relationships. It implies that anti-bullying strategies, if implemented effectively, can make a difference. However, both *Heathers* and *Mean Girls* sanitise the process of dealing with bullying and offer idealised, fairy-tale endings. In *Heathers*, the monster is dead and marginalised Martha has a popular friend. In *Mean Girls*, Cady has tamed the high school jungle (more easily than Rick Dadier did his blackboard jungle), even to the extent that Regina George is reformed and finds a worthwhile avenue for her aggression and intimidation.

The television series we examined presented a less optimistic, perhaps more realistic, appraisal of school life, highlighting the social disruption, personal distress and complexity of bullying. Even in the British animated series *Bromwell High* (Channel 4, 2005), Keisha, a dominant school prefect, resorts to bullying rather than admitting she likes another student. Gripper Stebson is expelled from Grange Hill, but he is unreconstructed, and we presume his racist philosophy and violence will oppress his neighbours and the wider community in the future. Similarly, in *BtVS* both Marcie Ross and Jonathan Levenson are enticed towards evil as a result of the oppression of others. The implication is that, like Alex and Eric in *Elephant*, theirs is an extreme reaction to the desperation and impotence of their everyday lives. On the one hand, it is a causal relationship between being treated badly and behaving badly in response: suffering has eroded personal values and warped characters. On the other, it is an unrefined social model which does not offer any hope that the bullied might transcend their misery and despair. Many song lyrics, particularly in rap, paint the latter, bleak picture, in which aggression is the only mitigation against a society and education that institutionally oppress individuals, and the only retaliation against those who persistently intimidate and assault others.

There is no simple solution to bullying. Popular culture has the capacity to raise its profile, highlighting the perspectives of different players, but it does not purport to be a sociological thesis nor a psychological treatise. Although popular culture can trivialise bullying and ignore its complexity, it does constitute an acknowledgement of its existence, an admission that it happens. For many, that recognition is important. Perhaps it is up to the audience to engage critically and reflectively with whatever is offered; to interrogate its circumstances and specificity while recognising it is not an individual, gender or racial issue but part of the human condition, and a social and cultural phenomenon that none of us should ignore. If we were bullies, bystanders or victims as children or young people, who at the time did not speak up appropriately or with sufficient force, at least as adults we now have another chance to resist, dismiss and condemn bullying.

7 We don't need no education?

As a thinker one should speak only of self-education. The education of youth by others is . . . something unworthy.

(Friedrich Nietzsche, *The wanderer and his shadow*, quoted in Fitchett, 1999)

Introduction

The diversity of popular cultures, and the many contradictory messages that emerge from them, makes generalisations dangerous. None the less, there is a clear preponderance of representations of schools and schooling that are in some way hostile. This may be explained in part by the fact that significant elements of popular culture, and the majority of those that feature representations of education, have been driven largely by oppositional youth cultures. It may also be that the energies of the counter-cultures of the 1960s are, in various subtle ways, still at work in the mainstream of cultural production. Sixties radicalism was often expressed in the context of educational institutions; it was, very largely, a 'student movement'. Guy Debord's (1995) *Society of the spectacle* was published for the first time in 1967, and became a key text for the protagonists of student protest in 1968. In the US during the 1960s there was a move to desegregate schooling, and across the US and Europe social protests were often campus based. Education was not merely a context for radical movements but generally a major part of their political programmes, as visions of new liberation pedagogies took hold. Radical libertarian ideas found expression in the anarchistic 'Free Schools Movement', and schools such as Summerhill (based on A. S. Neill's child-centred pedagogy: see Neill, 1968) enjoyed a new high profile. 'Cultural events' in the UK, such as the 'Schoolkids' edition of the *Oz* underground magazine, published in May 1970 and the subject of an Old Bailey obscenity trial, captured the headlines. The following year saw the publication in Britain of *The little red school book* (Hansen and Jensen, 1971), a guide designed to empower schoolchildren, and, to much tabloid press ballyhoo, declared obscene by a London magistrate. Reports on educational disputes, mostly arising from moral panics about educational progressivism – for example, the William Tyndale School dispute in London and the subsequent official inquiry and its associated reporting (1974–1976) – were common in the popular press. Popular culture, however, especially film, had been representing education long before the 1960s. This chapter will consider selected 'negative' and 'positive' instances of education in popular culture, focusing primarily on some examples from the cinema, popular music and television.

The late twentieth-century explosion of television output, accelerated by globalisation, satellite broadcasting, and the emergence of new technologies such as video and DVD, was accompanied by certain synergies in which different forms of marketing linked to sell cultural products. A successful film would be likely to have 'tie-in' products such as a soundtrack CD, a novel and associated character figures or other toys. A particularly strong link was formed between the pop song and the pop video, with the rise of the MTV music channel based on this potent creative and commercial alliance. MTV was also the home of the animated characters Beavis and Butt-head.

Examining *Beavis and Butt-head* for signs of life

The ostensibly banal characters Beavis and Butt-head offer some utility in the consideration of negative representations of education and teachers. The following discussion explores aspects of the stereotypes and behaviour represented in the *Beavis and Butt-head* series and briefly analyses some possible interpretations of these images. *Beavis and Butt-head* is an American cartoon series that has been widely dismissed as 'moronic'; its primary purpose is to provide light entertainment for a largely teenage audience.

The characters Beavis and Butt-head first appeared on the US rock music-dedicated television channel MTV in September 1992. Regular transmission by MTV America of a one-hour, five-nights-a-week *Beavis and Butt-head* series began on 8 March 1993. In April 1994, the programme first appeared on British terrestrial television on a Channel 4 'late slot'. By the mid-1990s the series had been broadcast in seventy-one countries and in five languages (Doyle, 1996). In the spring of 1997, the animated feature film *Beavis and Butt-head Do America* went on general release in the UK following huge pre-release marketing hype and strong indications of box-office success in the USA. There has also been a Marvel comic wholly devoted to the antics of the pair as well as an associated small industry of comic books, annuals, CDs, videos and T-shirts.

According to their creator, Mike Judge, the Beavis and Butt-head characters represent fourteen-year-olds. Young (1993, p. 9) quotes an MTV Europe press release which describes them as 'metal-heads who amuse themselves with obser-vations on important things like girls, TV shows and rock stars'. The daily existence of Beavis and Butt-head, like that of much of their audience at the time, is based primarily on a couch in front of a television, watching and com-menting inanely on a succession of banal rock music videos. When they venture forth from this entertainment, it is often to their school, Highland High, where they are involved in a permanent state of war against their teachers Mr Buzzcut and Mr Van Driessen, the other students and each other. Young (*ibid.*) outlines the predictably negative reaction to the cartoon of America's anti-violence lobby, one member of which described it as 'pure societal poison, glorifying losers, violence and criminality'.

Beavis and Butt-head are deeply impressed by, and under the influence of, the (often violent and/or sexist) images that they see on television. Young (*ibid.*), however, argues that those who regard the pair as symptomatic of an anti-political-correctness backlash have missed the point that, by depicting the two chief characters as immature fools, the programme cannot be accused of endorsing their attitudes. At the same time, he accepts that the complicated satirical framework of the programme is likely to be lost on the majority of its mostly teenage audience. According to Stallabrass (1996, p. 203), though:

> *Beavis and Butt-head* is a direct critique and simultaneous endorsement of what has been dubbed 'yob culture'. These cartoon adolescents spend most of their time watching television and – unless you really are endowed with the mental equipment of the protagonists – the link between their viewing habits and their ignorance, smuttiness and arbitrary acts of violence is obvious. Such shows are ironic celebrations of their subjects and their audience in which celebration and irony have become absolutely inseparable.

In a chapter titled 'Looking glass TV', Stallabrass reviews some of the cultural debates surrounding the social consequences of television. Quoting Adorno, he suggests (*ibid.*, p. 199) that, under its influence: 'The predominant social character becomes a "subjectless subject", marked by a "scattered, disconnected, inter-changeable and ephemeral state of informedness", which one can see erased at the very next moment to be replaced by a new formation.' Certainly, this pessimistic view of modern society might be taken as an effective description of the delinquent cartoon characters represented by Beavis and Butt-head.

Visually, the cartoons are very basic, the backdrops are minimal and the characters move in a shaky motion that is incongruent with the sophisticated capabilities of modern animation. The juxtaposition of this crude quality of animation with the often very high production values of the rock music promotional videos which punctuate the show serves to amplify the mundane quality of the 'world of Beavis and Butt-head', while privileging the spoken dialogue. The Beavis and Butt-head characters are drawn with disproportionately large heads and decidedly 'boyish' bodies (they always wear short trousers). The dialogue and pacing, however – with the exception of the frequent 'trademark' punctuation by demented staccato laughter (Beavis: 'Heh heh heh heh'; Butt-head: 'Huh huh huh') – are intended to be relatively naturalistic (Dessau, 1994). The 'plots' of the cartoons are lacking in any strong narrative. Beavis and Butt-head idle, watch TV, have puerile fantasies, show a strong interest in matters scatological and masturbatory, and fool about in class. The entertainment, the humour and the satire are primarily contained in the nuances of the dialogue and in the nature of the various stereotypes that appear, prime among these being the two male teachers.

The messages which may be read from the *Beavis and Butt-head* representations of teachers are inevitably more resistant to a straightforward reading in that there are a great many of them, and because they are placed in a context of a postmodern irony where ambiguity, contradiction and fluidity of meaning are at the centre of the genre. In *Beavis and Butt-head*, both the traditional teacher and the progressive teacher are scorned by the 'heroes/anti-heroes', who themselves are subjects of ridicule. It is clear that, for Beavis and Butt-head, teachers' hegemony, of whatever type, 'sucks'. It is also evident that, for these two characters, anti-school, anti-learning, anti-societal attitudes are 'cool'. It is less clear what meaning the audience – or, more correctly, the audiences – extracts from and invests in this obviousness.

By appearing on a music video channel that specialises in rock music, the *Beavis and Butt-head* multi-product phenomenon was, in 1997, momentarily at the nexus of a cluster of cultural forms which constantly transforms in a way that epitomises the diffused and porous nature of postmodern culture. (For a relatively early, but still persuasive, account of the social effects of globalisation and the concentration of the ownership of forms of cultural production, see Stallabrass, 1996).

Two kinds of teacher

The *Beavis and Butt-head* series features archetypal representations of a traditional teacher (Mr Buzzcut) and a progressive teacher (Mr Van Driessen). Both teachers are literally extreme caricatures in terms of both appearance and behaviour, as the genre demands, and both are held up as objects of derision for students (Beavis and Butt-head) who are also objects of derision for an audience (the viewers) who, presumably, are not objects of derision to themselves. That the *Beavis and Butt-head* audience may be capable of 'knowing' aspects of opposing cultures/values/regimes within the practice of teaching is suggested by the following extracts from 'letters home', which appeared in *MTV's Beavis and Butt-head: this book sucks* (Johnson and Marcil, 1993, n.p.):

Letter from Mr Buzzcut
Regarding: Extreme Disciplinary Breakdown of Students Beavis and Butt-head

Parent or Current Occupant:
A discipline condition has been ongoing re: Beavis and Butt-head dating from 9 September 1993. This condition is characterised by chronic actions of gross insubordination such as the following selected incidents:

Incident: Partial immolation of Beavis's work station.

Cause: Disposable butane incendiary device. 9-9-93

Incident: Random bursts of individual condiment packets – mustard, ketchup – throughout hallway, classroom sectors. 17 bystanders sprayed. 9-15-93

[Six other incidents are outlined.]

Recommendations: Barring neutralization with Extreme Prejudice, this teacher recommends corporal punishment: i.e. flogging, solitary confinement, and hard labor detail . . .

Letter from Mr Van Driessen

Dear Care Provider,

I want to share with you my feelings about your son's self-esteem problem. When a student sticks a pencil in his eye or sets fire to the other children's homework, it's clear that he doesn't respect his own self-hood.

I've tried and tried to 'stay positive' and guide your son toward a loving relationship with himself. But today, when I asked him to write a song in class, he surreptitiously inserted some sort of entrail into the sound hole of my guitar. I respect the impulse to create by challenging the rules established by society. That's what the revolution was all about. But that guitar was autographed by Pete Seeger, and it may never be completely rid of the smell.

If the behavior of your child does not change for the better immediately I'm going to have to strongly urge that you find a healer for him. Perhaps an energy redirection therapist . . .

The characteristics which may be identified with the positions represented by the Buzzcut and Van Driessen characters are generally as follows:

Buzzcut	*Van Driessen*
Traditionalist	Progressive
American	Un-American
Macho	Effeminate
Disciplined	Undisciplined
Smart appearance	Scruffy appearance
Insensitive	Sensitive
Uncaring	Caring
Military	'Hippy'
Violent	Non-violent
Conservative values	Alternative values
Upholding society	Changing society

For Beavis and Butt-head, both teachers 'suck'; both are 'uncool'. A possible message is that, for the Generation X which Beavis and Butt-head are intended to represent, a generation seemingly condemned to a future of uncertain employment in a labour market where often only fast-food retailing offers an immediate job opportunity, all teachers 'suck' because the point of education is no longer evident. Buzzcut and Van Driessen are, of course, both representations of Americans. They are both also products of the US popular culture which has come to dominate youth culture throughout the developed world and beyond. Judge (1995, p. 262), in a paper which provides a cross-national study of the images of teachers, claims the American school functions primarily as a locus of assimilation within a pluralist society and suggests that in the USA, despite the new economic realities of the 1990s, the persistent image of the teacher is . . . of an individualist preparing children for lives in a competitive world in which it is possible for the talented citizen to progress in one generation from the log cabin to the White House. Such a teacher must, in principle, welcome all pupils, whatever their social or ethnic origins and be prepared to offer them what will suit them best. The teacher must ensure that the pupil is, to use a distinctively American expression, 'comfortable'.

Judge (*ibid.*, p. 263) contrasts this well-established American image of the teacher as an individualist assimilator to perceptible shifts which have occurred in the images of teachers in France ('from transmitter of culture towards animateur') and England (from 'guardian of tradition towards agent of change'). There is a sense in which the Buzzcut and Van Driessen characters might effectively represent the English stereotypes of preserver of tradition and catalyst of values transition, respectively, though both are essentially products of the mass popular culture which is sometimes seen as assimilating the youth of the world to the 'American Way' of individuality and the supremacy of the market.

A type of student: alienated/powerless and laughing

Conciliatory laughter is heard as the echo of an escape from power; the wrong kind overcomes fear by capitulating to the forces which are to be feared. It is the echo of power as something inescapable.

(Adorno and Horkheimer, 1972, p. 140)

The problem of alienated and disruptive students in schools is not new, though their increasing presence in the further education system in England is something that has been a source of some comment. As with traditional and progressive teachers, a series of the stereotypical characteristics of the reluctant student springs easily to mind. Such students might be regarded as low academic achievers, incoherent, lacking respect for their teachers, destructive, and having a potential for random 'mindless' violence; their 'cultural' interests would be considered unlikely to extend beyond trash music and pornography. Beavis and Butt-head represent this well. The behaviour that they exhibit is antisocial but ineffectual; it offends but it offers no challenge because it contains no critique. In this sense, perhaps, it presents an interesting metaphor through which to consider the problem of student perceptions as well as the problem of perceptions (stereotypes) of students. Guy Debord's notion of the 'society of the spectacle' – that is, of a society where the advanced technology of the media of communication perpetuates individual infantilism as a form of control – may offer a partial explanation:

[W]hen images chosen and constructed by someone else have everywhere become the individual's principal connection to the world . . . these images can tolerate anything and everything . . . The flow of images carries everything before it, and it is similarly someone else who controls at will this simplified summary of the sensible world; who decides where the flow will lead as well as the rhythm of what should be shown, like some perpetual, arbitrary surprise, leaving no time for reflection . . . In this concrete experience of permanent submission lies the psychological origin of such general acceptance of what is; an acceptance which comes to find in it, ipso facto, a sufficient value.

(Debord, 1988, p. 8)

The recurring laughter motif (Butt-head: Huh huh huh; Beavis: Heh heh heh heh) is an important element of the *Beavis and Butt-head* formula, performing a similar function to a stand-up comedian's 'catchline', but also underlining stupidity, insolence and, at the same time, social impotence. Paul Willis' (1977, p. 29) seminal study of male working-class youths in a secondary modern school identifies 'having a laff' as being of 'extraordinary importance in the counter school culture', suggesting that the utility of the 'laff' comes from its ability to 'defeat boredom and fear, to overcome hardship and problems'. Indeed, the profanity and violence of the 'real world' of alienated youth which Willis' study so evocatively describes finds more than an echo in the cartoon capers of Beavis and Butt-head. The increasing pervasiveness of the broadcast media means that the possibility of life, at some point and in certain spheres, imitating 'art' becomes all the more likely.

Signs of life?

Weber and Mitchell (1995) have suggested the potential which images of teachers might have in the training of the profession, providing a means by which teachers might be able to 'see themselves' as a basis for 'self-interrogation'. They argue (*ibid.*, p. 130) that 'through multiple readings of our own reactions to teacher images in popular culture, we enter into a dialectical relationship with the polarities, ambiguities, and tensions within the social matrix of teaching'. *Beavis and Butt-head*, then, provides yet another opportunity for a teacher to engage in a reflexive learning relationship with the cultural/media artefacts of society, and perhaps to go beyond this to act as a kind of 'teacher-deconstructor' by deploying an 'ironic attitude' which might facilitate the ability to read what Parker (1997, p. 142) has referred to as the 'unstable, dynamic oscillation of the rhetorical forces of deconstruction and position, or reactivity and creativity [which] is the signature of the postmodern voice and a central characteristic of emancipation in postmodernity'. A particular appeal, in this respect, of the commodities which spin off the pop/rock production line is that, unlike modern literature, children's stories and the work of overtly political cartoonists whose drawings appear in newspapers, they are a major part of the daily cultural diet which is consumed and enjoyed by the same young people who constitute the most problematic constituency in the education system: the teenagers who directly experience disaffection, alienation and powerlessness. This inertia is evident in the following dialogue from the *Beavis and Butt-head* comic book cited earlier (Johnson and Marcil, 1993, n.p.):

VOCATIONAL/DIAGNOSTIC TEST

Talk about an important day in your life.

BUTT-HEAD: It was the day that Beavis tried to kiss me, but I kicked his ass. That's why it was an important day. 'Cause it was the first time I completely shredded Beavis.

BEAVIS: Shut up, bum wipe. I wasn't trying to kiss you. I tripped. Besides, I kicked your ass. But that's not important. My important day was when I kidnapped Buzzcut and brought him to my torture chamber and made him talk. I burned his pants.

BUTT-HEAD: I'm afraid that never happened, Beavis.

BEAVIS: No. Uh, wait. No.

For the fictional cartoon characters Beavis and Butt-head, victory consists of minor insubordinations. Major acts of rebellion remain a fantasy. That was not to be so in the cases of Eric Harris and Dylan Klebold, the perpetrators of the Columbine High School massacre.

Popular music: pro- and anti-education

The potency of popular music as a commodity has, despite various market blips and 'technological revolutions', been sustained for more than half a century. As (primarily) a youth product, it has been widely associated, particular in sub-genres such as heavy metal, punk and rap, with certain kinds of rebelliousness, nihilism or negativity. Lee Cooper (2001, p. 73) has provided an analysis of 'recordings from the early Rock Era that illustrate adolescent disenchantment with institutionalized learning'. Many songs that feature lyrics concerned with education fit into that category, but there is a significant number that do not.

Be true to your school

For 1950s American teenagers, the high school was a community where there were social spaces that afforded the opportunity to experience a sense of collective youth identity. The escape from domestic hierarchies and parental control enabled the freedoms of post-war prosperity to be exercised in a climate more liberal than that which might have been found in British schools and colleges at the same time. The high school movie genre that represented this milieu in a significant way was preceded by the advent of rock 'n' roll music. Bill Haley's '**ABC Boogey**', a happy, upbeat song about a school combining 'boogey' with learning, was recorded in 1954. It would be another four years before the film *High School Confidential* would open with Jerry Lee Lewis performing the song of the same title. Bobby Rydell's song 'Swingin' School' (1960) was effectively celebrating an established 'at the hop' ethos of school as a locus of fun. When, in 1979, the film *Grease* placed its fun-loving students in Rydell High School, it was clear that the genre had become knowing and self-referential.

Inter-school competition, especially through sports, has long been established on both sides of the Atlantic. Having pride in school was the major theme of the Beach Boys' hit **'Be True to Your School'** (1963). Such songs reflect positive experiences of school from a student perspective, while others nostalgically reminisce about how enjoyable school life really was. Stevie Wonder's **'I Wish'** (1978) refers to illicit smoking, writing graffiti on walls and being sent to the principal's office, then, from an adult perspective, admits that such behaviour was wrong and yearns to be back at school. Others regret their lack of application while at school and send out a pro-school message in a less than direct way. The rap artist Mac's **'My Brother'** (1998) provides an example of this, with a school miscreant making a hero and role model of his more compliant brother.

School has been represented as fun because of great times with friends, as exemplified in many of the early high school songs and later work, such as Cat Stevens' **'(Remember the Days of the) Old Schoolyard'** (1968) and Paul Simon's **'Me and Julio Down by the Schoolyard'** (1972). It can be fun as a place of romance (as discussed in Chapter 4); or because of the joy of learning, as in New Edition's **'School'** (1990). There may be fond memories of a specific teacher, as in Frank Sinatra's **'The Old School Teacher'** (1945); or it can be seen positively as a place of self-improvement. So pop music *has* celebrated school, but its negative representations of the institution have most caught the imagination of the public.

'School's Out'

Alice Cooper's classic, anarchic anti-school anthem **'School's Out'** was a major chart success in 1972. This song is perhaps the most powerful of its kind and became both embedded in the consciousness of those who were listening to rock music in the early 1970s and well known to a wider audience. Performed by the cane-wielding, make-up-wearing stage persona of shock-rock legend Alice, it sounded apocalyptic, especially when compared to the Beach Boys' 'Be True to Your School' from only nine years earlier. But by the US election campaign of the summer of 2004, Cooper was strongly criticising those rock stars and celebrities who were condemning President George W. Bush and his policies. Cooper is an iconic artist who has created a brand of theatrical rock which has influenced numerous others, most notably Marilyn Manson. He is also one who is aware that the oppositional postures of rock music can be highly symbolic, and this applies strongly in relation to school.

Some songs complain about what can be seen as the sometimes stifling routine of school. Chuck Berry's **'School Day'** (1957) evokes compressed spaces and pressured time before breaking free at the end of the day, finding a jukebox and being liberated by the new noise of rock 'n' roll. This scenario would later also be evoked by Bruce Springsteen's **'No Surrender'** (1984). Paul Simon, a Brooklyn Law School drop-out, through his song **'Kodachrome'** (1973), also questioned the value of what he had learned. For those who stayed in school rather than 'bunking off' (truanting), there was the prospect of alienation, as expressed in Mott the Hoople's **'(I'm the) Teacher'**. In 2003, **'Mad World'**, expressing a similar sentiment, was an unlikely Christmas number one for Gary Jules. The UK pop charts of December 2005 also had a surprising anti-school theme song at number one, in the form of Nizlopi's engaging and gently subversive '**JCB Song**', featuring a five-year-old narrator who is pleased to be riding on his dad's JCB, away from the teachers and the bullies at school.

Perhaps the strangest UK Christmas number one, in terms of an overtly serious and political song, dealt explicitly with education. In 1979, Pink Floyd's '**Another Brick in the Wall, Part 2**' boomed through living rooms across Britain courtesy of the Christmas Day special edition of *Top of the Pops*. The chorus on the record had been sung by pupils of Islington Green Comprehensive School, which was conveniently situated close to the group's Britannia Road studios in north London. Its adoption as an anthem by South African school students during the Soweto riots would lead to a ban on its sale and broadcast in apartheid South Africa. The lyrics and the dynamics of the music, especially when combined with the visual images of totalitarian 'marching hammers' and educational institutions as 'human meat grinders', made the song perhaps the most iconic and powerful anti-schooling statement ever made in popular music. It presented a view of education as a process of social control that very much accorded with the Althusserian accounts which had much academic currency in the 1970s.

The idea of oppressive teachers is the theme of the Smiths' '**The Headmaster Ritual**' (1985). In this case, the band's lyricist Morrissey decides, as so many before and after him have, that he wants to leave education for good. Bennett (2001, p. 160) has referred to the way in which society has sought to regulate pop through censorship, casting youth as 'cultural dupes'. He points out that young people produce and consume music 'as ways of making sense of everyday life and that this has to be seen against a backdrop of postindustrialisation and related problems such as rising youth unemployment, the casualisation of labour and the resurgence of fascism in countries throughout the world'. A chronology of pro- and anti-school songs would, with some notable exceptions, roughly approximate to wider fluctuations in the economy and in social optimism. A similar trend is evident in cinema.

The Guinea Pig

The British, and perhaps even more so the English, private (generally known as 'public') boarding school has spawned a genre of fiction in the form of books (generally) aimed at younger readers. This is especially true of schools for boys. Well-known examples, as mentioned earlier, include Thomas Hughes' classic *Tom Brown's school days* (1857) through to Richmal Compton's *Just William* stories and Anthony Buckeridge's *Jennings* series. Billy Bunter, the overweight, greedy and cowardly boy at Greyfriars School, was the creation of Frank Richards (the best known of the many pen names of the prolific Charles Harold St John Hamilton) and has become firmly lodged in the national imagination. Bunter first appeared in the *Magnet*, a 'boys' paper' published between 1908 and 1940, but, through many books and ultimately a BBC television series (*Billy Bunter of Greyfriars*,

1953–1961), he survived its demise. This kind of literature has not been directly discussed in any extended way in our study, partly because there is a sense in which, in the post-war period, it has tended to be read mainly outside the mainstream of adult popular culture. It has, however, influenced representations of popular culture in many powerful ways. For example, many of its themes emerge in the *Harry Potter* novels. Also, many of the powerful values associated with this form of education have been both celebrated and challenged in other media, such as film. The values in question might be summarised as a Victorian worldview that was based on British imperialism. The ethos was essentially religious, fostering a division between the mind and the body that tended to relegate the cerebral as secondary to the physical; this has been termed 'muscular Christianity' (Riordan, 1991). It was an education that often served to reinforce class, racial and gender stereotypes, as did much of the associated literature. This ethos would prevail until relatively late in the twentieth century, when there was what many, from the perspective of the 1960s, might have regarded as an unlikely surge in the popularity of private education after many private schools, responding to the growth of higher education and increasing credentialism in British society, focused their energies on success in public examinations and won a new market among the increasingly affluent and growing middle classes. In the immediate post-war years, however, there was a political recognition that the public school tradition was under attack, and that it would need to make an accommodation of sorts with a society that was likely to be more consensual and more egalitarian than that of the inter-war years.

The British film *The Guinea Pig* (directed by Roy Boulting and briefly examined in Chapter 2) appeared in 1948, so it is an early post-war instance of a film taking education as a major theme. In 1944 Parliament had passed the Butler Education Act, and the political climate was one in which the election by a landslide of a Labour government seemed to indicate the potential for unprecedented social change. Aldgate and Richards (1999) outline how the film was based on a play by Warren Chetham Strode that itself had been inspired by the Fleming Report. What follows is indebted to their account. In 1942, Minister of Education Rab Butler set up a committee under Lord Fleming which two years later recommended that 25 per cent of public school places could beneficially be allocated to children selected from the state education system by local authorities. The scheme never came to fruition, but *The Guinea Pig* explores the idea by placing 'working-class' boy (he is actually the son of shopkeepers) Jack Read in a privileged public school as part of an experimental scholarship scheme. The film depicts Jack on a journey from uncouth boy with bad table manners and an 'inappropriate' accent to his emergence as a young toff who has acquired both social graces and an education and who, courtesy of another generous scholarship, is on his way to Cambridge. Jack learns to cherish the values of the school, and he is socially transformed by an education that has survived for centuries and will, by strong implication, survive for many more. *The Guinea Pig*, like so many British films, is primarily about social class. As Aldgate and Richards (*ibid.*, p. 116) state, it 'aims to show that both sides can learn from each other, a classic consensual stance, but the evidence suggests that it is the poor boys who do most of the learning'.

For Aldgate and Richards, pre-war cinema's perspective on public schools is summed up by the wistful and celebratory *Goodbye, Mr Chips* (1939). By 1951, *The Browning Version* was showing a repressive dimension to such schools. By the 1960s, films such as *Spare the Rod* (1961), *Term of Trial* (1962) and *To Sir with Love* (1967) had put secondary modern education on the British big screen. In between, however, there was a contrasting cinematic depiction of school life that is worthy of some consideration.

St Trinian's

For an excellent overview of the St Trinian's films, see Alan Foale's 'The St Trinian's cycle and British film comedy' (1993). An informative and insightful discussion of the films from a feminist perspective is provided by Ju Gosling (1998). The discussion that follows is indebted to both of the accounts.

Both Foale and Gosling trace the genesis of the St Trinian's films from the popular cartoons of Ronald Searle, which initially appeared in magazines and were ultimately published in books that sold well in the early 1950s. Foale (1993, p. 4) quotes Searle as stating: 'A St Trinian's girl "would be sadistic, cunning, dissolute, crooked, sordid, lacking morals of any sort and capable of any excess. She would also be well spoken, even well mannered and polite."' These contradictions form the basis of most of the humour in the cartoons and the films. For Gosling (1998, 8.ii, p. 3),

> The joke was that, contrary to the popular image of the quiet, well behaved, 'honourable' British boarding-school girl which had dominated from the beginning of the century until the Second World War, the girls were in fact violent, even demonic, gin-swigging, cigar-smoking and out of control. Rather than being 'innocent' and worthy of respect – the pre-war ideal – the girls were worldly wise and to be feared. The fear of girls' school and of lesbianism had, of course, been the motivating factor for attacks on the genre from as early as 1915. While the post-war critics became more overt in their attempts to repress the genre, the post-war parodists became more overt in revealing the reason for these fears.

Gosling (*ibid.*, p. 9) quotes Siriol Hugh-Jones, who reveals that, for men, the appeal of Searle's cartoons lay in the way in which, having a

> profound fear and distrust of women . . . particular the canny ones liable to grow up into astute turf accountants, or demon barristers, . . . men can safely laugh themselves insensible at the Searle girls, at the same time proving their point that females are basically jungly and out to kill, and if you can't beat them you can at least lock them away.

Gosling adds to this analysis the fact that, as Searle himself attested, the characters of the teachers concealed 'plenty of lesbianism', thereby touching on a cultural nerve about women teachers in girls' schools.

The success of the St Trinian's series built on that of 1950's *The Happiest Days of Our Lives*, a Frank Launder comedy starring Joyce Grenfell and Alastair Sim. In the earlier movie, a girls' school is relocated by error during the Second World War to a building used by a boys' school. Sim would subsequently play the main character, headmistress Millicent Fritton, as well as her 'no good' turf accountant brother Clarence Fritton, and Launder would direct the 1954 classic comedy *The Belles of St Trinian's*, the first and generally acknowledged to be by far the best of five films based on Searle's cartoons. The other four films were *Blue Murder at St Trinian's* (1957), *The Pure Hell of St Trinian's* (1960), *The Great St Trinian's Train Robbery* (1966) and *The Wildcats of St Trinian's* (1980). As the series progressed, the films became progressively less connected to the cartoons and less critically acclaimed, with 'St Trinian's' becoming something of a by-word for the 'jolly hockey sticks' view of English girls' schools (although the concept is allegedly based on St Trinnean's School in Edinburgh). Given the indelibility of the St Trinian's image, an announcement in 2004 of a remake to be set in a rundown boarding school came as no surprise; the new film, titled simply *St Trinian's*, finally appeared in 2007. One of the early scenes from *The Belles of St Trinian's* shows railway staff and others fleeing in terror from the prospect of the approach of the train carrying St Trinian's girls returning to school for the start of a new term. Gosling (1998) suggests that this tendency to associate instances of 'girls behaving badly' with St Trinian's may have been a factor in Searle's decision to end his cartoons of the girls in 1952.

The plot of *The Belles of St Trinian's* features a school under threat of bankruptcy and saved by its students. All St Trinian's films are peopled by incompetent and crooked teachers, a dithering but unscrupulous headmistress, spivs, cardboard cut-out police officers and criminals and, above all, the pupils (though the latter are rarely characterised). St Trinian's girls in the films are of two basic types: wildly anarchic 'fourth formers' (year 10), who usually appear as a collective force; and 'sixth formers' (years 12 and 13), who are generally played by women in their early twenties. The latter did not feature in Searle's cartoons, appearing only in the films and becoming increasingly sexualised as the series progressed. All the girls fully justify the claim of Miss Fritton in *The Belles of St Trinian's* that 'Most schools merely teach their girls and send them out, unprepared into a merciless world. But when our girls leave here, it is the merciless world that has to be prepared.'

Like the cartoons that inspired them, the St Trinian's films raise interesting questions about girls in schools and women in society. Not surprisingly, the filmed St Trinian's rather than the cartoon version features stronger in the public imagination. The films are, however, open to a huge range of readings. They clearly parody the formula of the classic girls' school story. Progressive educational ideas are espoused by the excessively tolerant headmistress and depicted through such scenes as girls distilling gin in chemistry classes. The Ministry of Education was satirised as incompetent. There are racist stereotypes. According to Gosling (1998), Sim's performance as Millicent Fritton satirises single women headteachers as 'unfeminine', and shows them as needing male qualities to succeed. For Gosling, while the fourth formers are independent in spirit and deed, the sixth formers succeed by means of their (hetero)sexuality. The teachers are either sexless and therefore doomed to St Trinian's or sexual and therefore able to escape by means of catching a man. Quoting Hugh-Jones again, however, Gosling (*ibid.*, p. 12) acknowledges that 'Searle's girls were strong young women, united around their school – which, as in the school stories, was the focus of their lives – against the rest of the world.' She points out that as the series progressed the St Trinian's girls became more sexualised and passive, she sees the humour of the films as both reactionary and intended for an adult male audience, and she feels this is the enduring St Trinian's image. It is interesting to note, though, that when fifty schoolgirls were involved in a violent disturbance at New Beckenham railway station in south London in May 2004, media reports (for example, McGowan 2004) quoted a police officer as saying: 'These girls were acting like screaming banshees . . . St Trinian's had nothing on them.'

Foale sees St Trinian's as encompassing the contradictory elements of both the 'sinister egotism' present in Searle's cartoons and elements of a 'humanistic girls' boarding school'. He points to the splendid school building and grounds, the diverse curriculum that features the theoretical and the practical, and the 'service roles' allocated to the few men. The St Trinian's films can be regarded as trivialising the privileged world they represent and thereby defusing critiques of private schooling. As previously noted, though, they are susceptible to many other readings. Certainly, St Trinian's is a school that is full of energy: while presented as a place apart from the world, it is more than a match for that world. This school is not by any means an idyll, but it is a place of creativity and, in our view, it projects a strong sense of 'girl power'. That this 'progressive dimension' should be seriously compromised in various ways is not surprising, bearing in mind both the historical context and the fact that St Trinian's was, ultimately, a comedic device.

Gosling (1998, p. 4) discusses the situationist-inspired way in which during the 1980s, postcard companies such as Recycled Images juxtaposed illustrations from pre-war publications with 'knowing' ironic captions that served to critique the values associated with the images. While the cards were progressive in politics, Gosling feels that they ultimately reinforce the view that the genre of school stories is 'only fit to be laughed at'. It is possible, however, that such cards have changed the ways in which the St Trinian's films are sometimes read, perhaps moving them beyond slapstick and superimposing a more ironic consumption. Foale (1993, p. 10) observes that the St Trinian's texts 'Do not pretend to be realist works,' while Gosling (1998, p. 10) points out that 'there have been no similar parodies of boy's schools and school stories'. This may be the case, but *If* is certainly of interest because it is equally surreal and perhaps even more apocalyptic in its exploration of the world of the English boys' boarding school.

If

If offers a far darker vision of the English public school than does St Trinian's. The film is surreal and, while it uses humour, it is essentially bleak in its vision both of public schools and of the wider British society. Directed by Lindsay Anderson and released in 1968, the film depicts a brutal regime of regimentation, militarism and floggings that finally leads to violent rebellion. Filmed at Cheltenham College, the film is very much a product of the late 1960s. With a script based on an unpublished play (*Crusaders*) by David Sherwin and an anti-hero in Mike Travis, played by Malcolm McDowell, the school depicted is one of rigid hierarchy enforced by prefects.

Like *The Belles of St Trinian's*, *If* begins with the start of term. A new boy is introduced to the arcane rituals and codes of the school, and quickly learns to obey and serve the whims of 'the whips' (as the prefects in the film are known). Vicious punishments are meted out to transgressors. Aldgate and Richards (1999, p. 205) point out that the masters play a relatively insignificant role in the film, and that 'almost all are eccentrics, perverts or ineffectual nonentities . . . The headmaster . . . is a bland, self-satisfied, platitudinous pseudo liberal, a caricature of the liberal house tutor, Nigel Lorraine, in *The Guinea Pig*.' *If* reeks of repression. The boys find solace in furtive smoking, drinking and homosexuality. The finale of the film is the school prize-giving at which an old boy, now a distinguished general, addresses the school with a speech that encapsulates all the privilege and tradition that the message of the film opposes.

During the speech, Travis and his small gang of rebels ignite a fire beneath the stage. When smoke begins to fill the hall, the assembled parents, dignitaries, boys and masters escape into the school grounds, where they are met by mortars and machine-gun fire from the rebels. The headteacher, when appealing for calm and telling the rebels that he understands them, is cold-bloodedly executed by a bullet in the forehead fired by a young waitress who has joined the rebellion after meeting Travis in her roadside café. Aldgate and Richards (*ibid.*, p. 208) astutely make the point that

> She is the only working class character in the rebel band, and she is the only woman. She stands for female equality, unrepressed sexuality, and youthful revolt. But, even more significantly, as the film ends, the school forces rallied by the Bishop and the old boy General counterattack, and Mick turns his gun on the audience.

If met with huge critical acclaim when it was released, though some more recent reviewers have criticised it on the basis of perceived manipulation, political naïvety and a wish to shock.

Class realities and violence

John Lennon's song **'Working Class Hero'** (1970) evokes the way in which the working-class experience of school can be negative and brutalising – a form of symbolic violence. *The Guinea Pig*, the St Trinian's series and *If* are all films with a concern with social class. *The Guinea Pig* hardly constitutes 'gritty social realism', though in its day some aspects were considered 'shocking', in particular the use of a swear word, and the film did contain some violence in the form of beatings and fights. The world of St Trinian's is essentially absurd, but there are high levels of violence (torture, explosions, beatings with lacrosse sticks). *If* has violence as a central theme, though the surreal nature of the film partially mitigates its impact. All of these films place education in highly privileged institutions, but for most people educational institutions are not places of privilege. For most, they are 'ordinary places' – although the theme of violence, as indicated in Chapter 6, is not uncommon.

The idea that violence is endemic within the education system, that the educational process has historically committed violence (through beatings, canings and other corporal punishment), is not really contentious. There is also an argument that education is a process that commits symbolic violence. The work of Bourdieu and Passeron (1977) is most associated with the idea that education reinforces and reproduces class divisions. In 2004, only 9 per cent of University of Cambridge students were from the 'lowest social classes' (those whose parental occupation is non-skilled manual, semi-skilled or unskilled), while even in a vocationally orientated former polytechnic such as the University of Huddersfield the figure was only 37 per cent (*Sunday Times* University Guide, 12 September 2004). Why does the working class fail to achieve in the education system? Is 'natural ability' likely to be so unevenly distributed between the social classes? Bourdieu and Passeron (1977) argue that education, by favouring certain ways of behaving (dispositions) and certain ways of using language, is biased towards dominant groups in society. It favours certain kinds of cultural capital.

When Ken Loach's film *Kes*, which was set in Yorkshire, appeared in 1969, the dialect was so strong that many audiences, even in the UK, complained that they had difficulty understanding what was being said. According to Derek Malcolm (2000), *Kes* is 'undoubtedly one of the most remarkable films about education, or the lack of it, ever made'. The plot revolves around a boy, Billy Casper, from a broken, poverty-stricken and socially excluded home who finds a young kestrel and, through his interest in rearing and training the bird, learns in ways that his teachers never thought possible. What the film evokes strongly, however, is the atmosphere of a down-at-heel 1960s northern secondary modern school that contains good as well as bad teachers. Clearly a cluster of endemic factors keeps Billy down, but the greatest of them is being who he is, where he is. In Bourdieu's terms, he occupies a *'linguistic habitus'* where his use of language and forms of speech reinforce uneven power relations. Billy's school seems redolent of that which would later be described in Paul Willis' (1977) classic study *Learning to labour*. Willis (*ibid.*, p. 128) explains that Bourdieu and Passeron 'have argued that the importance of institutionalised knowledge and qualifications lies in social exclusion rather than in technical or humanistic advance. They legitimate and reproduce a class society.' This, perhaps, is the central message of *Kes*.

When working-class students succeed in the educational system, and it is acknowledged that many do, there is often a breaking of bonds and a leaving behind of class, community and culture (see, for example, Chapter 8). If social surveys generally describe class by occupation, as Medhurst (2000, p. 20) has pointed out, it is also the case that class is 'not just an objective entity, but also (and mostly?) a question of identifications, perceptions, feelings.' In *Education and the working class* (Jackson and Marsden, 1962), a classic early sixties study of eighty-eight working-class children who had passed through Huddersfield grammar schools, Brian Jackson and Dennis Marsden explored some of the familial and community tensions to which working-class educational success can be heir. Almost forty years later, Medhurst (2000, p. 20), rejecting 'fashionable postmodern indeterminacy' and 'triumphalist celebrations of fluidity', reminds us 'that being unfixed, mobile, inbetween, can distress as much as it liberates'.

A relatively recent American film that deals with the question of social class and education is *Good Will Hunting* (1997, directed by Gus Van Sant from a screenplay by actors Ben Affleck and Matt Damon). Will, played by Damon, is a psychologically troubled young man with a history of having been abused as a foster child. By the age of twenty, he is prone to aggression and easily gets into fights. He is, however, also highly gifted in the field of mathematics and has a photographic memory. (This combination of psychological issues and advanced mathematical ability was later echoed in the film *A Beautiful Mind* (2001, directed by Ron Howard), based on the life of John Forbes Nash, in which a Nobel Prize-winning Princeton mathematician fights mental illness.) In *Good Will Hunting*, while working as a caretaker at the Massachusetts Institute of Technology, Will's extraordinary abilities are spotted by a tutor when he answers mathematical problems left on boards as challenges to students. Following an assault charge, Will undertakes counselling and has to come to terms with what to do with the rest of his life.

One educational theme in the film is the difference between intelligence and the learning of facts. A more prominent one relates to the problems and issues that might be faced by the exceptionally gifted. Of specific interest here, however, is the way in which Will's learning appears to have taken place outside the educational mainstream. Yet, the choice of 'making something of his life' rather than 'wasting it' involves breaking free from his community and his friends. A particularly powerful scene occurs near the close of the film, when Will takes a break with his friend Chuckie and they drink beer while working on a construction site. Chuckie asks Will about his girlfriend, who has left for medical school in California. He then asks about the therapy meetings Will has been attending. The crux of the scene is that when Will indicates that he wants to stay with his friends in the community where he grew up rather than 'move on in life' and exploit the opportunities that are now available to him, Chuckie becomes angry. He argues that if Will does not take advantage of his opportunities then he will be letting down his friends, who do not have the same choices. The film ends with Will making the big leap and setting off to be with his girlfriend in California, with the intention of making a career using his talents. He has chosen upward mobility, and his traumas are seemingly resolved.

There is a sequential progression from symbolic violence, through violent confrontations in schools, to violent death in schools and colleges. Death on a large scale through 'accidents/natural disasters' is rare but does occur, and in

Britain the Aberfan disaster of 21 October 1966, when a slag heap enveloped a junior school with the loss of 144 lives, including 116 children, still resonates in the national collective memory. For different reasons, associated with political dissent and state violence, the campus protest at Kent State University on 4 May 1970, which saw four students shot dead by Ohio state troopers, is lodged in the US national consciousness.

Violent death perpetrated by intruders periodically occurs: for example, the Dunblane massacre of 13 March 1996 saw 16 children between four and six years of age and one teacher shot dead in a Scottish primary school by Thomas Hamilton. In the US, the West Nickel Mines Amish School in Pennsylvania was the scene of the killing of five girls when a lone gunman, Charles Roberts IV, entered the premises on 2 October 2006. Two years earlier, the Beslan school massacre in Russia saw 344 civilians, at least 172 of whom were children, murdered by terrorists. Hundreds more were wounded. Popular culture sometimes deals with such events, but there appears to be more focus on those instances when death is inflicted on educational institutions by the students themselves.

On 19 January 1979, sixteen-year-old Brenda Spencer used a .22 rifle to wound nine (eight students and a police officer) and kill two (the principal and a custodian) at San Diego's Grover Cleveland Elementary School. Her infamous alleged remark that she did it because '**I don't like Mondays**' inspired the Boomtown Rats song of the same title. A series of similar incidents followed, the most infamous being the Columbine High School massacre of 1999, where Eric Harris and Dylan Klebold murdered many of their classmates and a teacher. Gus Van Sant's *Elephant* (2003) is a bleak portrayal of 'motiveless' high school mass murder. In this film, as observed in Chapter 6, two high school students commit acts of violence against their fellow classmates in a way which directly mirrors the events of the Columbine tragedy in a fictional setting. The two boys order assault weapons over the Internet before systematically and emotionlessly gunning down students and teachers. In the prelude, the film captures the tedium of the school, with its endless corridors, dull classrooms, functional refectories, empty sports fields and echoing gymnasium. It shows nothing in the way of emotion and offers no explanations. There is little characterisation, and the killers, Alex and Eric, are shown to be 'ordinary' rather than demonic.

Wernick (1999) acknowledges the scandal that might arise from attempts to attach micro-political meaning to Columbine, yet argues that there is meaning to be gained from considering the tragedy as a form of 'contestative transgression', suggesting that this would 'enable us – against all diabolising and reifying – to recover a sense of agency with regard to the actors [Eric Harris and Dylan Klebold] at its centre'. For Wernick, Columbine encompassed two symbolic events: the subsequent 'copycat' killings in other schools; and the 'reparative ritual' of accusations of evil, of prayer and policy initiatives through which the 'school, the locale and "the nation"' were 'healed and restored'. As Wernick relates, those seeking reasons for the atrocity have pointed to the fact that Harris had been medicated for anger management, and that he had failed his entry to the marines, disappointing the expectations of his father. Klebold, meanwhile, was an 'obsessive anti-Semite' who, Wernick suggests, was probably responsible for choosing Hitler's birthday as the day of the massacre. Although both were bullied, Wernick warns against reading the attack as 'victim's revenge' or as some form of white, right-wing, male atrocity. He describes the pair as having an 'equal opportunity hatred . . . They hated everything and everyone they encountered,' and contends, from analysis of what happened on the day, that their botched plan had been to kill everyone at the school, including themselves.

The moral panic of campaigns to reduce violence, increase school security rituals and introduce emergency drills, and the sense of community that was created through the rituals of grief were amplified and mediated by the media. As Wernick states, Columbine and its tragedy became 'a celebrity event', with Harris and Klebold enacting

> a replay of the plot of *Heathers*, the dress-up recalled *The Matrix*, the shootings repeated the mannerisms of *Quake* and *Doom*. A year before, in a media arts exercise, they had even made a video of themselves playing out the scene of what they actually did. It was a hall of mirrors, and their action only repeated what it reflected back. There was, though, a crucial difference. This repetition translated celluloid and the digital back into the embodied real. The simulacrum became flesh.

For Wernick, the symbolic event at Columbine conjures up something of the social contradictions and tensions that last stirred 'in the thickets of '68', which is where this chapter started. Now, it may well be appropriate to recall Debord's (1995, p. 73) dictum, 'a lie that can no longer be challenged becomes a form of madness'.

8 School for grown-ups
Lifelong learning in popular culture

Introduction

There is little in popular culture that focuses on the older learner or on vocational further education compared with the volume of school-based stories. Yet adult education, reconceptualised as lifelong learning, is central to the educational agendas of Western governments, concerned with new technologies, the ageing workforce and the need to keep people working for longer, to counteract an anticipated pensions shortfall. The only aspect of the post-compulsory sector that competes with school for coverage in popular culture is university education.[1]

This introduction touches on some of the key thinking that has shaped adult education research and practice in recent decades, to provide a context for the analyses of popular texts. In a limited space, there is not the opportunity to offer in-depth discussion of these issues and their mediation through popular culture. They do need addressing, however, as the textual analyses attempt to show how the discourses embodied in popular culture relate to these academic and professional concerns.

Valuing learners' experiences

It is generally accepted that adults need a pedagogical approach that values life experience. There are numerous testaments from practitioners and researchers reporting the frustration of adult learners whose experience is not valued and the high-quality learning that develops when it is (Cairns and Merrifield, 2001; Van Stralen, 2002; Edwards, 1993). The extensive writings on transformative learning in adulthood suggest that, even when experience provides contradictions and difficulties, it can lead to valuable learning (Brookfield, 2000; Mezirow and Associates, 1990; Mezirow, 2000; Taylor, 2006). There is a political dimension to the emphasis on valuing experience. Given adult education's traditional role in working with social groups whose voices are less dominant, it is thought to be important to recognise and acknowledge people's grounded realities, rather than impose theoretical models that may appear to negate lived experience. It follows that if students' experience is to be respected, the relationship between teacher and student cannot be one in which the teacher knows everything and the student nothing. The transformation and democratisation of the relationship between teachers and learners have long been central goals of radical adult education. The influential Brazilian educator Paulo Freire (1972) argued that relationships which treat learners as objects of other people's knowledge rather than subjects capable of making their own are damaging to both teachers and students.

Epistemology

This approach to experience and to the dialectical creation of knowledge between students and teachers is incompatible with a positivist view of knowledge. Freire's (1972) formulation of this is perhaps the best known, rejecting 'banking' education in which the teacher's knowledge is used to fill up students' heads and championing a 'problem-posing' approach in which teachers and students work together to understand the world. Empirical work (King and Kitchener, 1994; Belenky *et al.*, 1986) suggests that learners' epistemology develops with age and education, moving from a simplistic view of knowledge and right and wrong to one that understands it to be constructed (Hobson and Welbourne, 1998).

Political questions

Adult education has always been concerned with questions of resources, justice and inequality, in terms of educational opportunities and social and political power. It has a strong radical tradition from its origins in the UK in organisations like the Workers' Educational Association (WEA) and the Mechanics' Institutes that stressed working with communities and individuals towards empowerment and increased agency. Radical, liberal and postmodern adult educators have addressed issues relating to diversity, focusing on class, poverty, gender, race and disability (Benn *et al.*, 1998; Leicester, 1993; Thompson, 2000; Trifonas, 2003; Newman, 2006). Because adult education has often been concerned with reaching groups less well served by conventional schooling and higher education, it has also been interested in workplace education and workers' education. It therefore has a foot in vocational further education and in workplace learning, recognising that these are often more readily available to disadvantaged groups. Both are currently central to much UK policy for adult/higher education.

The texts

This chapter features texts that reflect these themes and ideas. It first considers the film *Educating Rita* (1983, directed by Lewis Gilbert). Although this film is over twenty years old, it remains one of the few examples of popular culture where the education of an adult is central to the plot and characterisation. Next, *Buffy the Vampire Slayer*'s critique of institutional lifelong learning, including work-based learning, is explored. This leads to a discussion of one aspect of lifelong learning that does feature in films: learning on the job, with a particular emphasis on the relationship between trainee and supervisor/mentor, considered here through the film *Boiler Room* (2000, directed by Ben Younger). Tom Sharpe's *Wilt* books offer a rare instance of fiction set in the further education sector, affording an interesting glimpse into vocational post-compulsory education in the 1970s, and revealing underlying attitudes that persist today. These attitudes can be found in the analysis of two episodes of the US animation series *The Simpsons* that completes the chapter. They foreground, through humour, beliefs about adult education that may help to explain its relative lack of glamour, and therefore limited exposure in popular culture.

Educating Rita

This film, based on Willy Russell's play (2001, first published in 1980), traces the development of Rita, played by Julie Walters, a hairdresser and Open University[2] student, and her relationship with her tutor, Frank, played by Michael Caine. It is particularly interesting for its representation of class and gender, although today, when almost half of the UK population has some experience of higher education and there are more mature part-time students in some universities in the UK than there are eighteen-year-olds, the film's presentation of Rita as an unusual university student has dated. Even in 1983, it presented a picture of higher education, adult learners, particularly women learners, and working-class life that bore little resemblance to contemporary experience. Nevertheless, it is worth considering because its clichéd view of higher education and of the adult learner is still prevalent, in spite of widespread experience of the reality of university life.

Higher education: privilege and cultural exclusivity

The higher education that Rita experiences looks more like the world of *Brideshead Revisited* than of Margaret Thatcher's 1980s, with its emphasis on vocational education and value for money. Everything connected with the northern, provincial red-brick university[3] Rita visits is presented to connote privilege and culture. Going to university involves procuring a lifestyle as much as an education. The opening sequences show elegant buildings with classical façades and pleasant lawns in quad-like developments reminiscent of Oxbridge colleges. Students sit contemplatively under shady trees. The male protagonist, lecturer Dr Frank Bryant, works in his office, a room larger, one suspects, than the entire ground floor of most academics' houses and entirely unrepresentative of the facilities accorded to most university staff. Its furniture suggests upper-middle-class taste and wealth: it has huge leather sofas, an antique desk and space for all the bookcases one could desire. Frank's students call him Dr Bryant. In response to Rita's question, 'What do they call you round here?', he replies, 'Sir.' There is so much deference towards the academic staff that although Frank is rude to his students, often drunk and cannot be bothered to teach them properly, they challenge him nervously and politely. He feels entitled to be openly contemptuous of them. Although they complain about his drunkenness, the relationship between students and staff bears no resemblance to the consumer culture that exists today in higher education, and was beginning to develop even when the film was released. There has been a major cultural shift in the UK in the last twenty years. The impetus to develop higher education as an arm of economic development, begun by the Conservative government of the eighties, has become an almost unquestioned orthodoxy. Universities are expected to prepare people for roles as productive workers; courses that exist solely to develop the mind, critical thinking, the imagination or an appreciation of culture are denigrated. Former UK Chief Inspector of Schools Chris Woodhead's attacks on 'Mickey Mouse' degrees are well known, while New Labour's Secretary of State for Education Charles Clarke was notorious for declaring that he didn't mind 'There being some medievalists around for ornamental purposes, but there is no reason for the state to pay for them.'

Rita is invited to Frank's house. He lives in a beautiful, large, Georgian building, probably well beyond the financial reach of any UK university lecturer living on their salary, even then. His social life is devoted to dinner parties with other academics, to the accompaniment of classical music. Altogether, the portrayal of university life implied by Frank and his students is that higher education confers not only cultural capital on its participants but social and financial capital. Whereas teachers are frequently portrayed unrealistically in popular culture as rather sad, ignorant losers (see Chapter 3), university lecturers are often presented equally unrealistically as established and rather leisured members of a stereotypical upper middle class.

Education, culture and the working class

The film capitalises on the contrast between the middle-class world of the university and hairdresser Rita's life. Its drama and humour depend on marked class distinctions. If Frank's lifestyle offers an exaggerated view of the cultural and financial benefits of a university education, that of Rita's electrician husband Denny underestimates the earning capacity of a skilled tradesman. Rita and Denny live in a small terrace house, rather than the more spacious and attractive property a skilled craftsman might have comfortably afforded. Their life and that of their neighbourhood presents a reductive image of working-class life, which provides some of the justification for Rita's desire to escape. Their spare time is spent in the local pub, where they meet her mum and dad and younger sister for a sing-song. Rita gives an impassioned speech about how she does not belong to this, any more than she belongs to Frank's, world. She uses the words her mother spoke about the songs to indicate that her whole life is unsatisfactory: 'There must be better songs than this.' The impression given is that working-class life is intellectually and culturally impoverished, yet emotionally rich – a world of loving, close-knit families, busily stifling ambition in their members for fear they will escape. Denny is trying to improve the home by knocking through two small downstairs rooms. Symbolically, Rita, irritated with the slow pace of improvement offered by the cautious Denny, takes a sledgehammer to the wall and causes major structural damage. To make progress, Rita must destroy what she already has, which is what her education helps her to do.

The film shows the working class as a homogeneous group. But the concept of class is problematic. It has been argued that there is no longer a working class following the demise of the big manufacturing industries that had taken place some time before *Educating Rita* was made (Gorz, 1997), let alone a clearly definable group like that shown here. Even in the 1980s society was relatively fractured, with distinct youth cultures (Giroux, 2002). Hoggart's (1957) influential analysis of working-class life and culture is relevant here. The older class stereotypes that appear in the film echo Hoggart's observations from the 1950s. His description of 'the neighbourhood' (*ibid.*, p. 38) could equally apply to the sequences following Rita through her home streets: 'They are understandably depressing, these massed proletarian areas; street after street of shoddily uniform houses intersected by a dark pattern of ginnels and snickets [alley-ways] and courts; mean, squalid, and in a permanent half-fog; a study in shades of dirty grey.' Hoggart (*ibid.*, pp. 72–101) perceives a dramatic distinction between 'them and us', between those with status and authority and the working classes, just as Rita talks about Frank's world as though it were another dimension. Above all, perhaps, he describes the phenomenon of the 'uprooted and anxious'. In an era when very few members of the working classes were educated beyond the age of fourteen, those who were might well feel ill-at-ease with the 'well-polished, prosperous, cool, book-lined and magazine-discussing world of the successful intelligent middle-class which he glimpses through doorways' (*ibid.*, p. 302). By the 1980s, however, distinctions were much less marked, and a far higher proportion of people had further and higher education and white-collar jobs, so Rita's sense of dissonance has a historical feel.

A Hoggart-like attitude towards popular culture is also reflected in the film. Hoggart views mass culture as debased and inauthentic, contrasting it with an earlier vision of working-class culture that was not commercial but, he felt, a true expression of their experiences. Frank tells Rita that 'devouring pulp fiction is not being well read'. Much of Rita's motivation is drawn from her passion for 'art'; her community is presented as ignorant of 'truth and beauty' and seduced by the cheap and tacky. Thus, education is seen as a way of accessing a better culture; escaping an unenlightened inheritance. Although the film reveals that the middle-class world to which Rita aspires is flawed (Frank is a cuckolded drunk; the flatmate she admires is depressed and suicidal), it is not mocked. But the lives of the workers are. Cheap laughs are garnered from the ignorance shown by Rita and her family and neighbours, such as this typical exchange:

FRANK: Do you know Yeats?
RITA: The Wine Lodge?

The film assumes anyone undertaking manual work will be ignorant, and it was sufficiently confident that this would generally be accepted by cinema audiences to build much of its drama and humour on this. Changing class and culture is still shown to be part of getting a degree, and the adjustments Rita has to make are presented as worthwhile. The idea that she could remain in her own neighbourhood and still be an educated person is unthinkable. Education in *Educating Rita* is about personal development and progress: moving up in the world and away from your roots. This portrayal of adult learning ignores the extrinsic goals that motivate many adult students. Limited economic prospects often drive adults to education. Although they may well become engaged with learning for its own sake, as Rita is, it is important to recognise that this delineation of the adult learner driven by a desire for personal growth is only a partial picture.

Women learning

Rita's apparent unsuitability for university comes not only from her class, but from her gender. The expectations of the working class for women cause her most frustration. She gives her reason for wanting to study as the desire to learn more about herself, rather than have a baby. Her husband and father both put pressure on her to start a family; her father humiliates her in public; and Denny burns her books and her work. In the end, Denny insists that she must choose between her course and her marriage. There are documented parallels from this period of women returners experiencing similar pressures from partners and families (McGivney, 1993; Edwards, 1993). Feminist adult educators during that era discussed the role of adult education in raising women's awareness of the wider structural implications of their personal relationships and the situations they faced (Thompson, 1983; Keddie, 1980). Rita's situation is representative, therefore. Her response is always apolitical, however. She does not challenge the assumption that women's primary interest should be child-rearing; her education seems to offer her no insights. Instead, she accepts that this is an individual matter – she just happens to want something different.

Although the film champions her personal journey, it would be misleading to suggest it celebrates the achievements of Rita as a working-class woman. The film presents the working-class woman as a victim and a joke. She totters into the university in a tight pink skirt and stiletto heels, tripping over. Her make-up and elaborate coiffure betray her origins, and part of her development is learning to dress and speak differently. This exaggerated stereotype insults the many women returners whose commitment to learning has been the mainstay of adult education for decades. In spite of Rita's resistance to her community's attempts to limit her horizons and her feisty criticisms of middle-class life, the film has a conservative view of adult education. It develops as a narrative of self-actualisation that suggests adult education exists to benefit special individuals who are somehow worthier, more sensitive and more intelligent than the rest of their class. Her education does not equip her to recognise the factors that construct the limitations that have been placed on her as a woman and as a member of a specific social group. It lacks the development of 'critical consciousness' that is an integral part of liberatory and feminist pedagogies. The focus is on enrichment through an accumulation of knowledge about elite/legitimate culture (Bourdieu, 1986), not on empowerment through the development of a political consciousness. The adult education shown here supports the status quo by removing a dissatisfied minority from their class of origin. By contrast, *Buffy the Vampire Slayer* offers a more critical and radical view of adult learning.

Buffy the Vampire Slayer

This section is particularly relevant to three areas discussed in the introduction: the teacher–student relationship, the view of knowledge this implies and the role of workplace learning. *BtVS*'s central characters are committed to self-directed learning, often at considerable personal cost. The institutional adult education they experience, however, is generally demeaning and dehumanising. (Any reader coming to this section without a knowledge of the series should perhaps first read the brief description in Chapter 3.)

The university system Buffy and Willow enter does not take account of students' increased maturity by offering more equal relationships. Teaching takes place in large, impersonal lecture theatres; professors are unapproachable. There is a wonderfully ironic portrayal of a class on social constructivism, in which the students compete to give the 'right' answers to the professor's questions. Maggie Walsh, the psychology professor, one of the few teachers who knows about the world of demons and vampires, does not share knowledge creation in the way Buffy and her friends do when they collectively research demon activity. Instead, she maintains a secret military outfit, 'the Initiative', that captures and studies non-humans. Buffy is coopted into the Initiative. This organisation serves a metonymic function in season four. Its passivity and unquestioning obedience exemplify a static and hierarchical world order in which knowledge is uncontested and scientific; professors have absolute authority and students accept this (Daspit, 2003). From the beginning of season one, however, Buffy has resisted attempts to control her access to knowledge or indeed to force knowledge upon her. That resistance commonly manifests itself through linguistic subversion and an exploitation of the dissonance created by her overt femininity, as evidenced in the analysis by Jarvis (2005). When financial and family reasons mean that Buffy is unable to continue as a university student, she finds that workplace learning can be even more dehumanising.

Learning on the job

To support her family, Buffy takes a job in a fast-food outlet, the Doublemeat Palace ('Doublemeat Palace', 6.11, written by Jane Espenson, directed by Nick Marck). Throughout *BtVS*, the class and financial constraints on education are clear (see 'The Zeppo', 3.13, written by Dan Vebber, directed by James Whitmore Jr.). School experience is dictated by class and income bracket; income as much as ability dictates choice of HE institution. Buffy's experiences at Doublemeat show the kind of education available to those at the bottom of the pile and parody 'customer care' training through the development of a spoof horror story that plays on our expectations about the dubious ingredients of fast food.

Persuading employers to invest in the education of their staff has long been an objective for adult educators, but there are anxieties about complicity with new forms of employee oppression (Fenwick, 2003). Cruickshank (2002, pp. 147, 141), for example, argues that for many in Canada 'lifelong learning (read learnfare) forces welfare recipients into dead-end training programmes, which keep them trapped in poverty' as part of an ideological shift in lifelong learning that has it 'now tied solely to skill acquisition'. Forrester (2002, p. 52) argues that the prominence of human resource management as an organisational model can lead to an alliance between corporate organisations and education and training that redefines education and knowledge to result in workplace learning that can be used to add to 'new forms of work intensification'. He sees the emphasis in human resource management/education on developing employee commitment as particularly significant.

Buffy's training at the Doublemeat Palace exemplifies these anxieties. She is shown a video clearly designed to create 'commitment'. It begins with a 1950s-style sepia-toned picture of a fast-food restaurant. This, combined with the narrator's comforting voice telling us that Doublemeat Palaces are found across the American West in people's own small towns or cities, associates the company with nostalgic images of American values. It celebrates the thrill of working behind the counter as a part of the Doublemeat experience (at this point the picture of smiling employee and customer blossoms into colour). We then see a series of happy employees claiming to be part of the experience, topped by ludicrous images of a happy cow and a happy chicken that are also part of this communal experience. The juxtaposition of happy employees and happy cow and chicken suggests that all participants should be happy to make the ultimate sacrifice for Doublemeat. Buffy's later discovery in the mincer of the finger of an employee who left suddenly intensifies the notion that employee identity is consumed by the company. Intellectual curiosity, the essential component of any good student's make-up, is stifled by an atmosphere of fear. Her reasonable questions about exactly what the special ingredient in Doublemeat might be are met with the sinister reply that it is a 'meat process'. Echoes of many a horror film resound in the scene where the manager catches her looking in the freezers for the secret ingredient.

Following the induction video, Buffy is shown around the kitchen by the manager, Manny. Observing an employee producing consistently round meat slices, she remarks how identical they all seem. Manny assumes she means the employees, who, he says, all begin to look alike to him. It is comically presented, but makes the point that the company training system does not acknowledge individuality. Buffy's co-worker Gary tells her to stop being funny, as Manny believes that humour robs the company of employee time. Humour is subversive because it turns people into individuals who might take time for themselves; it also relies on ambiguity and ambivalence – on making interpretations and connections between disparate entities. As such, it challenges Doublemeat's approach to education, in which truth is absolute, a far remove from the kind of constructivist approach to knowledge that is generally thought to be characteristic of good practice in adult education. Manny asks a seemingly casual question about why Buffy wants to work at Doublemeat. She begins to explain her financial situation, but, reading his face, she pauses and realises that this is a test. Searching for the right answer, she stumbles on the fact that she is meant to claim she wishes to be part of the Doublemeat Experience. Manny smiles and nods, indicating that there is only one 'right' answer to this apparently open question. The training is about instilling commitment, not creating knowledge or exploring experience.

Boiler Room

Boiler Room (1999, directed by Ben Younger) also presents workplace learning as limiting, but it occupies a slightly different political space from *BtVS*. The latter is concerned with the limitations of workplace learning resulting from the limited collective goals of the organisation. *Boiler Room* is set in a less globally powerful organisation, but shows how individual development is equally damaged by the emphasis on individualism and competition within a postmodern, communications-driven company. They are similar in that they both suggest the profit motive is incompatible with effective education. Although little appears to have been written about adults' experiences of institutional education beyond the university, workplace learning is a common theme in contemporary popular culture, including films such as *Training Day*, *Private Benjamin*, *The Firm* and innumerable television dramas, soap operas and situation comedies. It forms an integral part of the popular narrative's preoccupation with individual adjustment to a new culture and environment: the first job, the change of career, the adjustment to big-city or small-town life. Its popularity may be linked to its capacity to show the central character's response to the challenge of learning in an environment where failure would be economically and socially costly. The character has to fit in; s/he also has to cope with the personal relationships involved in learning in what is often a claustrophobic and exposed environment. These texts often focus on the relationship between the employee/student and his/her mentor.

The central character in *Boiler Room*, Seth, has dropped out of university, motivated by a desire to be part of something he can hardly name: 'I just wanted in.' He is hungry to make big money and cannot see the point of formal education. He also believes this perspective is part of a cultural shift: 'Nobody wants to work for it any more. There's no honour in taking that after-school job and making Ds. Honour's in the dollar, kid.' In a culture that values consumerism and wealth and insists on linking education almost exclusively to economic growth and individual financial success, education has no instrinsic merit. It becomes devalued: if its only purpose is to help people make money, they will perceive that there are quicker and easier routes. Seth's quick fix may be different from that of many school refusers, who turn to crime to fulfil their ambitions, but the link is there: 'I took the white boy's way of slinging crack rock. I became a stockbroker.'

The culture of J. T. Marlin, the company that employs Seth as a trainee stockbroker, has much in common with that of a boys' public school[4] when the teachers are not watching. The brokers are noisy, riotous bullies, keen to pick fights with outsiders. Their table manners are appalling – they dive on the food at a convention with an obsessive greed that represents their hunger for all things material. They have a strict hierarchy: trainees are at the bottom and treated with contempt. The atmosphere is macho: they will not even 'pitch the bitch' (sell stocks to women). Their director addresses them as 'boys'. Also reminiscent of public school, is the competitive approach and the emphasis on public humiliation. When a senior broker's trainee fails to soften a lead sufficiently for the broker to seal the deal, he is yelled at in front of the entire floor – 'You happen to suck fat arse rhinoceros dick' – an insult worthy of *South Park* elementary school character Cartman. The control and overt institutional values of public school have been removed, leaving its hidden curriculum: the survival of the fittest.

The training manager, Jim, is a highly successful broker. His main concern when training new staff is that no one should 'waste my time'. He needs to get back to making money. Unlike the idealised teacher explored in Chapter 2, he does not encourage the students to confide in him or come to him for support; he is not interested in their perspective. His group interview is described as a 'Hitler Youth rally'. The training method throughout, consisting of arbitrary injustice and consistent abuse, punctuated by promises of unimaginable wealth, is modelled during the group interview for the traineeships. He dislikes a remark from one candidate, who is told, 'Get the fuck out of here.' Another, who has already passed his stockbroker examinations, is summarily dismissed for knowing too much: 'That's it, Skippy, pack your shirt, let's go.' He talks *at* them, and his main objective is to convey the core values of the firm, which are about excessive work and excessive money. They should not 'ask about vacations' because (contemptuously): 'If you want vacation time, go teach third-grade public school.' This, in itself, positions a career in teaching in opposition to success, where success is measured in terms of money. As he says, 'They say money can't buy happiness – look at the smile on my face.' When he meets them again, after their first few weeks in the job, he is supposed to be preparing them for their Series Seven examinations. This consists of tossing the booklets at them and taking three hundred dollars from each of them. Passing an examination is not seen as an achievement: 'If you study, you'll pass.' Instead, Jim concentrates on teaching the trainees things that are important to the culture of work. These are characterised by their superficiality. 'Most of you dress like shit,' he tells them, and insists they buy at least one good suit. They do not meet customers; however, this is merely to keep up the aesthetic values of the firm, which are clearly based on signalling that you have money. His big message is based on a slogan: they must all 'Act "as if"'.

When Seth starts work he is assigned to Greg, who is supposed to show him the ropes, while Seth works for him. The weakness of this mentor-based learning on the job is revealed when it becomes apparent that the selfish and competitive Greg is not giving Seth even the basic information that is necessary and is jealous of his ability. At their first meeting, the broker begins by issuing instructions at great speed. Seth interjects, 'Morning,' and is ignored – there is clearly no time for social niceties. There is no time to reflect, either. Every failure is public. Greg stands by the phone as Seth makes calls and insults him as he does so. He is critical and unsupportive, fuelled by a personal vendetta, even when Seth becomes good at the job. The relational and reflective learning that research has shown to be so important is impossible. Learning by doing, under the aegis of a mentor, may be excellent with a good mentor. Two aspects of capitalist culture militate against this, however. First, the primary target is profit, not individual growth and development. Therefore, the trainee's learning will always be subordinate to the need to make the next dollar. Second, the competitive, individualistic atmosphere means that the trainee's success may not be in the interest of the mentor. This contrasts with most formal, state education, where the individual's learning is the whole point of the business, where the culture usually emphasises helping everyone to achieve their potential, and where it is unequivocally in the interest of the teacher (sometimes even in their financial interest) for the pupil to succeed.

Although Seth has rejected school and the values of his middle-class parents, he is amazed by the emptiness of the lives of his rich colleagues. Greg is more useful as a cultural mentor than as a work mentor, and explains that the brokers spend all their money and have no capital. Moreover, they do not know what to buy. They visit a colleague's huge house. Seth walks through vast empty rooms before eventually finding all the brokers in one room, clustered on a single sofa, watching a film about stockbrokers. They have bypassed conventional liberal education and made money, but they have also bypassed their own imaginative and cultural development, so they cannot make the most of the income they have.

Wilt

Training for work also takes place off-the-job. The world of Tom Sharpe's comic novels featuring Henry Wilt, a further education lecturer, is recognisable to anyone familiar with FE in the 1970s. However, an analysis of the first novel in the series, *Wilt* (published in 1976 and subsequently made into a film, 1988, directed by Michael Tuchner), reveals themes and issues that help to explain some contemporary preoccupations within this sector. Henry Wilt reappeared in three more novels, most recently *Wilt in nowhere* (Sharpe, 2004). The latter uses the Wilt family as the basis for a series of comic escapades. It is set some time after 2001, but does not attempt to offer any critique of contemporary post-compulsory education, and the action does not take place in the college. Indeed, Sharpe does not seem to be aware of the significant changes that have taken place in lecturers' working lives, and instead assumes they are on leave all summer and still report to the Local Education Authority. But the novel's interest lies elsewhere, and it makes no claims to focus on education, whereas the early novels offer scope for reflection on perceptions of the post-compulsory sector.

The FE sector is almost synonymous in some quarters with vocational education. At the time of *Wilt*, FE colleges predominantly trained young people, especially young men, for craft and technician work. This was partially funded by employers, who supported the training by releasing employees to attend college. The curriculum included an element of liberal studies, the subject taught by Wilt. This was meant to offer young people a broad understanding of the world to complement the work-related training. It took various forms. The Technician Education Council and Business Education Council developed curricula, but academic staff had considerable latitude to develop their own programmes (Fisher, 2003b, 2004). These could consist of any of the social science/humanities subjects – literature, history, sociology – or topics related to developing a broader understanding of the vocational area the students were entering – the study of buildings and the environment for bricklayers, for example. The subject no longer exists, but various strands can be seen in today's curriculum in ideas like citizenship and key skills.[5]

Liberal studies was always a contentious area of the curriculum. There were exciting and successful developments, with a strong emphasis on democratic classrooms and critical thinking skills. In many cases, however, it was difficult to get young people who had left school and taken up a practical trade to accept the value of continuing to study subjects not directly linked to work. Furthermore, many employers resented releasing their workers unless they were learning skills of immediate use. Liberal studies staff fought internal battles for space on the timetable, were often landed with the worst slots in the day (three to five o'clock on Friday afternoons, for example) and, as the novel suggests, their work was taken less seriously than that of the vocational teachers. At the end of the 1970s, vocational training in the UK was being revolutionised by the introduction of employer-driven national vocational qualifications. These were based on the assessment of job performance, and left no incentive for colleges to consider the development of the whole person. Changes in funding ensured there was no space to include teaching not directly linked to obtaining qualifications. Liberal studies was replaced initially, as Wilt himself suggests at the end of the novel, by the more practical social and life skills and communication skills. But these still met with resentment from students and employers. Much of the humour in *Wilt* comes from exploiting the resentment of students, vocational teachers and employers at the expectation that students should undergo a broad, more academic education post-sixteen. The perspective of the book is one that accepts the premise that this is pointless. The central character's failure is based on the fact that he, too, accepts that the work he does has no value.

Wilt contributes to two complex discourses concerning further education, which continue to be prominent in the twenty-first century. First, it reveals anxiety about controlling FE teachers and the FE curriculum; second, it focuses on the battle between vocational and non-vocational further and adult education.

Out of control: the teachers and the curriculum

There were no precise requirements for the training of FE or HE staff in 1976. In practice, most FE teachers were well qualified and often had considerable industrial or commercial experience, and many took advantage of in-service teacher-training courses. However, there was not the centralised, government control of FE teacher subject specialist qualifications or teacher training that applied to schoolteachers. The curriculum, more so in some areas than others, was left to the discretion of these professionals. Some of the anxieties upon which *Wilt* capitalises, therefore, are those that have driven policy developments in this area over the last three decades: the need to regularise and standardise the curriculum and the wish to establish tight controls over entrants to the profession. The head of catering opposes Wilt's promotion and challenges the assertion from the head of liberal studies that Wilt is 'committed'. His comments reveal his suspicion that liberal studies teachers use the curriculum as a front for political radicalism: 'Committed to what? Abortion, Marxism or promiscuity? It's bound to be one of the three. I've yet to come across a liberal studies lecturer who wasn't a crank, a pervert or a red-hot revolutionary' (Sharpe, 1976, p. 12).

Descriptions of Wilt's teaching, however, make it clear that there is no radical politicisation going on in his classroom. There is very little learning of any kind, in fact:

> For ten long years he had spent his days going from classroom to classroom with two dozen copies of *Sons and Lovers* or Orwell's *Essays* or *Candide* or *The Lord of the Flies* and had done his damnedest to extend the sensibilities of Day-Release Apprentices with notable lack of success.
>
> (*Ibid.*, p. 8)

His goal is to get through the day in the least painful way possible. He allows his class of butchers to continue, under semi-controlled conditions, the drunken conversation they were having before he arrived. They accept some degree of order in the conversation when the sanction for complete disorder is a return to reading the set book, *The lord of the flies* ('Either we hear what Peter has to tell us about the effects of the Pill, or we get on and read about Piggy'). The consequence of this is that their educational experience lacks focus and relevance:

> Meat One ranged far and wide about vasectomy and the coil and Indians getting free transistors and the plane that landed at Audley End with a lot of illegal immigrants and what somebody's brother who was a policeman in Brixton said about Blacks and how the Irish were just as bad and bombs and back to Catholics and birth control.
>
> (*Ibid.*, p. 16)

The curriculum comes under attack from the media, too. The newspapers distort the discovery of a blow-up doll in the college grounds and add it to investigations about teaching in the college, culminating in the headline: 'Sex Lectures Stun Students'. After reading this, the principal expresses his concern about its claims that fitters and turners study *Last exit to Brooklyn* and nursery nurses are taught to wear Dutch caps at all times. Although the storyline is farcical, the suspicion and anxiety surrounding the delegation of responsibility for the curriculum to staff rings true. Everyone – from the management, to the media, to the employers – assumes staff must be teaching material that is subversive or, at best, pointless. The novel appears to support the view that FE is largely pointless.

Vocational versus non-vocational education

Academic education supposedly has higher status than vocational education, and successive governments have expressed concern about this. There are competing discourses in this arena, though, and the novel presents them very well. First, we see that there is an academic snobbery at work, even in Fenland College of Arts and Technology. The principal, the academic board and the promotions board are obsessed with raising their academic status a little by offering higher education and eventually becoming a polytechnic.[6] This distorts everything the college management does: where it places resources, who gets promoted and how it responds to publicity and a police investigation.

At the same time, within the college itself, another discourse prevails. While the wider context may privilege academic work, the subculture of the vocational college embraces vocationalism and denigrates the academic. Thus, liberal studies is regarded with suspicion, further reducing the likelihood of Wilt's promotion. All the other subjects are more important. Moreover, the attitude of his students towards all teachers is characteristic: 'Work? You lot don't know what work is . . . All you do is sit at a desk all day and read. Call that work. Buggered if I do and they pay you to do it' (*ibid.*, p. 23). In this particularly macho environment, real work is physical while intellectual work is pretence. The conclusions of Willis' (1977)[7] influential study of young males and their attitude to work and education are embodied in the attitudes of these students. They are not successful academically, so they choose to classify academic achievement as valueless.

There is also a presumption that non-academic youngsters are a problem and those who have to deal with them are somehow diminished by association. Wilt's own head of department, Mr Morris, says, 'Anyone who is prepared to teach the sort of bloody-minded young thugs we get can't be entirely sane' (Sharpe, 1976, p. 202). The following scene makes the point. The principal is concerned that the bad publicity resulting from Wilt's arrest for murder and the subsequent investigation into teaching at the college will lead to budget cuts:

> The fact that we have been providing a public service by keeping, to quote Mr Morris, 'a large number of mentally unbalanced and potentially dangerous psychopaths off the streets' unquote, seems to have escaped their notice.
> 'I presume he was referring to the day-release apprentices,' said Dr Board, charitably.
> 'He was not,' said the Principal. 'Correct me if I am wrong, Morris, but hadn't you in mind the members of the Liberal Studies Department?'
> (*Ibid.*, p. 202)

What to do with non-academic young people, particularly males, has always been a cause for concern. Governments worry about their potential for crime and disruption, and the huge decline in the developed world of unskilled work to absorb and exhaust them has exacerbated concerns. Education and training have been expected to resolve this. The book presents the working classes as rather nasty.

Wilt's students, with their identities taken entirely from their vocations (Meat One, Printers Three and so on), reinforce every stereotype of the working-class male. They use crude language, have right-wing responses to law and order and are extremely sexist. Some of his students are very callous. Printers Three relish the fact that their current teacher is off sick, possibly because he cannot bear to teach them, and a previous lecturer gassed himself.

Championing the underdog

The hero's name, and the prominence this gains from also being the book's title, indicates that teachers in the post-compulsory sector are not going to be presented as any more glamorous than schoolteachers. 'Wilt' suggests impotence and the novel reveals that Wilt does indeed fail to satisfy his wife Eva both sexually and in terms of the social status he can offer her. This impotence is indicative of a general powerlessness and failure. He has failed to achieve promotion for several years running because he teaches the wrong subject. He earns no respect from his students and has no sense of pride in his work. The college principal has not heard of him until he is accused of murder.

The general ambiguity relating to teachers' professional status is even more marked when considering FE staff. Inspector Flint makes his view of the status of FE staff clear when he states: 'If you are a professional man, and in spite of what some people may say lecturers in technical colleges are members of a profession if only marginally . . .' (*ibid.*, p. 147). His sergeant expresses a common prejudice about lack of standards for teachers when he says, 'You know they can't sack lecturers' (*ibid.*, p. 141).

We do discover that Wilt has developed cunning through coping with his demoralising job and his sad social and personal life. When arrested and subjected to extended questioning by the police, he manages because: 'For ten years he had sat in front of classes answering irrelevant questions . . . By comparison with Bricklayers Four, Sergeant Yates and Inspector Flint were child's play' (*ibid.*, p. 117). Nevertheless, the overall picture is conservative, refusing to value education for the less well off and less academic. It presents students engaged in non-academic further education as almost sub-human, insensitive thugs. Teachers are incompetent and unprofessional, not fit to have control of the curriculum. The radical agenda that historically inspired much work (from Mechanics' Institutes onwards, through the WEA and other bodies) and formed the origins of adult and further education is presented as pointless. The conclusion, which does not seem to be intentionally ironic, is that the (now successful) Wilt will institute an entirely functional curriculum for working-class youth:

> In future Gasfitters One and Meat Two would learn the how of things not why. How to read and write. How to make beer. How to fiddle their income tax returns. How to make an incompatible marriage work . . . After all, you didn't require a degree in English Literature to teach Gasfitters the how of anything.
> (*Ibid.*, pp. 220–221)

Wilt implies that working-class people should be educated only to operate within given parameters. The above quotation clearly states that those teaching less academic students do not themselves need academic ability. Thirty years later, this kind of instrumentalism still dominates further education policy.

The Simpsons

The US cartoon series *The Simpsons* frequently locates the action in Springfield Elementary School and tackles many educational issues, such as home–school relations, teacher disaffection, disruptive behaviour, bullying, poor teaching and unequal resources (Kantor *et al.*, 2001). School is the primary focus for the series' educational satire. Occasionally, however, it turns its attention to the education of its adult characters. This section considers two episodes, 'Homer Goes to College' and 'Secrets of a Successful Marriage'. Both reveal conflicting attitudes towards adult education, adult students and their teachers. And both feature Homer Simpson. Homer (in spite of his resonant name) is preoccupied with the material: donuts, Duff beer and cable TV. His ignorance, stupidity and gullibility are constantly paraded. We know from flashback episodes that he did poorly at school. He is therefore in need of adult education. Unlike his daughter Lisa and wife, Marge, he evades informal education, such as museum visits or participation in the arts, preferring undemanding, commercialised entertainment. In 'Homer Goes to College', an inspection of the nuclear power plant where he works (or sleeps, mainly) reveals he is dangerously underqualified for his role, so he has to pass a university course in nuclear physics in order to keep his job.

Higher education and the working man

Marge says, 'This is a great opportunity, you could learn so much' but his son Bart, who is already part of the male, blue-collar, anti-intellectual culture that pervades the show, mocks him. Homer failed to complete the application for a guaranteed college place when he was at school because he left the school guidance counsellor's room for the more immediate gratification of chasing a dog that had stolen some meat. He calls this 'fate' and fails to realise that his preference for easy and immediate distraction repeatedly stops him achieving. Once enrolled in the university, he prefers insulting the professor to listening; sleeping and eating to studying; partying, drinking and playing pranks to revising. Unsurprisingly, he fails his examinations, but his new nerdy friends change his grade on the computer. Although Marge, a woman of integrity, insists he retakes the course, it is clear he will not work any harder next time.

Homer's understanding of university life is based on popular cultural representations. He explains to Marge that he is watching a 'programme about campus life' which turns out to be a film called *School of Hard Knockers*. This and everything else he has seen leads him to tell Marge that students at college are either 'jocks' or 'nerds', and it is the jocks' role to abuse the nerds. In spite of his beer belly and obvious lack of athleticism, Homer is convinced he is a 'jock' and sets out to undermine the university's academic and intellectual objectives. His behaviour resembles that of Bart at school. Both set themselves up in opposition to their respective educational institutions and believe it is the student's role to undermine the work of the staff. Homer is disappointed that his fellow students do not want to trick or insult the faculty. He ignores the fact that the dean is young, kind and cool (he is an ex-bass player with the Pretenders), and persists in seeing him as old and embittered. In this way the programme initially undercuts Homer's media-based beliefs about higher education. Like Rita in *Educating Rita*, Homer comes from a background where higher education was both revered as something for the elite (he shouts, 'I'm a college man, I am so smart,' when he gets a place) and mocked (not real work).

Characteristically for this series, the assumptions it has built for us are quickly reversed. Having established that Homer's pop culture views of education are nonsense, we are then introduced to three postgraduate students whom he approaches for extra tuition, and they live up to every popular cliché about the nerdy science student. They share an insular world of in-jokes, based on science fiction and fantasy, are brilliant at maths, physics and computing, and are so unfit to cope with life outside the university that they hand their wallets over to Nelson, a schoolboy bully, when he claims to be the 'wallet inspector'. They have no friends and no social life.

As an older, blue-collar male, Homer is a misfit at university. Respect for the student's experience is at the heart of much adult education theory, and failure to recognise this is often thought to be the cause of student disaffection. Government policy has driven the growth of Accreditation of Prior Experiential Learning (APEL) systems to give adults academic credit for experience gained at work or in life, but this episode has no time for such an idea. At one point, Homer tries to assert the importance of experience, challenging the nuclear physics lecturer on the grounds that he, Homer, has actually worked in a nuclear power plant. If the value of experience were to be portrayed, this should be the moment when the working male's experience is valorised, while the academic tries to denigrate him. Rather than belittle him, however, the professor invites him to show what he knows, and Homer manages to blow up the building. Homer may have had years of experience, but he has learned nothing from it, suggesting that experience *per se* is not superior to academic knowledge.

Homer may seem unworthy of education, but the system itself has flaws. He almost fails to gain entry to university this time round too because he cannot think of any books he has read to form the basis of the essay he must write in his application, so instead he sends a picture of himself eating cake. The admissions tutors cannot even be bothered to take the 'seconds' required to read his application and judge him entirely on the basis of the photograph. His acceptance is due to the influence of his boss, the corrupt Mr Burns, revealing the HE system's vulnerability to the influence of the rich.

Adult education

In 'Secrets of a Successful Marriage', Marge advises Homer to 'take an adult education class' when he is depressed by the (long-overdue) realisation that his friends and family think he is 'slow'. Homer's contempt for education comes through in his reply: 'Oh, and how is education supposed to make me feel smart? Every time I learn something new, it pushes some old stuff out of my brain.' However, he agrees to go to the adult education centre. Its slogan, 'We take the "dolt" out of "adolt" education', sets the tone for an episode portraying adult learners as stupid and lazy.

Instead of registering as a student, however, Homer is appointed as a teacher and feels immensely proud. He boasts to all his acquaintances and jumps red lights, shouting, 'I'm a teacher, let me through.' Initially, it would seem that the show is indicating that adult education tutors have a relatively high status in society. Homer's pride is undercut for the audience, however, by their awareness of how he came to be appointed and by the subsequent representation of the adult education centre. It seems that anyone can become a tutor. For instance, Homer's spinster sister-in-law, always unlucky in love, is teaching the 'How to turn a man to putty in your hands' class. Homer is shocked to find such entirely unsuitable people working as teachers so applies to be a tutor instead of joining a class. The administrator is concerned only with filling classes and with getting someone who is still breathing to stand in front of them, so Homer merely has to mention that he is happily married to find himself in charge of a class on marriage. His fellow tutors are drunks, incompetents and down-and-outs. Adult education is therefore presented as an amateur business staffed by the dregs of society.

Prospective students surge from class to class until they find the most amusing option. The idea that adult education offers easy, unchallenging subjects is epitomised by the 'Orange eating' class. Learning from life experience is savaged in the treatment of Homer's marriage class. Struggling (unsurprisingly, given his lack of knowledge and training) to think of anything to do with his students, Homer resorts to telling stories about his own married life. The students adore this, and beg for more details. So the whole idea of storytelling and of building on experience is represented simply as an excuse for gossip and prurient curiosity. Just as the tutors are shown to be amateurs, the curriculum is shown to be trivial and knowledge-free, an excuse to chat and extend social interaction. Homer's lack of knowledge and education becomes apparent the moment his intitial teaching approach ceases. The students are presented as consumers rather than seekers after knowledge. Statements like 'I can't believe I paid ten thousand dollars for this course. What the heck was that lab fee for?' imply that adult education is exploitative and poor value for money, and that the students themselves contribute to this by demanding an essentially recreational service.

The sublime and the ridiculous

These two *Simpsons* episodes offer excellent illustrations of some popular beliefs about adult education; beliefs that appear to have had some influence on policy.

'Homer Goes to College' offers a mixed view of university education. The portrayal of callous and corruptible admissions tutors indicates a lack of faith in the fairness and integrity of individuals and processes relating to the opportunities HE can offer. On the other hand, the physics professor is knowledgeable and prepared to put in extra time to review the course content with students. He is also willing to listen to Homer. His teaching style might be didactic and unimaginative, but he is clearly a committed professional, as is the kindly dean. HE, though flawed, therefore comes across as a desirable institution.

By comparison, the more widely available adult education is treated with contempt in 'Secrets of a Successful Marriage'. The staff are not only ignorant but unprepared. The discussion above, relating to the FE faculty in *Wilt*, has some relevance here in that the historical lack of any formal requirement for qualifications in further and adult education, especially in comparison with schoolteaching, clearly creates suspicion about the credibility of such tutors. It is interesting to note, though, that there is no statutory requirement for a minimum qualification for HE lecturers, either. But their knowledge and education are rarely challenged in popular culture, which appears to prefer the stereotype of the overeducated boffin.

The programme also raises questions about curricula. The HE curriculum goes largely unchallenged. It is self-evidently worthwhile to study nuclear physics if you are responsible for the safety of a power plant. But the adult education curriculum is absurd and indefensible. The main target for this satire is non-vocational adult education, which has been under attack for decades. Since the 1992 FE/HE Act in the UK, it has been increasingly difficult to secure any state funding for this, with funds primarily targeted on vocational education for sixteen–nineteen-year-olds, and literacy and numeracy provision for adults. The series reflects the suspicion and lack of respect for popular adult education that led to this withdrawal of funding in the UK. Adult education has always been popular, but adults do not always wish to study subjects that accord with governmental economic development plans. Many adult educators believe that studying a subject that interests the individual has intrinsic value and that education should not be restricted to the merely utilitarian. This is clearly a matter for debate, but 'Secrets of a Successful Marriage' certainly sustains a popular view of adult education as pointless and recreational. Similarly, no value whatsoever is attributed to the extensively researched, proven through practice and well-argued perspective that adult learners do best when the curriculum builds on and values their experience. Indeed, both episodes are elitist in their assumption that adults' experiences have little value. They mirror the impression offered by the limited range of representations of adult education in British comedy, such as the ITV series *Mind Your Language* (1977–1986), which derived much of its humour from the failings of foreign students trying to learn English and from a stereotypical representation of a successful woman (the college principal) as a dragon, and Radio 4's *Night School* (first broadcast in 2002). The latter, a vehicle for the comedian Johnny Vegas, might be meant to be ironic, but it reinforces the idea that adult education teachers are failures (Johnny supposedly teaches a night-school class in pottery because he failed as a Butlin's Redcoat), and adult education students are the problem-ridden dregs of society.

HE students in the *Simpsons* episodes defy stereotypes of students as rebellious, political, lazy or addicted to wild living. They all appear to be well behaved, respectful and intent on studying hard, reflecting perhaps the large sums they have to invest in their education. Their weaknesses are insularity and an inability to cope in the world. Also, in spite of Homer's many faults, the audience may well identify with him in his desire to have some fun and feel that there is something wrong when the youthful spirit appears to have been knocked out of a generation. Although, as indicated earlier, the university system *The Simpsons* portrays does not operate entirely fairly, the programme does not locate the blame for failure entirely with that system. A great deal is attributed to individual responsibility. Homer is unwilling to do anything that requires effort and is incapable of thinking beyond his immediate comforts. In its dealings with schools, the series does show the inequalities and lack of opportunities that arise from the unequal and inadequate resourcing of state schools (Kantor *et al.*, 2001), but the two episodes discussed in this chapter do not focus on this with respect to adult education. Instead, they support the idea of a meritocracy. Individuals need to be able to defer gratification, employ self-discipline with respect to their studies and self-control with respect to their pleasures in order to succeed. No excuses are offered that might explain Homer's inability to do this. The stereotype of the blue-collar worker that Homer embodies is related to the craft apprentices Tom Sharpe portrays in *Wilt*. The implication is that education is wasted on such people. The view of adult education and its students that informed movements like the WEA and the Mechanics' Institutes is entirely absent. There is no sense that adult education might make individuals politically aware and enable them to change society. It is either a practical necessity (nuclear physics) or pointless recreation. In general, the perspective is extremely conservative, in spite of some iconoclastic humour.

Summary

This chapter has considered adult learners and their teachers in different contexts: in UK and US higher education, in further education, in the workplace and in adult education classes. It has drawn on film, television drama, books and cartoons. In spite of this diversity, some dominant discourses emerge that can be related to some of the key ideas that preoccupy adult educators.

Higher education

Higher education in popular culture takes place in an elite and rarefied environment; entry is determined by class and wealth. In all three texts featuring university life, we see the campus, staff and students through the eyes of individuals who feel they do not really belong. They see students they assume to be highly intelligent and somehow better than themselves. Homer and Rita, as working-class adults, believe that they are different from the people who inhabit this world. In *Educating Rita*, Rita's life experience is shown as a humorous barrier to her success as a student; in *The Simpsons*, Homer's is downright dangerous. Only later, when Rita has left her working-class home, does she develop the wisdom to challenge her teacher. The university is presented as a repository of high culture compared with the degraded mass culture of the working-class student. All of this might not be surprising given a British 1970s setting, but the two contemporary texts from the US, where there is a mass HE system, also portray universities (and these are provincial state universities: UC Sunnydale and Springfield State University) as frighteningly intellectual, elite institutions. It is true that the low level of working-class participation in higher education concerns governments and has been the focus in the UK of widening participation policies. However, popular culture exaggerates this, portraying an upper-middle-class elite as the mainstay of university life, whereas many universities would close without the lower-middle/upper-working-class students who constitute the majority of the student population.

Staff are highly qualified and respected by students and society at large. They may be flawed – alcoholic in Frank's case; mad in Maggie Walsh's – but their learning and right to dictate the curriculum are never questioned. Indeed, their weaknesses are part of the stereotype: Frank is a poet, and drunkenness has often been excused as part of the artistic temperament; Maggie epitomises the mad scientist. The HE curriculum is traditional and its delivery assumes clear demarcations between students and teachers. The value of the subjects on offer and the challenging nature of those subjects are not questioned. Only *BtVS* challenges the didacticism.

Adult and further education

Adult and further education receive none of this respect from popular culture. There are complex and contradictory discourses surrounding this area that we do not have the space to unravel here. Researchers and practitioners have long presented adult education as a serious and socially purposeful field of work that can have an important impact on individuals, communities and society as a whole. Successive governments have championed the kind of vocational education in which further education colleges specialise. On the other hand, these areas continue to be funded at a lower level than schools or universities, and their staff have lower pay and increasingly lower status. Concerns about the quality of provision and staff are aired by agencies such as Ofsted. Attendance at adult education or further education college often lacks the status accorded to university or even sixth-form education.

If popular culture's treatment of this sector of the educational world either reflects or helps to produce a general popular perception of the work done here, it may help to explain why it is politically possible for such a vital sector to be treated as second rate. In *Wilt*, *The Simpsons*, *Night School* and *Mind Your Language* the adult and further education curriculum is presented as undemanding intellectually and fairly pointless. Members of staff are losers, and often underqualified. Elements of teaching and learning celebrated by this sector, such as breaking down barriers between students and teachers and respecting students' life experiences, are ridiculed. The barriers may be down, but this comes from a complete lack of respect for the staff. Experience may be used, but it does not lead to learning.

Workplace learning

Popular culture is generally critical of the potential for exploitation offered by workplace learning. Relationships between employees, even when there is a mentor–mentee arrangement, are hierarchical and often difficult. The consensus seems to be that this is a far from ideal way to learn. Neither J. T. Marlin nor the Doublemeat Palace take account of their workers' views or life experiences, cutting them off when they try to bring any elements of themselves as people into the workplace. Both *Boiler Room* and *BtVS* take a critical stance towards this dehumanising behaviour. They seem to reject the limited and narrowly focused experience of the trainers. Thus, although the use of learners' experiences is belittled in texts featuring further and adult education, and the democratic nature of staff–student relationships is shown to engender lack of respect, in texts featuring workplace learning the opposite perspective seems to be taken. The lack of respect for students' personal feelings and experiences and the autocratic nature of relationships are shown to be exploitative.

Popular education

Although HE is not as elite as it is represented in these texts, it is nevertheless open to a smaller section of the population than schools, further and adult education and workplace learning. The latter represent the kinds of education open to the greatest numbers of people, and it would appear that familiarity breeds contempt and an unwillingness to value underpinning educational principles. The value of HE, on the other hand, is less frequently challenged. It is almost as though in most instances the mass of the population believes that non-HE tertiary education cannot be very good because they learn and teach in it. It is rather like the Groucho Marx joke: 'I would not want to be a member of any club that would have me in it.'

9   (In) conclusion

We said in the opening chapter to this book that we planned to focus on a range of discourses about education that could be found in popular culture. We have attempted to link these to wider professional, public and political debates about educational issues. These have included such issues as teacher performance, standards and expectations, social class and gender, and the effect of these on teachers' experiences and behaviour. We have looked at the connections with discourses about pupil behaviour, control and management; bullying and violence in schools; young people's moral and social education and their values and beliefs; and students' opportunities and attitudes towards education. We have also considered the way popular culture intersects with debates concerning curriculum content and control, particularly the vocational academic divide and the inflexibility of state-determined programmes. In so doing, we have attempted to show how popular culture both reflects and constructs our experience of education in ways that sometimes reinforce official educational perspectives and sometimes resist, challenge and undermine these in surprising ways. This can best be summarised, perhaps, by considering the treatment of teachers, students and the curriculum in turn.

Teachers

As we have discussed elsewhere, teachers have been cast as both 'saints' and as 'sinners', as powerful authority figures and as 'failures'. More recently, heightened consciousness in relation to issues of child protection have made teachers more vulnerable than previously to allegations of abuse (McWilliam and Jones, 2005). The discourses we considered constructed teachers in a number of ways that were often contradictory. The UK government's recent teacher recruitment drive included an advertising campaign that showed individuals from other professions explaining how they could not do the things that teachers have to do. The emphasis was on the personally and emotionally challenging nature of the job, suggesting that teachers need to be strong, sensitive and flexible individuals. This contrasts with the language used by the state when discussing or defining teaching in other contexts. Its quality reports and documents and its teacher-training requirements emphasise a much more instrumental approach to the profession, where teachers are expected to know and implement state policies and national curricula, and to demonstrate a predetermined set of qualities.

The image of teaching offered by the advertising campaign bears a strong resemblance to many images of teachers in popular culture. However, some popular culture undoubtedly appears to establish a counter-discourse to that purveyed by the recruitment campaign and the broader state/professional agenda. Far from showing teachers as people who are doing a job that others could not do, teachers in popular culture are often shown as failures – people who really wanted to be something else (sportsman/woman, musician and so on) or whose main career is over. This is particularly true of male teachers in popular culture. They are frequently presented as pompous individuals of limited ability who are working with children because they can have an authority and status in that situation that they could never achieve in the adult world. Even if they are presented as good people, male teachers are still frequently presented as failures. This seems to reflect both the relatively low status of teaching and the social construction of masculinity in terms of power, wealth and status.

The teaching profession for women was also frequently constructed by popular culture not as a positive choice but as something they did because they lacked an essential womanliness. Teachers such as those in romantic novels, Miss Toby Geist and Ms Stoeger in *Clueless*, and Miss Burke in *The Faculty* often lack the ability to attract men. The teen flick, in particular, makes this capacity a defining quality of female success. Where teachers are presented positively, professional practice is often conflated with being a good and very altruistic person. In this way, it becomes disconnected from skill, experience and specialist knowledge. This suggests that in many respects the discourse of the good teacher remains highly gendered. It is seen to be coterminous with being caring and nurturing, which in turn are presented as female traits – worthy of suspicion in a man and indicative of no special talent (because it is merely part of her nature) in a woman.

Overall, we found little evidence in popular culture of teaching as a high-status, successful profession, except in the case of higher education 'dons'. The relationship between popular culture and other discourses of teaching is more complicated than this, however. In popular culture, teachers are sometimes presented as precisely the kind of individuals the advertisements describe – people who can solve desperate and intransigent emotional and behavioural problems, cope with emergencies and behave calmly and with excellent judgement under intense pressure. Popular culture, however, suggests that this is incompatible with being the kind of teacher constructed through the quality and standards discourse. (This irony is simply ignored by the advertisements.) These marvellous teachers in popular culture do not acquire their talents through their training or by meeting the standards set down by the state. In many cases, they seem able to do their job only by acting in *opposition* to all such expectations, resisting authority and ignoring the frameworks within which they should be working.

Popular culture often relies on a dramatic tension between the individual character and charisma of the teacher and what is presented as the dead hand of the system. In this way, it draws our attention to the contradictory expectations

170 (In) conclusion

we place on teachers: the expectation that they will be creative and dynamic is confounded by the requirement that they adopt practices prescribed by educational policy and directives. Popular culture is driven by a complex set of factors. It is, to some extent, shaped by the requirements of narrative and characterisation, relying on a standard plot in which the individual fights the system in a superficially radical tale that need not be about teaching, but could be a Western, a tale of business and corruption or a political story. At the same time, it also appears to reflect the expressed concerns of teachers and students about the way in which teachers' behaviour is increasingly disciplined by the state, leading to restrictive instrumentalism that many teachers feel de-professionalises them, and leaves students feeling they are not treated as individuals but as cogs in a system. This perception is worsed by ironically named initiatives such as 'individual learning plans' and 'personalised learning' which in reality constrain individuals within government-determined targets. It would be naïve, however, to run away with the idea that popular culture offers a radical alternative to state definitions of good teaching. Rather, it seems to privilege an individualistic concept of the teacher that is just as de-professionalising in its own way. In popular culture, it is the teacher's essential charisma and personal passion that count, not their training, knowledge, intelligence, skill or political awareness.

Popular cultural discourses about teachers circumvent the political and structural factors that make up the modern teaching profession. In spite of the fact that many aspects of teacher identity and teachers' roles are constructed by the state, teachers in popular culture operate outside these frameworks, on a liberal, individual plane where the quality of their work is determined by personal character. In this way, popular culture contributes to a climate that can all too readily blame the teachers for any student's failure, and even for society's ills as a whole. Individuals will carry the blame in the mind of the public, for it is not the fault of the education system: 'It is Sir's fault.'

Bad teachers in popular culture are often constructed as mind-deadening agents of the system – the ones who have absorbed the targets, league tables, regulations and tips on good practice only too well. In this respect, they operate in opposition to dominant state and professional discourses about teaching. Yet, good and bad teachers also appear to reflect deep-seated fears and desires that presumably draw on our common experiences of school and teachers. Repeated images of teachers as evil reflect the impossibility of the job: everyone will have a school memory of being unfairly criticised, feeling victimised, ignored, belittled, irrespective of whether the teacher was even aware of the sense of grievance. In popular culture, these fears become exaggerated for dramatic purposes until teachers appear monstrous sadists. Moreover, teachers are in constant close proximity to adolescents with raging hormones and all the fantasies, fears and miseries these produce. As adults who are not parents, and with whom the students often have a close relationship, they can become objects of desire, of disgust and of fantasy. Unsurprisingly, popular culture picks up on this, presenting some teachers as depraved sexual predators and others as objects of lust, with all the implications for classroom power dynamics that these roles imply.

Students

It is possible to distinguish broadly between popular cultural texts in which the perspective is, or appears to be, primarily that of young people and those in which the young are shown principally through the eyes of teachers or society more generally.

Dangerous and endangered youth – the external perspective

Some of the texts we have considered seemed to present young people as 'other', almost as a different species, irrational and impossible to understand. The openings to *Lean on Me* and to *Class of 1999*, showing violent, out-of-control young people in school, and the film *Elephant*, where no attempt is made to humanise the killers by exploring their perspectives, are good examples of this. Even entertainment as light-hearted as the St Trinian's films fall into this category: the fourth-form girls are presented as an incomprehensible mob whose behaviour cannot be predicted beyond the certainty that it will be destructive. More recently, in the TV series *Teachers*, the children are weird creatures, to be approached with caution. In texts like these, we are never really offered the perspective of the child; instead, they seem to represent, often through humour or horror, wider social anxieties that young people are a threat to order, life and property. While it is not surprising that the adult world should be concerned about the socialisation, protection and development of its young, the extreme objectification and scapegoating evident in some of these representations may be indicative of a recognition that we have failed convincingly to create a world that offers meaningful identities to many young people.

The fear of youth verges on paranoia if the youth in question is working class and male. (This phenomenon is also evident in texts that deal with young people outside school, and, as Giroux (2002) has noted, the fear intensifies when the working-class male in question is also black.) In the 1960s British TV comedy *Please Sir*, a beleaguered and idealistic teacher (played by John Alderton) in a secondary modern school[1] tried to civilise 5C, the class destined for employment in local factories or for the dole queue. They were led by Duffy, whose dominance as a working-class male was signified by his large size and physical maturity. In spite of the apparent toughness of the students, this gentle comedy habitually reassured its audiences that these strange, rough creatures, the working classes, were really thoroughly decent and could be relied upon to perform their menial tasks for their betters, thereby becoming the backbone of society. *Wilt* and its sequels, discussed in Chapter 8, offer a much less sympathetic view of working-class youth, giving them no redeeming features and implying that education is wasted on them. As Willis (2003) has indicated, economic and social changes have dramatically altered the life courses of working-class youth. The removal of much traditional manufacturing work in the UK, together with the skilled and unskilled manual jobs it offered, has led to a growing concern about the development of an underclass and the loss of working-class male identity. This, coupled with the realisation that girls have begun to outstrip the academic performance of boys in schools (McGivney, 2004), is reflected in the way government policies and funding initiatives (such as widening participation targets in HE) have shifted from a concern for women and ethnic minorities to an almost exclusive focus on young people from working-class areas.

As well as images of school comprising, at times, hysterical and/or contemptuous views of the students, some portrayals also show students as victims of sinister controlling forces: education is presented as a tool for ensuring that the young conform to societal norms and expectations. Pink Floyd's 'Another Brick in the Wall, Part 2' is perhaps the best-known, classic statement of this position, with its insistence that education does not provide liberation or broaden the mind, but rather is a form of 'thought control'. The song allies itself firmly to an Althusserian view of education as an ideological state apparatus imposing itself on young people's impressionable minds in order to maintain the social structure. This perspective contrasts with that offered by texts like *Lean on Me* and *Dangerous Minds*, in which school is presented as something benevolent that can offer difficult and dangerous youngsters a chance to lead a fulfilling life, or even *Please Sir*, where school is at best an oasis of civilisation for a group of young people already resigned to a dead-end future. *Dead Poets Society* and *Mona Lisa Smile* offer images of the operations of such an apparatus for those destined for a place in the higher echelons of society. The violence of *Elephant* and *If* are located in schools that resonate with anomie, suggesting that the price we might pay for using education to promote conformity is the souls of the children themselves.

Buffy the Vampire Slayer often defies categorisation and here it seems to span both this section and the previous one. Although it primarily reflects the perspective of young people, like the texts that operate from the perspective of adults and authorities it often also shows students as non-human and schools as places dedicated to the suppression of youth. In *BtVS*, young people might be vampires, werewolves, demons or possessed by hyena spirits – all of which act as metaphors for the potential young people possess for violence, cruelty, sexual and anti-social behaviour. By showing this from the students' point of view, including the viewpoints of those who are monsters, the series suggests that these qualities are not unhuman but rather parts of the human psyche. It also offers a representation of school and teachers as deadening forces, but unsuccessfully so: the young people themselves are far more resourceful than their elders and resist in surprising ways.

'The kids are all right'

Popular cultural texts are often presented as though they originate from young people in school or college, but this does not necessarily mean that they reflect such perspectives; they are still the constructs of writers, directors, producers, musicians and actors. Nevertheless, they tell stories through the eyes of youth. This is indeed the norm with mainstream teen flicks, with British television programmes like *Hollyoaks*, and with popular teen fiction such as *Point Horror*,

Sweet Valley High, Cate Tiernan's *Wicca* novels and Cathy Hopkins' *Mates, Dates* series. While it is true that these products are not created directly by school or college students, they are mainstream and hugely popular with young audiences. This suggests that they do indeed tap into issues upon which the young want to focus; and, to some extent at least, they are reflections of youngsters' interests and preoccupations.

These kinds of school stories often have little to say about formal learning. Education does not seem terribly important, but school is. It is, above all, the centre of identity formation: the stories often depict the negotiation of a sense of self that is based on a struggle between the categorisation and acceptance/rejection of others and some undefined sense of inner integrity. Stories consider the attitude of various cliques to the protagonists and the protagonists' response to them. A common theme concerns the relative status of the hero or heroine with respect to the rich, popular and beautiful girls who are depicted as the pinnacle of the school's social hierarchy. In such contexts, fashion, music, style and body image are important signifiers of identity.

Part of the process of identity formation concerns the development of friendship and explorations of the concept of trust. This is particularly so with respect to stories that focus on girls. The stories tend to show boys who have mates, who may be good company, but may also humiliate and tease you (*South Park, American Pie, Dude Where's My Car, The Simpsons, Road Movie*). Being a good friend is consistently defined as an important characteristic of the mature heroine (*Clueless, Mean Girls, BtVS, The Princess Diaries*). Stories often focus on the tensions between romance and friendship (the *Wicca* series, for example) and even seem to suggest that the heroine will not capture the hero unless she behaves well towards her friends. To some extent, stories construct female identity in terms of the development of strong social ties and networks. This is a recognition, perhaps, that heterosexual partnerships may not sustain girls through life, and they will need to develop skills and loyalties outside the nuclear family in order to survive.

Having said that, the majority of these stories are romances in some form or another, and they rely on conventional romance motifs: less obviously glamorous girls with good souls win popular boys; plain girls are transformed by make-overs; the arrogant alpha-male turns out to have a soft side and falls for the feisty heroine. Boys desperately want to have sex, but they fall in love instead. Today's films and stories are contemporary in their recognition of the ambitions, intelligence, independence and determination of schoolgirls, but also place the development of a heterosexual relationship centre stage in their lives. Gay students are occasionally shown, but they do not feature as heroes or heroines in mainstream popular culture about schools and colleges.

Stories like these, told from the students' perspective, are often relentlessly optimistic. They acknowledge, sometimes to great comic effect, the existence of class, race and gender differences in education, and the impact these have on social cohesion, hierarchies and life chances. This acknowledgement seems to exist only to be overcome, however, not by social or political action but through individual redemption. In this respect, they provide both a vehicle for expressing dissatisfaction with the status quo (with its inequalities, spite, bullying, hierarchies and general unfairness) and the comfort and reassurance of easy resolution. They imply that society's ills can all be resolved by individual decency; there is no need to tackle underlying structural inequalities (*Clueless, Ten Things I Hate About You, She's All That, She Has to Dance, Crazy/Beautiful, American Pie*). The poor, white trailer trash can do well at school; the black guy and the white girl will readily resolve the cultural and familial tensions caused by their relationship; and sexist males will learn to be sensitive and relate to girls as real human beings. The individuals in question have to learn and grow up for all this to happen. This is a process that seems to involve developing more liberal and inclusive values, but the infrastructure is not challenged.

More challenging texts like *The Simpsons, South Park* and *BtVS* shift perspective – sometimes we see through the eyes of the school student; sometimes through other eyes – enabling the development of ironic or multiple perspectives. Thus, when Bart Simpson's parents are chastised by the school because of Bart's weak academic performance and delinquent behaviour, we are presented with a fantasy sequence that shows how he will become a despised male stripper, but could become a judge in the Supreme Court if only his father took more responsibility for him. The hyperbole undermines the whole premise and critiques the tendency to blame educational failure on individuals alone.

Curriculum

Teachers in the UK do not control the curriculum. A national curriculum (NC) for schools was introduced in 1992 and has since been refined. The NC determines what children should know and do at different ages and stages and it is reinforced by standardised national tests. Even at the early primary school level (ages five–seven), where there used to be flexibility to allow for the development of confidence and a recognition of different degrees of readiness to learn, there has been an increase in time devoted to literacy and numeracy and some prescription with regard to method that concerns many teachers. Many teachers feel they have lost the opportunity to encourage children to enjoy stories and creative play. The post-sixteen vocational curriculum is constrained by national occupational standards and national vocational qualifications. Higher education teachers have perhaps more input into curriculum design than teachers in other sectors, although this has declined considerably in recent years. Subject benchmarks and a national qualifications framework set expectations about the content of degree subjects and are used by the Quality Assurance Agency (QAA) in the UK as part of the basis for its inspection regimes, so that teachers designing curricula depart from these at some risk. Moreover, although teachers themselves design and submit courses for validation, there is an almost unchallenged orthodoxy that curriculum design should be outcomes-based.

There are advantages to students in some standardisation of the curriculum. It makes transfer between schools less disruptive and it provides a framework for weaker teachers that tries to establish some minimum levels of teaching for everyone. There are advantages to some employers in the increased emphasis on skills and vocational know-how rather than academic knowledge and cognitive development: they are more likely to find a narrowly competent and compliant workforce. It means, however, that important decisions about what counts as knowledge are not taken by the people most directly affected by the decisions – the students and teachers themselves. The exclusion or inclusion of topics and subjects from the curriculum has the potential to shape a generation's understanding of the world and what counts within it.

Vocationalism and basic skills have been at the top of the state's agenda in the UK, shaping curricula across the age ranges. There is simply less time in the curriculum for imaginative and creative subjects. Music, in particular, has become little more than a private extra in some parts of the country; physical education has declined; English literature is often no longer a subject in its own right. The recommendations of the Tomlinson Report on fourteen–nineteen curriuclum and qualifications reform (Department for Education and Skills, 2004) were influenced by the Secretary of State for Education's insistence that it focus particularly on strengthening vocational education; its core concerns have been with equipping students for work and the nature of vocational qualifications. Sports and the arts, subjects known to engage young people, remain optional extras. Our emphasis is on UK education, yet our knowledge and understanding of North American and Australian education systems indicate a similar increase in central control and a shifting focus away from the academic and imaginative towards performative versions of the vocational.

Popular culture, however, is often blind to these statutory frameworks. Frequently, popular texts assume the curriculum is in the control of the teacher. Set curricula are shown to be dull and disconnected from students' lives. The blame for this, though, is placed on the institution, its senior staff or the rest of the faculty. It can be changed by a charismatic teacher who is likely to come into conflict with the hierarchy of the individual organisation rather than the state apparatus. The charismatic teacher's revision of the curriculum often involves the arts, as was shown in Chapter 2. S/he reaches out to the students through art, music, literature or drama, as in *Dead Poets Society, Mona Lisa Smile, Freedom Writers* and *Mr Holland's Opus*. Even when there is no specific teacher involved, it is the artistic curriculum that is shown to engage the disaffected/different/inadequate student (such as photography in *Crazy/Beautiful* and *American Beauty*, and art in *She's All That*).

On the one hand, popular culture's cavalier disregard for the exigencies of the curriculum evades real issues facing teachers. It does not acknowledge the de-professionalisation of teaching that means teachers are no longer the people who decide what should be learned. It ignores the wider social and political implications of a system in which the curriculum is geared to the needs of the economy and the workplace, rather than the more general development of mind and imagination. Indeed, this may explain the popularity of texts set in private institutions and historical contexts, where it is easier to ignore the role of the state.

Nor does popular culture engage with the discourse of needs, entitlement and social mobility that informs contemporary curricula. It certainly does not face up to the possibility that students may need to learn things they do not enjoy in order to cope with life. In other words, a complex debate, with powerful arguments on both sides, is largely ignored in the search for a simple story that pits the teacher of integrity against the curriculum of doom.

On the other hand, popular culture does offer the start of a critique of current practice and it draws attention to contradictions in current curriculum discourse. It can show how the rhetoric of meeting individual learning needs is contradicted by curricula that define needs only in terms of vocational and technical-rational requirements. Similarly, the rhetoric of caring and fulfilling potential is under-mined by the categorisation of students' interests and capacities, forcing children into vocational or academic programmes. The repeated emphasis popular culture places on the creative and imaginative subjects and on their capacity to change people's lives seems to speak to a deeply felt concern about the failure of the technical-rational curriculum to engage our hearts and souls and develop fully rounded human beings. Indeed, popular culture offers an intensely felt and stimu-lating critique of the status quo, as long as we are not looking for a considered, fully rounded picture.

More about popular culture in education

Earlier in this book we acknowledged the work of Weber and Mitchell (1995, and, as Mitchell and Weber, 1999). Keroes (1999), Joseph and Burnaford (2001), Daspit and Weaver (2000) and Edgerton *et al.* (2005) are four more books that have interested us and, in their various ways, have influenced our thinking in relation to representations of education in popular culture. Similarly stimulating is Ellsmore's (2005) study of 'the charismatic teacher in film'. Those who have found the subject of this book to be of interest may wish to explore all or some of these earlier titles.

Interrogating popular culture can, we argue, open a window on issues such as gender, which, as Miller (1996) has pointed out, has been relatively absent from histories and from 'policy talk'. For Miller, this is paradoxical in that women have often been excluded from education and yet have been important as educators, a situation which she characterises as being 'there and not there' (*ibid.*, p. 1). In popular cultural representations of education, women are definitely there, though not necessarily in the roles that feminists would choose. Audrey Osler's (1997) study of the identities and lives of black teachers in the UK made a similar point about 'invisibility', and this too has been addressed by representations in popular culture through films such as *To Sir with Love* (1967) and the BBC TV series *Hope and Glory* (1999–2000). Sexuality, and in particular the way in which the dominant narrative of heterosexuality and the associated 'regimes of truth' exist alongside the hidden and 'dangerous' status of homosexuality in educational contexts, has been discussed in Epstein and Sears (1999). Again, we suggest, popular culture has, besides reflecting the dominant narrative, offered challenging alternative discourses.

Our argument, it should be stressed, is not that the study of popular cultural representations of education should replace empirical study of the 'real world' of the school or of the daily lives of teachers and learners, but rather that it can and should inform that reality which it constructs and by which it is constructed.

Thinking about teacher professionalism and values

Since the 'great debate' initiated by Prime Minister James Callaghan's speech at Ruskin College, Oxford, in 1976, and more particularly since the ascendancy of New Labour's vaunted priorities of 'education, education, education', teachers in the UK have been subject to inspection, regulation and the imposition of 'standards' in a push for 'school improvement'. The background to and the detail of these interventions will not be explored here, but those seeking a relatively recent examination of how they apply to schools in England are referred to Green (2004).

The concept of teacher professionalism can simultaneously serve a number of differing and sometimes opposing positions. On the one hand, the mantra of being 'professional' and adhering to professional standards can serve as a management rallying call that essentially seeks to generate compliance. On the other, teachers and their union representatives have sometimes employed the term as a lever to attempt to enhance status and, along with that, pay and conditions. More than a decade ago, Michael Eraut (1994) provided an authoritative account of professionalism as a form of ideology and outlined the concepts of professional knowledge, competence, qualifications and accountability. He concluded his study by stating that:

> organisations in the public sector are finding it increasingly difficult to attend to their own definitions of quality or even those of their immediate clients. Practices are increasingly changed to maximise performance on external inspections and performance indicators, causing increasing alienation of professional workers and weakening commitment to moral accountabilities.
>
> (*Ibid.*, p. 241)

Throughout and since the 1990s, the 'quality, audit and inspection' industry has grown in British society, but perhaps especially so within the education sector, even invading the more secluded realms of academe as represented by some of the more elite universities, which might have been imagined to be impervious to 'the inspector's call'. The strength of the ideology of professionalism lies in its appeal to concepts that tend to bridge the classic management–worker divide as well as some right versus left antagonisms. There is now a very large body of academic literature that relates to teacher professionalism, and those interested in pursuing this further may wish to seek out some of the following contributions that cover the spectrum from school to HE: Avis (1998, 2000a, 2000b, 2002, 2003); Barnett (2003, 2005); Bottery (1996); Carr (2003); Carr and Hartnett (1996); Clow (2001); Goodson (1997, 2003); Goodson and Hargreaves (1996);

Helsby (1995); Hoyle and John (1995); Hyland (2002); Lawn (1996); McFarlane (2003); Randle and Brady (1997); Robson (1996); Robson *et al.* (2004); and Walker (2001).

One of the most obvious utilities of the study of education in popular culture is the way in which the myriad dominant, emergent and 'subversive' discourses are represented over time. In other words, texts in popular culture provide a potent source of both contemporary and historical thinking on education. There are a number of **statements or codes of professional practice and values for teachers in England**. These statements are likely to be of particular interest to practising teachers and to those involved in teacher training. Indeed, trainee teachers are invariably invited to 'reflect' on their learning and professional experiences in relation to such statements and codes. We believe that the critical consideration of representations from popular culture offers considerable potential for the articulation of individual thinking and the development of group discussions on the basis that it both dramatises the issues and liberates the participants from both the inhibitions and the boundaries of their particular personal circumstances. The codes provide templates of 'professional aspiration' and typologies of ideal teacher characteristics that in addition to serving as a basis for individual reflective practice offer the possibility of systematic individual and group interrogation of cultural representations of teachers and learners. Moreover, the contemporary consensual interpretations of 'correct behaviour and values' that are both explicit and implicit in the statements themselves are open to critical scrutiny and discussion.

Teaching and critical reflection

> The critical project in education proceeds from assumptions that pedagogic practices are related to social practices, and that it is the task of the critical intellectual to identify and address injustices in these practices.
>
> (Popkewitz and Fendler, 1999, p. xiii)

The notion of 'reflective practice' has long had currency across a wide range of professions, and that this continues to be the case is underlined by the fact that in February 2000 Carfax launched a new refereed journal titled *Reflective Practice*. The influence of reflective practice has been particularly strong within teacher training, where it has been the philosophical basis of many pre- and in-service programmes of initial training in the UK.

During the 1990s, many Certificate in Education and Postgraduate Certificate in Education programmes in the UK were designed around primarily competence-based models. These had the appeal, as Ecclestone (1996, p. 147) suggested, of having clear statements about what learners were expected to achieve and offering '"authentic" assessment based on actual performance' that could be successfully counterpoised against 'allegations of "academic", "elitist" and "irrelevant" theory and "unnecessary" knowledge'. Those designing competence-based programmes sought to avoid the deeply reductionist and authoritarian essence of the model by welding it to a prescription for 'reflective practice'. Ecclestone outlines Schön's (1983) conceptions of 'reflection in action' and 'reflection on action'. She suggests that Schön's emphasis on individual 'intuition' and 'artistry' has been a large part of the appeal of reflective practice but questions the epistemological efficacy of reflective practice in the context of the complexities of everyday professional practice. In practice, Ecclestone suggests, the implementation of reflective practice has privileged technical enquiry (in the tradition of technical rationality) and practical enquiry (focused on the improvement of practice to produce a 'technology') over that of critical enquiry. This arises from an absence of debate about the 'purposes and underlying values in forms of reflection' (Ecclestone, 1996, p. 156). We would very much concur with this criticism, and it is our belief that the sensitive and appropriate use of texts from popular culture, far from simplifying the complexities of professional practice, can enrich reflection by taking participants beyond their experience and by liberating them from the often inhibiting process of 'writing up' aspects of their personal experiences.

The general 'intensification' of teachers' work that was discussed in the mid-1990s by Hargreaves (1994) is continuing to generate pressures of its own which need to be addressed through the provision of new skills (often of a broadly management/business nature) for those who are already experienced practitioners. Here again, we feel, the analysis of popular cultural representations of teachers and learners offers the potential to 'go beyond' competence and reflection on practice in the training and continuing professional development of the teacher and the lecturer of the future.

Trier (2005) has described the way in which a project with pre-service teachers in the US revealed the extent to which their preconceptions of inner-city teaching had been (negatively) shaped by cinematic representations. Following their practical experience of working in such schools, they were able to use cinematic representations (focusing specifically on issues of race) as a framework for critical analysis, highlighting the discrepancies between representation and lived reality as a means to deepen their understandings. In illustrating the usefulness of film as a teaching medium for teachers in training, Trier (*ibid.*, p. 187) suggests the 'taking up of a wide variety of texts beyond films and television programs: music videos, animation features, magazine images, newspaper articles and so on'.

It is our conviction that 'the good teacher' is also a critical intellectual, though this premise appears to be absent from recent political understandings of what a teacher is supposed to be, and, to some extent, the profession itself appears to have lost the confidence to reassert its *academic* identity. Given the wider context of social changes in the late twentieth century and currently in this one, this is, perhaps, unsurprising. Carlson and Apple (1998, p. 12) refer to Foucault's employment of the concept of 'normalisation' in relation to 'a complex set of processes involved in defining modern norms of self-discipline, rationality and instrumentalism'.

The educational research community has engaged in debate about the way in which the media has propagated panics about education (see, for example, the dialogue between Warmington *et al.*, 2005, and Pollard, 2005 in *Research*

Intelligence). We believe that these kinds of crises, typically focusing on standards and performance, while most recognisable at the surface level, are also embedded in the discourse of popular culture, and it is at that level that they more insidiously become part of commonsense understandings.

There are many ways in which the influence of popular culture studies have impacted on pedagogic practice and on the development of disciplines (for a US perspective on this latter point and on the uses of popular culture in teaching the humanities and social sciences, see Browne, 2005). In the UK, teacher education has, over the last thirty years or so, moved from a curriculum based on a combination of the key disciplines of psychology and sociology, together with smaller components of educational philosophy and history that were used to inform and underpin the practical matter of classroom teaching, towards something that is far more prescribed and performative and which focuses more on technicist notions of what it is to be a teacher. Hartley (1997, p. 105) refers to a 'curricular, pedagogical and technical fix'. That this has coincided with a deep crisis of the status of the teacher is not coincidental.

The death of disciplines in UK teacher education has been noted elsewhere. Goodson (2003, p. 7) argues for the development 'of teachers' professional knowledge, the joining of "stories of action" to "theories of context"', and claims that 'Without this kind of knowledge, teaching becomes the technical delivery of other people's purposes.' The US-based work of Cameron White (2003, p. xv) and others offers ideas 'for integrating popular culture and critical social efficacy as the driving themes in the teaching and learning process'. White sees popular culture as providing a possible powerful vehicle for 'transdisciplinary teacher education' in the USA. Flores-Koulish (2005, p. 1), also writing in the US context, argues for the need for teachers to develop 'media literacy', pointing out that the average American 'spends 9.2 hours each day engaged in media information/ entertainment' and asserting that 'This level of media exposure has created a powerful influence within our lives, one that far exceeds and is vastly different from the democratic values being taught in many schools.'

Finally . . .

We have argued above that teachers must be recognised as academics and intellectuals. We are conscious, however, that our discussions in early chapters have not addressed in any significant way the impact of the development of the internet on popular culture and learning. This is not a deficiency which will be 'made good' at this point, but it is one that we wish to acknowledge and provisionally explore. Information technology is now relatively cheap and pervasively plentiful. The various associated media have permeated popular culture in many complex ways. A fundamental issue is the extent to which the applications of information technology may prove to be ultimately negative or positive for society as a whole. Popular culture will be a major conduit for these 'cultural flows' and education will be a major constituting element at several levels.

Carr (2003, p. 241) has pointed to the potential danger that action research, with its empirical focus and locatedness in the immediate sphere of teacher experience, 'may appear to be not just instrumentalist but also narrowly pragmatist, if not actually anti-intellectual'. He argues that to 'insulate the concerns of the classroom teacher from the wider educational questions at least entertained by more general philosophical, sociological or psychological enquiries' may contribute to the process of de-professionalisation. Certainly, as indicated above, we would wish to argue that practitioner reflection on and research into education should go beyond immediate experience and should be enriched by 'other stories'. Weaver and Daspit (2000, p. xiv) point out the 'potential for multiple readings of popular cultural texts, the contradictory and shifting meanings of texts, and the shifting power struggles over control of texts'. Kate Myer (2004) utilises 'real life case studies' as a basis for professional development around issues of sexual ethics between teachers and learners. 'Real life' is, of course, reported on, represented in and created by culture.

Brottman (2005, p. 139), in her application of 'high theory' to 'low culture', states that her main interest in popular culture arises from 'consideration of how such culture functions as a source of aesthetic pleasure'. In our view, it is this aesthetic potency that gives it power as a means by which education and the associated processes can be analysed. The pleasures of 'low culture' are, for Brottman (*ibid.*),

> full of comedy, humor, and irony, suggesting that these forms are profanely productive and deathless, infected with the spirit of process and inconclusiveness, and liable to break up the otherwise often grim atmosphere of 'conventional' culture and society. Many forms of 'low culture' . . . contain a carnivalesque creativity and vitality far from fatalism and pessimism, and it is this basic force of pleasure that gives these cultural forms their great power, and affirms the ways they link to the real and the textual, discourse and desire, the spectacle, the gesture, and the body.

McCarthy (2004) has convincingly argued that aesthetic practices are now deeply embedded in the daily practices of 'ordinary people' and are no longer something associated with cultural elites. In his discussion of Paul Willis' (1977) classic *Learning to labour*, he suggests (McCarthy, 2004, pp. 159–160):

> Categories and metaphors that have been relied on in the past to unscramble social relations and dynamics now seem challenged by the new circumstances of contemporary education, work and leisure . . . The framework of analysis that linked education to capitalist employers, to factories, to the nation-state, and so forth is no longer serviceable, as the co-ordination of economic and symbolic production is now rearticulated along multiple sites.

The landscapes of social class, gender, race and sexuality have been radically transformed in the UK since the 1970s. So have conceptions of teaching and learning, and of what it is to be a teacher or a learner. It is our conviction that representations of education in popular culture, while containing few easy remedies or easy guidelines to practice, enable us to identify the important questions that, although arising from the sphere of fiction, impact directly on the terrain of lived experience.

Notes

8 School for grown-ups

1 The terms 'college', 'school' and 'graduate' are used differently in the US and the UK. In the UK, 'college' is most likely to refer to further education provision, with a strong emphasis on technical and vocational education. These institutions traditionally trained sixteen–nineteen-year-olds in trades and technical skills, although they now have large numbers of adult students and work with HE institutions to offer higher as well as further education. 'College' is also used to describe sixth-form colleges, which focus almost exclusively on sixteen–nineteen-year-olds and generally have a more academic focus, and colleges of higher education, which serve the eighteen-plus market, usually offering teacher training and a range of degree and sub-degree courses. 'School' in the UK is a term confined to the four–eighteen sector, whereas in the US, university students are described as being 'in school'. 'Graduate' in the UK is someone with a degree; pupils do not graduate from school. Someone undertaking study that requires a degree for entry is doing postgraduate work; in the US, they are doing graduate study and may be in 'graduate school'.

2 The Open University in the UK operates primarily through distance learning, but allocates students to tutor counsellors for support.

3 The assumption is that it is the University of Liverpool, although the film was shot in Dublin.

4 UK public schools are fee paying (i.e., private); free schools are called state schools.

5 General studies remains as a GCE AS and A level subject, and is often taken as an almost automatic extra by students on A level courses or those undertaking level 3 national vocational programmes, particularly in sixth-form colleges. However, these are not normally taken by young people on level 2 courses training directly for jobs or doing apprenticeships. Many institutions attempt some broadening of the post-sixteen curriculum by offering enrichment programmes. Again, these rarely reach the students on the most directly vocational programmes, on day-release, in-service courses, whose timetables are devoted to job-related training.

6 UK polytechnics were HE institutions that focused on vocational courses. As HE institutions they had more status than FE colleges. They ceased to exist as polytechnics in 1992 when they were granted independent degree-awarding powers and the right to use the title 'university'.

7 He brings this up to date in his 2003 study in the *Harvard Educational Review*.

9 (In) conclusion

1   At that time in England and Wales, education from the age of eleven was determined by results achieved in an examination known as the 11+. Approximately 20 per cent of students were selected for an academic education in grammar schools; the rest received a different curriculum in secondary moderns.

Useful websites

For lists of films, popular fiction and popular music containing representations of education, please visit the Education in Popular Culture Lists site at the University of Huddersfield: www.hud.ac.uk/edu/edpop
Friends Reunited: www.friendsreunited.co.uk
The General Teaching Council for England: www.gtce.org.uk
The Higher Education Academy: www.heacademy.ac.uk
The Institute for Learning: www.ifl.ac.uk
The Training and Development Agency for Schools: www.tda.gov.uk

Bibliography

Adorno, T. W. and Horkheimer, M. (1972) *Dialectic of enlightenment*, New York: Continuum.

Aldgate, A. and Richards, J. (1999) *Best of British: cinema and society from 1930 to the present*, second edition, London: I. B. Tauris.

Allen-Mills, T. (2005) 'Child rape teacher weds her victim', *Sunday Times*, 22 May, p. 3.

Almack, J. C. and Lang, A. R. (1925) *Problems of the teaching profession*, Boston: Houghton Mifflin.

Althusser, L. (1969) 'Ideology and ideological state apparatuses (notes towards an investigation)', in Althusser (1971) *op. cit.*

—— (1971) *Lenin and philosophy and other essays*, London: NLB.

American Civil Liberties Union (ACLU) (2001) 'Student suspended over sex song', www.aclu.org/studentsrights, accessed 6 January 2003.

Armstrong, E. G. (2001) 'Gangsta misogyny: a content analysis of the portrayals of violence against women in rap music, 1987–1993', *Journal of Criminal Justice and Popular Culture*, Vol. 8, No. 2, pp. 96–126.

Armstrong, L. (1994) *Trial by marriage*, London: Mills and Boon.

Aronwitz, S. and Giroux, H. (1987) *Education under siege: the conservative, liberal and radical debate over schooling*, London: Routledge.

—— (1991) *Postmodern education: politics, culture and social criticism*, Minneapolis: University of Minnesota Press.

Atkinson, E. (2002) 'Education for diversity in a multisexual society: negotiating the contradictions of contemporary discourse', *Sex Education*, Vol. 2, No. 2, pp. 119–132.

—— (2003) 'Sexualities and resistance: quer(y)ing identity and discourse in education', paper presented at the second Discourse, Power, Resistance Conference, University of Plymouth, UK, 6–8 April.

Austen, J. (2003) *Emma*, London: Penguin.

Avent, J. E. (1931) *The excellent teacher*, Knoxville, TN: Author.

Averill, L. A. (1939) *Mental hygiene for the classroom teacher*, New York: Pitman.

Avis, J. (1993a) 'A new orthodoxy, old problems: post-16 reforms, *British Journal of Sociology of Education*, Vol. 14, No. 3, pp. 245–260.

—— (1993b) 'Post-Fordism, curriculum modernisers and radical practice: the case of vocational education and training in England', *The Vocational Aspect of Education*, Vol. 45, No. 1, pp. 3–14.

—— (1998) '(Im)possible dreams: post-Fordism, stakeholding and post-compulsory education', *Journal of Education Policy*, Vol. 13, No. 2, pp. 251–263.

—— (2000a) 'Policing the subject: learning outcomes, managerialism and research in PCET', *British Journal of Educational Studies*, Vol. 48, No. 1, pp. 38–57.

—— (2000b) 'Policy talk: reflexive modernisation and the construction of teaching and learning within post-compulsory education and lifelong learning in England', *Journal of Education Policy*, Vol. 15, No. 2, pp. 185–199.

—— (2002) 'Imaginary friends: managerialism, globalisation and post-compulsory education and training in England', *Discourse: Studies in the Cultural Politics of Education*, Vol. 23, No. 1, pp. 75–90.

—— (2003) 'Re-thinking trust in a performative culture: the case of education', *Journal of Education Policy*, Vol. 18, No. 3, pp. 315–332.

Ayers, W. (2001) 'A teacher ain't nothin' but a hero: teachers and teaching in film', in Joseph and Burnaford, *op. cit.*

Bailey, S. M. (2002) 'Foreword', in Jossey-Bass, *op. cit.*

Ball, S. J., ed. (1990) *Foucault and education: disciplines and knowledge*, London: Routledge.

Barnett, R. (2003) *Beyond all reason: living with ideology in the university*, Buckingham: Society for Research into Higher Education and Open University Press.

—— (2005) *Reshaping the university: new relationships between research, scholarship and teaching*, Buckingham: Society for Research into Higher Education and Open University Press.

Barreca, R. and Denenholz Morse, D., eds (1997) *The erotics of instruction*, Hanover, NH: University Press of New England.

Barrett, M. and Phillips, A., eds (1992) *Destabilising theory*, Cambridge: Polity Press.

Barthes, R. (1964) *Elements of semiology*, New York: Noonday Press.

Bauer, D. M. (1998) 'Indecent proposals: teachers in the movies', *College English*, Vol. 60, No. 1, pp. 301–317.

Bauman, Z. (1992) *Intimations of postmodernity*, London: Routledge.

Belenky, M., Clinchy, B., Goldberger, N. and Tarule, J. (1986) *Women's ways of knowing*, New York: Basic Books.

Belsey, C. (1994) *Desire: love stories in Western culture*, Oxford: Blackwell.

Benn, R., Elliott, J. and Whaley, P. (1998) *Educating Rita and her sisters*, Leicester: NIACE.

Bennett, A. (2001) *Cultures of popular music*, Buckingham: Open University Press.

Berk, A. (1985) *Teacher's pet*, New York: Silhouette Desire.

Bernstein, A. (2002) 'The philosophical foundations of heroism', www.andrewbernstein. net/heros, accessed 10 October 2007.

Besag, V. E. (1989) *Bullying and victims in schools*, Milton Keynes: Open University Press.

Blyton, E. (1946) *First term at Malory Towers*, London: Methuen.

—— (1992) *Collection: the naughtiest girl in the school*, London: Dean and Son.

Boggs, C. (1976) *Gramsci's Marxism*, London: Pluto Press.

Bottery, M. P. (1996) 'The challenge to professionals from the new public management: implications for the teaching profession', *Oxford Review of Education*, Vol. 22, No. 2, pp. 179–197.

Bourdieu, P. (1986) *Distinction: a social critique of the judgement of taste*, London: Routledge.

Bourdieu, P. and Passeron, J. (1977) *Reproduction: in education, society and culture*, London: Sage.

Brehony, K. J. (1998) '"I used to get mad at my school": a representation of schooling in rock and pop music', *British Journal of Sociology of Education*, Vol. 19, No. 1, pp. 113–134.

Brontë, C. (2006) *Jane Eyre*, London: Penguin.

Brookfield, S. D. (2000) 'Transformative learning as ideology critique', in Mezirow and Associates, *op. cit.*

—— (2005) *The power of critical theory for adult learning and teaching*, Maidenhead: Open University Press.

Brottman, M. (2005) *High theory/low culture*, Basingstoke: Palgrave Macmillan.

Brown, C. (1981) 'Mothers, fathers and children: from private to public patriarchy', in Sargent, *op. cit.*

Browne, R. B., ed. (2005) *Popular culture across the curriculum: essays for educators*, New York: McFarlane & Co.

Buckingham, D., ed. (2002) *Small screens: television for children*, London: Leicester University Press.

Burke, L., Crowley, T. and Girvan, A. (2000) *The Routledge language and cultural theory reader*, London: Routledge.

Cairns, T. and Merrifield, J. (2001) 'Tales from the margins, learning beyond teaching', in West *et al., op. cit.*

Cameron, D. (1985) *Feminism and linguistic theory*, Basingstoke: Macmillan.

Carlson, D. and Apple, M. W. (1998) *Power/knowledge/pedagogy: the meaning of democratic education in unsettling times*, Boulder, CO: Westview Press.

Carr, D. (2003) *Making sense of education: an introduction to the philosophy and theory of education and training*, London: RoutledgeFalmer.

Carr, W. and Hartnett, A. (1996) *Education and the struggle for democracy: the politics of educational ideas*, Buckingham: Open University Press.

Chesney-Lind, M. and Hagedorn, J. (1999) *Female gangs in America*, Chicago: Lakeview Press.

Christian-Smith, L. (1993) *Texts of desire: essays on fiction, femininity and schooling*, London: Falmer Press.

Cirksena, K. and Cucklanz, L. (1992) 'A guided tour of five feminist frameworks for communication studies', in Rakow, *op. cit.*

Clarke, J., Hall, S., Jefferson, T. and Roberts, B. (1976) 'Subcultures, cultures and class', in Hall and Jefferson, *op. cit.*

Clow, R. (2001) 'Further education teachers' constructions of professionalism', *Journal of Vocational Education and Training*, Vol. 53, No. 3, pp. 407–419.

Coates, J. (1993) *Women, men and language: a sociolinguistic account of gender differences in language*, second edition, London: Longman.

Cocca, C. (2003) 'First word "jail", second word, "Bait"', *Slayage*, Vol. 10, www.slayage.tv, accessed 19 July 2007.

Codell, E. R. (2003) *Educating Esme: diary of a teacher's first year*, New York: Workman.

Cohen, S. (1996) 'Postmodernism, the new cultural history, film: resisting images of education', *Paedagogica Historica*, Vol. 32, No. 2, pp. 395–420.

Cohn, J. (1988) *Romance and the erotics of property*, Durham, NC: Duke University Press.

Coleridge, S. T. (2002) *Kubla Khan*, Reading: Two Rivers Press.

Collins, J., Radner, H. and Collins, A. P., eds (1993) *Film theory goes to the movies: cultural analysis of contemporary film*, New York: Routledge.

Connell, R. W. (1987) *Gender and power*, Cambridge: Polity Press.

Cowen, R. (1996) 'Performativity, postmodernity and the university', *Comparative Education*, Vol. 32, No. 2, pp. 245–258.

Crenshaw, K. (1991) 'Beyond racism and misogyny: black feminism and 2 Live Crew', *Boston Review*, Vol. 6, No. 6, www.bostonreview.net.BR16.6/crenshaw, accessed 19 July 2007.

Crick, N. and Bigbee, M. (1998) 'Relational and overt forms of peer victimisation: a multiinformant approach', *Journal of Consulting and Clinical Psychology*, Vol. 66, No. 2, pp. 337–347.

Cruickshank, J. (2002) 'Lifelong learning or retraining for life: scapegoating the worker', *Studies in the Education of Adults*, Vol. 34, No. 2, pp. 140–155.

Crum, S. (2000) 'Mind the gap', *Guardian Education*, 5 September, pp. 10–11.

Dalton, M. M. (1995) 'The Hollywood curriculum: who is the "good" teacher?', *Curriculum Studies*, Vol. 3, No.1, pp. 23–44.

Daspit, T. (2003) 'Buffy goes to college, Adam murders to dissect', in South, *op. cit.*

Daspit, T. and Weaver, J. A. (2000) *Popular culture and critical pedagogy*, New York, Oxford: Garland Science.

Daugherty, A. (2001) 'Just a girl: Buffy as icon', in Kaveney, *op. cit.*

Debord, G. (1988) *Comments on the society of the spectacle*, Sheffield: Pirate Press.

—— (1995) *The society of the spectacle*, New York: Zone Books.

Department for Education (DFE) (1994) *Bullying: don't suffer in silence*, London: HMSO.

Department for Education and Skills (DfES) (2004) *14–19 curriculum and qualifications reform: final report of the working group on 14–19 reform* [The Tomlinson Report], London: DfES.

de Pizan, Christine (2005) *City of ladies*, London: Penguin.

Dessau, B. (1994) 'Less is moron', *Vox*, Vol. 44, pp. 16–17.

Dixon, J. (1999) *The romance fiction of Mills and Boon 1909–1990s*, London: UCL Press.

Dolby, N., Dimitriadis, G. and Willis, P., eds (2004) *Learning to labour in new times*, London: RoutledgeFalmer.

Donald, J. (1992) *Sentimental education: schooling, popular culture and the regulation of liberty*, London: Verso.

Doyle, L. (1996) 'All they need to know they learned in Hollywood', *Rolling Stone*, Vols 750/751, pp. 34–40 and 214.

Dreyfus, H. and Rabinow, P., eds (1983) *Michel Foucault: beyond structuralism and hermeneutics*, Chicago: University of Chicago Press.

Dube, F. and Moore, N. (2000) 'The teachers' pets', *National Post*, 29 April, www.fact.on.ca./news/news0004/np00042m.htm, accessed 8 January 2003.

du Maurier, D. (2003) *Rebecca*, London: Virago.

Dwyer, P. and Wyn, J. (2001) *Youth, education and risk: facing the future*, London: Routledge.

Dyer, R. (1988) 'Children of the night: vampirism as homosexuality, homosexuality as vampirism', in Radstone, *op. cit.*

Early, F. (2002) 'Staking her claim: Buffy the Vampire Slayer as transgressive woman warrior', *Slayage*, Vol. 5, www.slayage.tv, accessed 19 July 2007.

Ecclestone, K. (1996) 'The reflective practitioner: mantra or model for emancipation?', *Studies in the Education of Adults*, Vol. 28, No. 2, pp. 146–161.

Edgerton, S., Holm, G., Daspit, T. and Farber, P., eds (2005) *Imagining the academy: higher education and popular culture*, London: RoutledgeFalmer.

Education Group, Centre for Contemporary Cultural Studies (1981) *Unpopular education: schooling and social democracy in England since 1944*, London: Hutchinson.

Education Group 2, Cultural Studies, Birmingham (1991) *Education limited: schooling and training and the new right since 1979*, London: Unwin Hyman.

Edwards, R. (1993) *Mature women students: separating or connecting family and education*, London: Taylor and Francis.

Elliott, G., ed. (1994) *Althusser: a critical reader*, Oxford: Blackwell.

Ellsmore, S. (2005) *Carry on, teachers! Representations of the teaching profession in screen culture*, Stoke-on-Trent: Trentham.

Epstein, D., Elwood, J., Hey, V. and Maw, J., eds (1998) *Failing boys? Issues in gender and achievement*, Buckingham: Open University Press.

Epstein, D. and Sears, J. T., eds (1999) *A dangerous knowing: sexuality, pedagogy and popular culture*, London: Cassell.

Eraut, M. (1994) *Developing professional knowledge and competence*, London: Falmer Press.

Evans, M., ed. (1982) *The woman question*, London: Fontana.

Farber, P., Provenzo, E. Jr. and Holm, G., eds (1994) *Schooling in the light of popular culture*, Albany, NY: Suny Press.

Fenwick, T. (2003) 'Dancing with the devil: towards a critical HRD', *Proceedings of the 44th Adult Education Research Conference*, San Francisco State University, June.

Fisher, R. (1997) '"Teachers' hegemony sucks": examining *Beavis and Butt-head* for signs of life', *Educational Studies*, Vol. 23, No. 3, pp. 417–428.

—— (2003a) 'The golden age of BTEC: the business education curriculum in 1980s further education', *The Curriculum Journal*, Vol. 14, No. 2, pp. 253–277.

—— (2003b) 'Gramsci, cyberspace and work-based learning', *Journal of Access and Credit Studies*, Vol. 4, No. 2, pp. 154–158.

—— (2004) 'From Business Education Council to Edexcel Foundation 1969–1996: the short but winding road from technician education to instrumentalist technicism', *Journal of Education and Work*, Vol. 17, No. 3, pp. 237–255.

Fitchett, A. (1999) 'There were punches that went to my head', www.tangents.co.uk/tangents/main/challenge, accessed 24 May 2001.

Flores-Koulish, S. A. (2005) *Teacher education for critical consumption of mass media and popular culture*, Abingdon: RoutledgeFalmer.

Foale, A. (1993) 'The St Trinian's cycle and British film comedy', *Electronic Journal of British Cinema*, www.shu.ac.uk/services/lc/closeup/foale9, accessed 15 August 2005.

Forrester, K. (2002) 'Work related learning and the struggle for employee commitment', *Studies in the Education of Adults*, Vol. 34, No. 1, pp. 42–55.

Foucault, M. (1972) *The archaeology of knowledge and the discourse of language*, New York: Pantheon.

—— (1976) *The history of sexuality*, Vol. 1, Harmondsworth: Penguin.

—— (1980) 'Prison Talk', in Gordon, *op. cit.*

—— (1983) 'The subject and power', in Dreyfus and Rabinow, *op. cit.*

—— (1991) *Discipline and punish: the birth of the prison*, Harmondsworth: Penguin.

Francis, B. (2000) *Boys, girls and achievement: addressing the classroom issues*, London: RoutledgeFalmer.

Frank, A. (1997) *The diary of a young girl: the definitive edition*, London: Penguin.

Freedom Writers with Gruwell, E. (1999) *The freedom writers' diary: how a teacher and 150 teens used writing to change themselves and the world around them*, New York: Random House.

Freire, P. (1972) *Pedagogy of the oppressed*, Harmondsworth: Penguin.

—— (1998) *Pedagogy of freedom*, Lanham, MD: Rowman and Littlefield.

French, M. (1994) 'Power/sex', in Radkte and Stam, *op. cit.*

Frith, S. and Goodwin, A., eds (1990) *On record: rock, pop and the written word*, London: Routledge.

Frith, S. and McRobbie, A. (1990) 'Rock and sexuality', in Frith and Goodwin, *op. cit.*

Gatens, M. (1992) 'Power, bodies and difference', in Barrett and Phillips, *op. cit.*

Gates, H. L. (1990) *Figures in black: words, signs and the racial self*, Oxford: Oxford University Press.

General Teaching Council for England (2007) 'Statement of professional values and practice for teachers', www.gtce.org.uk/gtcinfo/code.asp, accessed 4 June 2007.

Giddens, A. (1991) *Modernity and self identity: self and society in the late modern age*, Stanford, CA: Stanford University Press

Gilbert, F. (2004) *I'm a teacher, get me out of here!*, London: Short Books.

Giroux, H., ed. (1992) *Border crossings: cultural workers and the politics of education*, London: Routledge.

—— (1993) 'Reclaiming the social: pedagogy, resistance and politics in celluloid culture', in Collins *et al., op. cit.*

—— (2002) *Breaking into the movies: film and the culture of politics*, Oxford: Blackwell.

Goldberg, D. T. (1994) *Multiculturalism: a critical reader*, Oxford: Blackwell.

Goodson, I. (1997) '"Trendy theory" and teacher professionalism', *Cambridge Journal of Education*, Vol. 27, No. 1, pp. 7–21.

—— (2003) *Professional knowledge, professional lives: studies in education and change*, Buckingham: Open University Press.

Goodson, I. and Hargreaves, A. (1996) *Teachers' professional lives*, London: Falmer Press.

Gordon, C., ed. and trans. (1980) *Power and knowledge: selected interviews and other writing by Michel Foucault 1972–1977*, New York: Pantheon.

Gordon, R. (2002) *School of corruption*, London: New English Library.

Gorz, A. (1997) *Farewell to the working class: an essay on post-industrial socialism*, London: Pluto Press.

Gosling, J. (1998) 'Virtual world of girls', www.ju90.co.uk, accessed 6 August 2005.

Gramsci, A. (1971) *Selections from prison notebooks*, London: Lawrence and Wishart.

Green, H., ed. (2004) *Professional standards for teachers and school leaders: a key to school improvement*, London: RoutledgeFalmer.

Greene, M. (2007) *The public school and the private vision*, New York: New Press.

Greer, G. (1971) *The female eunuch*, London: Paladin.

Gregson, M. and Spedding, T. (2003) 'Constructing learning environments in initial and continuing post-16 teacher education in the UK', paper presented at the annual conference of the British Educational Research Association, Heriott-Watt University, 11–13 September.

Griffiths, M. and Troyna, B., eds (1995) *Antiracism, culture and social justice in education*, Stoke-on-Trent: Trentham Books.

Gruwell, E. (2007) www.freedomwritersfoundation.org, accessed April 2007.

Guaspari-Tzavaras, R. (1999) *Music of the heart*, New York: Hyperion Books.

Hall, S. and Jefferson, T., eds (1976) *Resistance through rituals: youth sub-cultures in post-war Britain*, London: Hutchinson.

Hampton, C. (1985) *Les liaisons dangereuses*, London: Samuel French.

Hansen, S. and Jensen, J. (1971) *The little red school book*, London: Stage 1.

Hargreaves, A. (1994) *Changing teachers, changing times: teachers' work and culture in the postmodern age*, London: Cassell.

Hartley, D. (1997) *Reschooling society*, London: Falmer Press.

Hebdige, D. (1979) *Subculture: the meaning of style*, London: Methuen.

Heller, Z. (2003) *Notes on a scandal*, London: Penguin.

Helsby, G. (1995) 'Teachers' construction of professionalism in England in the 1990s', *Journal of Education for Teaching*, Vol. 21, No. 3, pp. 317–332.

Hilton, J. (1984) *Goodbye, Mr Chips*, London: Coronet.

Hines, B. (1968) *A kestrel for a knave*, London: Penguin.

Hobson, P. and Welbourne, L. (1998) 'Adult development and transformative learning', *International Journal of Lifelong Education*, Vol. 17, No. 2, pp. 72–86.

Hoggard, L. (2004) 'The Spite Girls', www.film.guardian.co.uk/features/featurepages, accessed 21 July 2004.

Hoggart, R. (1957) *The uses of literacy*, London: Pelican.

Hoh, D. (1997) *The whisperer*, London: Scholastic Books.

Hollows, J. (2000) *Feminism, femininity and popular culture*, Manchester: Manchester University Press.

Hollows, J. and Moseley, R. (2005) *Feminisms in popular culture*, Oxford: Berg.

Holtby, W. (2003) *South Riding*, London: Virago.

Home Office (2006) *Positive futures: be part of something*, London: Home Office.

Hooper, C. (2002) *A child's book of true crime*, London: Vintage.

Hope, A. and Oliver, P., eds (2005) *Risk, education and culture*, Aldershot: Ashgate.

Hoskin, K. (1990) 'Foucault under examination: the crypto-educationalist unmasked', in Ball, *op. cit.*

—— (1994) 'Boxing clever: for, against and beyond Foucault in the battle for accounting theory', *Critical Perspectives in Accounting*, Vol. 5, No. 1, pp. 57–85.

Hoyle, E. and John, P. D. (1995) *Professional knowledge and professional practice*, London: Cassell.

Hughes, T. (1857) *Tom Brown's school days*, www.literature.org/authors/hughes-thomas/tom-browns-schooldays/chapter-06.html, accessed February 2007.

Human Rights Watch (2001) *Scared at school: sexual violence against girls in South African schools*, New York: Human Rights Watch.

Hunter, E. (1955) *The blackboard jungle*, London: Constable.

Hyland, T. (2002) 'Third way values and post-school education policy', *Journal of Education Policy*, Vol. 17, No. 2, pp. 245–258.

Ingham, R., Woodcock, A. and Stenner, K. (1991) 'Getting to know you . . . young people's knowledge of their partners at first intercourse', *Journal of Community and Applied Social Psychology*, Vol. 2, No. 1, pp. 117–132.

Irigaray, L. (1977) 'When our lips speak together', in Burke *et al.* (2000), *op. cit.*

Jackson, B. and Marsden, D. (1962) *Education and the working class*, Harmondsworth: Penguin.

Jarvis, C. (2001) 'School is Hell: gendered fears in teenage horror', *Educational Studies*, Vol. 27, No. 3, pp. 257–267.

—— (2005) 'Real stakeholder education? Lifelong learning in the Buffyverse', *Studies in the Education of Adults*, Vol. 37, No. 1, pp. 31–47.

Jefferson County Sheriff's Office, *The Columbine Report*, www.boulderdailycamera.com/shooting/report.html, accessed February 2007.

Johnson, L. (1992) *My posse don't do homework*, New York: St Martin's Press.

Johnson, S. and Marcil, C. (1993) *MTV's Beavis and Butt-head: this book sucks*, London: MTV Books/Callaway/Boxtree.

Johnson, T. S. (2005) 'The "problem" of bodies and desires in teaching', *Teaching Education*, Vol. 16, No. 2, pp. 131–149.

Jones, A. (2004) 'Social anxiety, sex, surveillance, and the "safe" teacher', *British Journal of Sociology of Education*, Vol. 25, No. 1, pp. 53–66.

Jones, K. and Davies, H. (2002) 'Keeping it real: *Grange Hill* and the representation of the "child's world" in children's television drama', in Buckingham, *op. cit.*

Jones, R. (1986) 'Mills and Boon meets feminism', in Radford, *op. cit.*

Joseph, P. B. (2001) 'The ideal teacher: images in early 20th century teacher education textbooks', in Joseph and Burnaford, *op. cit.*

Joseph, P. B. and Burnaford, G. E., eds (2001) *Images of school teachers in America*, second edition, Mahwah, NJ: Lawrence Erlbaum.

Jossey-Bass (2002) *The Jossey-Bass reader on gender in education*, San Francisco: Jossey-Bass.

Jowett, L. (2005) *Sex and the Slayer*, Middletown, CT: Wesleyan Press.

Judge, H. (1995) 'The images of teachers', *Oxford Review of Education*, Vol. 21, No. 3, pp. 253–265.

Kantor, K., Kantor, N., Kantor, J., Eaton, M. and Kantor, B. (2001) '"I will not expose the ignorance of the faculty": *The Simpsons* as school satire', in Joseph and Burnaford, *op. cit.*

Kaplan, C. (1986) *Sea changes: essays on culture and feminism*, London: Verso.

Kaveney, R., ed. (2001) *Reading the Vampire Slayer*, London: Tauris Parke.

Keddie, N. (1980) 'Adult education: an ideology of individualism', in Thompson, *op. cit.*

Kent, C. (1999) *Boys of Swithins Hall*, San Francisco: GLB.

—— (2002) *The real Tom Brown's school days: an English school boy parody*, San Francisco: GLB.

Keroes, J. (1999) *Tales out of school: gender, longing, and the teacher in fiction and film*, Carbondale and Edwardsville: Southern Illinois University Press.

Kidd, S. (2004) '"The walls were closing in and we were trapped": a qualitative analysis of street youth suicide', *Youth and Society*, Vol. 36, No. 1, pp. 30–55.

Kilgour, M. (1995) *The rise of the Gothic novel*, London and New York: Routledge.

King, K. and Kitchener, P. (1994) *Developing reflective judgement*, San Francisco: Jossey-Bass.

Kirschenbaum, H. and Henderson, V. (1990) *The Carl Rogers reader*, London: Constable.

Kureishi, H. and Savage, J., eds (1996) *The Faber book of pop*, London: Faber and Faber.

Larkin, J. (1994) *Sexual harassment: high school girls speak out*, Toronto: Second Story Press.

Lawn, M. (1996) *Modern times? Work, professionalism and citizenship in teaching*, London: Falmer Press.

Lee Cooper, B. (2001) 'Formal education as a lyrical target: images of schooling in popular music, 1955–1980', in Oliker and Krolikowski, *op. cit.*

Leicester, M. (1993) *Race for a change: in continuing and higher education*, Milton Keynes: Open University Press.

Levinthal, C. (2002) *Drugs, behaviour and modern society*, New York and London: Allyn and Bacon.

Little, T. (2003) 'High school is Hell: metaphor made literal in *Buffy the Vampire Slayer*', in South, *op. cit.*

Lloyd, R. (2002) 'Behind these "nice" school walls: a teacher's nightmare! A teenage jungle!', http://www.homeofhere.com, accessed 30 July 2007.

Lyotard, J.-F. (1984) *The postmodern condition: a report on knowledge*, Manchester: Manchester University Press.

Mac an Ghaill, M. (1994) *The making of men: masculinities, sexualities and schooling*, Buckingham: Open University Press.

McBride, L. (2000) 'The mindset list', in Crum, *op. cit.*

McCarron, K. (2000) 'The family's value: the parent and child in *Point Horror*', *Diegesis: Journal of the Association for Research in Popular Fictions*, No. 6, pp. 8–17.

McCarthy, C. (2004) 'Thinking about the cultural studies of education in a time of recession: *Learning to Labor* and the work and aesthetics of modern life', in Dolby *et al.*, *op. cit.*

McCourt, F. (2005) *Teacher man*, Glasgow: Fourth Estate.

MacDonald, M. (1995) *Representing women: myths of femininity in the popular media*, London: Hodder Arnold.

McFarlane, B. (2003) *Teaching with integrity: the ethics of higher education practice*, London: Routledge.

McGivney, V. (1993) *Women education and training: barriers to access, informal starting points and progression routes*, Leicester: NIACE/Hillcroft College.

—— (2004) *Men earn and women learn: bridging the gender divide in education and training*, Leicester: NIACE.

McGowan, P. (2004) 'This is London', *Evening Standard*, 14 May, www.thisisLondon.co.uk/news/article-10759616-details/girls+fought+like+banshees/article.do, accessed 10 May 2006.

McLuhan, M. (1964) *Understanding media*, London: Routledge and Kegan Paul.

McMillan, B. and Connor, M. (2002) 'Drug use and cognitions about drug use amongst students: changes over the university career', *Journal of Youth and Adolescence*, Vol. 31, No. 3, pp. 83–87.

McRobbie, A. (1982) '*Jackie*: an ideology of adolescent femininity', in Waites *et al.*, *op. cit.*

—— (1994) *Postmodernism and popular culture*, London: Routledge.

McWilliam, E. (1996) 'Seductress or schoolmarm: on the improbability of the great female teacher', *Interchange*, Vol. 27, No. 1, pp. 1–11.

McWilliam, E. and Jones, A. (2005) 'An unprotected species? On teachers as risky subjects', *British Educational Research Journal*, Vol. 31, No. 1, pp. 109–120.

Malcolm, D. (2000) 'Ken Loach: Kes', *Guardian*, 22 June, www.guardian.co.uk/Archive/Article/0,4273,403221,00.html, accessed 12 October 2006.

Malson, H. (1998) *The thin woman: feminism, post-structuralism and the social psychology of anorexia nervosa*, London: Routledge.

Mamet, D. (1993) *Oleanna*, London: Josef Weinberger Plays.

Marcus, G. (1992) 'Notes on the life and death and incandescent banality of rock'n'roll', *Esquire*, reprinted in Kureishi and Savage (1996), *op. cit.*

Marinucci, M. (2003) 'Feminism and the ethics of violence: Why Buffy kicks ass', in South, *op. cit.*

Marks, J. (2001) *Girls know better: educational attainments of boys and girls*, London: CIVITAS: Institute for the Study of Civil Society.

Medhurst, A. (2000) 'If anywhere: class identifications and cultural studies academics', in Munt, *op. cit.*

Melrose, M. (2000) *Fixing it? Young people, drugs and disadvantage*, Lyme Regis: Russell House.

Mezirow, J. (2000) *Learning as transformation: critical perspectives on a theory in progress*, San Francisco: Jossey-Bass.

Mezirow, J. and Associates (1990) *Fostering critical reflection in adulthood*, San Francisco: Jossey-Bass.

Miller, J. (1996) *School for women*, London: Virago.

Miller, L. (2001) 'Juvenile delinquency in films during the era of film noir: 1940–59', in Oliker and Krolikowski, *op. cit.*

Miller, M. (1990) *Seeing through movies*, New York: Pantheon.

Miss Read (1988) *The school at Thrush Green*, Harmondsworth: Penguin.

Mitchell, C. and Weber, S. (1999) *Reinventing ourselves as teachers: beyond nostalgia*, London: Falmer Press.

Mitchell, J. (1971) *Women's estate*, Harmondsworth: Penguin.

Modleski, T. (1990) *Loving with a vengeance*, London: Routledge.

Money, M. (2002) 'The undemonisation of supporting characters in *Buffy*', in Wilcox and Lavery, *op. cit.*

Moody, N. (1998) 'Mills and Boon temptations: sex and the single couple in the 1990s', in Peace and Wisker, *op. cit.*

Muggleton, D. and Weinzierl, R., eds (2003) *The post-subcultures reader*, Oxford: Berg.

Mulvey, L. (1975) 'Visual pleasure and narrative cinema', *Screen*, Vol. 16, No. 3, pp. 6–18.

Munt, S. R., ed. (2000) *Cultural studies and the working class: subject to change*, London: Cassell.

Myer, K. (2004) *Teachers behaving badly? Dilemmas for school leaders*, London: RoutledgeFalmer.

Nabokov, V. (1998) *Lolita*, London: Penguin.

National Commission on Education (NCE) (1993) *Learning to succeed*, London: Heinemann.

Neill, A. S. (1968) *Summerhill*, Harmondsworth: Penguin.

Newman, M. (2006) *Teaching defiance, stories and strategies for activist educators*, San Francisco: Jossey-Bass.

Newport Community Safety Partnership (2006) 'Crime and Disorder Audit 2001–2005', www.crimereduction.gov.uk, accessed April 2007.

Noble, C. and Bradford, W. (2000) *Getting it right for boys . . . and girls*, London: Routledge.

Oakley, A. (1990) *Housewife*, London: Penguin.

O'Day, R. (1982) *Education and society 1500–1800*, Harlow: Longman.

Ofsted (2003) *Bullying: effective action in secondary schools*, London: Crown.

Oliker, M. and Krolikowski, W., eds (2001) *Images of youth: popular culture as educational ideology*, New York: Peter Lang.

Olweus, D. (1980) 'The consistency issue in personality psychology revisited – with special reference to aggression', *British Journal of Social and Clinical Psychology*, Vol. 19, pp. 377–390.

Ortner, S. (1982) 'Is female to male as nature is to culture?', in Evans, *op. cit.*

Osler, A. (1997) *The education and careers of black teachers: changing identities, changing lives*, Buckingham: Open University Press.

Owen, M. (1990) 'Women's reading of popular romantic fiction: a case study in the mass media', unpublished Ph.D. thesis, University of Liverpool.

Parker, H., Bakx, K. and Newcombe, R. (1988) *Living with heroin: the impact of a drugs 'epidemic' on an English community*, New York: McGraw Hill.

Parker, S. (1997) *Reflective teaching in the postmodern world: a manifesto for education in postmodernity*, Buckingham: Open University Press.

Pasley, J. (2003) 'Old familiar vampires: the politics of the Buffyverse', in South, *op. cit.*

Paule, M. (2004) 'You're on my campus, buddy! Sovereign and disciplinary power at Sunnydale High', *Slayage*, Vol. 15, www.slayage.tv.

Peace, L. and Wisker, G. (1998) *Fatal attractions: rescripting romance in contemporary literature and film*, London: Pluto Press.

Pearson, M. (2005) 'Young people's attitudes to drug education', in Hope and Oliver, *op. cit.*

Perkins, A. (2001) 'When female teachers cross the line', *Eagle-Tribune*, 30 December, www.eagletribune.com/news/stories/20011230/FP_002.htm, accessed 8 January 2003.

Playden, Z. (2001) 'What you are, what's to come: feminisms, citizenship and the divine', in Kaveney, *op. cit.*

Pollard, A. (2005) 'Real and imagined crises: the construction of political and media panics over education: a response', *Research Intelligence*, No. 91, pp. 4–15.

Popkewitz, T. S. and Fendler, L., eds (1999) *Critical theories in education: changing terrains of knowledge and politics*, New York: Routledge.

Pryce, S. (2006) 'Sex and the cinema: what *American Pie* teaches the young', *Sex Education*, Vol. 6, No. 4, pp. 367–376.

Pryer, A. (2001) '"What spring does with the cherry trees": the eros of teaching and learning', *Teachers and Teaching: Theory and Practice*, Vol. 7, No. 1, pp. 75–88.

Qualifications and Curriculum Authority (QCA) (1998) *Can do better: raising boys' achievement in English*, London: QCA.

Rabine, L. (1985) 'Romance in the age of electronics: Harlequin Enterprises', *Feminist Studies*, Vol. 11, No. 1, pp. 39–60.

Radford, J., ed. (1986) *The progress of romance: the politics of popular fiction*, New York: Routledge.

Radkte, L. and Stam, H., eds (1994) *Power/gender social relations in theory and practice*, London: Sage.

Radstone, S., ed. (1988) *Sweet dreams, sexuality, gender and popular fictions*, London: Lawrence and Wishart.

Rakow, L., ed. (1992) *Women making meaning: new feminist directions in communication*, London: Routledge.

Randle, K. and Brady, N. (1997) 'Managerialism and professionalism in the "Cinderella service"', *Journal of Vocational Education and Training*, Vol. 49, No. 1, pp. 121–139.

Reay, D. (2001) 'Spice girls, nice girls, girlies and tomboys: gender discources, girls' cultures and femininities in the primary classroom', *Gender and Education*, Vol. 13, No. 2, pp. 153–166.

Renold, E. (1997) '"All they've got on their brains is football": sport, masculinity and the gendered practices of playground relations', *Sport, Education and Society*, Vol. 2, No. 1, pp. 5–23.

Rickels, L. (1999) *The vampire lectures*, Minneapolis: University of Minnesota Press.

Rigby, K. (2003) *Addressing bullying in schools: Theory and practice*, Trends and Issues in Crime and Criminal Justice series, no. 259, Canberra: Australian Institute of Criminology.

Rigby, K. and Slee, P. T. (1993) 'Directions of interpersonal relating among Australian school children and their implications for psychological well-being', *Journal of Social Psychology*, Vol. 133, No. 1, pp. 33–42.

Riordan, J. (1991) *Sport, politics and communism*, Manchester: Manchester University Press.

Robinson, T. (2001) 'Joss Whedon', *The Onion*, Vol. 37, No. 31, www.auclub.com/Content/node/24238, accessed 28 December 2007.

Robson, J. ed. (1996) *The professional FE teacher: staff development and training in the corporate college*, Avebury: Ashgate College.

Robson, J., Bailey, B. and Larkin, S. (2004) 'Adding value: investigating the discourse of professionalism adopted by vocational teachers in further education colleges', *Journal of Education and Work*, Vol. 17, No. 2, pp. 184–195.

Roddick, N. (2000) 'Feature article, *Cherry Falls*', *Preview on-line*, www.preview-online.com/may_june/feature_articles/cherry_falls/cherry_falls_pg1.html, accessed 9 November 2003.

Rogers, C. (1967) 'The interpersonal relationship in the facilitation of learning', in Kirschenbaum and Henderson (1990), *op. cit.*

Rousseau, J. (1993) *Emile*, London: Everyman.

Ruskin, J. (2002) *Sesame and lilies*, Cumberland: Yale University Press.

Russ, J. (1973) 'Somebody's trying to kill me and I think it's my husband: the modern gothic', *Journal of Popular Culture*, Vol. 6, No. 4, pp. 666–691.

Russell, W. (2001) *Educating Rita*, London: Methuen.

Rutherford, J., ed. (1990) *Identity: community, culture, difference*, London: Lawrence and Wishart.

Sargent, L., ed. (1981) *The unhappy marriage of Marxism and feminism*, London: Pluto Press.

Sarup, M. (1982) *Education, state and crisis: a Marxist perspective*, London: Routledge and Kegan Paul.

—— (1993) *An introductory guide to post-structuralism and postmodernism*, London: Harvester Wheatsheaf.

Schön, D. (1983) *The reflective practitioner: how professionals think in action*, New York: Basic Books.

Sewell, T. (1995) 'A phallic response to schooling: black masculinity and race in an inner city comprehensive', in Griffiths and Troyna, *op. cit.*

Sharpe, T. (1976) *Wilt*, London: Pan.

—— (2004) *Wilt in nowhere*, London: Arrow.

Shary, T. (2002) *Generation multiplex: the image of youth in contemporary American cinema*, Austin: University of Texas Press.

Sikes, P. (2006) 'Scandalous stories and dangerous liaisons: when female pupils and male teachers fall in love', *Sex Education*, Vol. 6, No. 3, pp. 265–280.

Simmons, R. (2002) *Odd girl out: the hidden culture of aggression in girls*, Orlando, FL: Harcourt.

Skelton, C. (1997) 'Primary boys and hegemonic masculinities', *British Journal of Sociology of Education*, Vol. 18, No. 3, pp. 349–369.

Smith, P. K. and Sharp, S. (1994) *School bullying: insights and perspectives*, London: Routledge.

South, J., ed. (2003) *Buffy the Vampire Slayer and philosophy: fear and trembling in Sunnydale*, Chicago and La Salle, IL: Open Court.

Stallabrass, J. (1996) *Garantua: manufactured mass culture*, London: Verso.

Stam, R. and Shohat, E. (1994) 'Contested histories: Eurocentricism, multiculturalism and the media', in Goldberg, *op. cit.*

Steiner, B. A. (1994) *The phantom*, New York: Scholastic.

Storey, D. (2001) *Cultural theory and popular culture: an introduction*, third edition, Harlow: Pearson Education.

Stubbs, M. (2003) *Ahead of the class: how an inspiring headmistress gave children back their future*, London: John Murray.

Sunday Times (2004) 'The *Sunday Times* University Guide', 12 September.

Taylor, E. W., ed. (2006) *Teaching for change: fostering transformative learning in the classroom*, San Francisco: Jossey-Bass.

Thompson, J. (1983) *Learning liberation*, London: Croom Helm.

—— (2000) *Women, class and education*, London: Routledge.

Thompson, J. L., ed. (1980) *Adult education for a change*, London: Hutchinson.

Thurston, C. (1987) *The romance revolution*, Urbana: University of Illinois Press.

Topping, K. (2004) *The complete Slayer: an unofficial and unauthorised guide to every episode of Buffy the Vampire Slayer*, London: Virgin.

Training and Development Agency for Schools (TDA) (2007) *Professional standards for qualified teacher status and requirements for initial teacher training*, London: TDA.

Trier, J. (2005) '"Sordid fantasies": reading popular "inner–city" school films as racilized texts with pre-service teachers', *Race, Ethnicity and Education*, Vol. 8, No. 2, pp. 171–189.

Trifonas, P., ed. (2003) *Pedagogies of difference: rethinking education for social change*, London and New York: RoutledgeFalmer.

Udovitch, M. (2000) 'What makes Buffy slay?', *Rolling Stone*, 11 May, pp. 60–65.

Usher, R. and Edwards, R. (1994) *Postmodernism and education*, London: Routledge.

Van Stralen, S. (2002) 'Making sense of one's experience in the workplace', in Yorks and Kasl, *op. cit.*

Vint, S. (2002) '"Killing us softly?" A feminist search for the "real" Buffy', *Slayage*, Vol. 5, www.slayage.tv.

Waites, B., Bennett, T. and Martin, G., eds (1982) *Popular culture: past and present: a reader*, London: Croom Helm.

Waldron, P. (1998) *The adventures of a lesbian college school girl*, New York: NBM.

Walker, M., ed. (2001) *Reconstructing professionalism in university teaching*, Buckingham: Open University Press.

Walkerdine, V. (1997) *Daddy's girl: young girls and popular culture*, Basingstoke: Macmillan.

Wall, B. and Zyrd, M. (2001) 'Vampire dialectics: knowledge, institutions and labour', in Kaveney, *op. cit.*

Wallace, M. (1992) 'West End riots, 1991: young people's perspectives', unpublished MA thesis, University of Northumbria, quoted in Skelton (1997), *op. cit.*

Warburton, T. and Saunders, M. (1996) 'Representing teachers' professional culture through cartoons', *British Journal of Educational Studies*, Vol. 44, No. 3, pp. 307–325.

Warmington, P., Murphy, R. and McCaig, C. (2005) 'Real and imagined crises: the construction of political and media panics over education', *Research Intelligence*, No. 91, pp. 12–14.

Weaver, J. A. and Daspit, T. (2000) *Critical pedagogy, popular culture and the creation of meaning*, in Daspit and Weaver, *op. cit.*

Weber, S. and Mitchell, C. (1995) *'That's funny, you don't look like a teacher'*, London: Falmer Press.

Weiner, G. (1994) *Feminisms in education: an introduction*, Buckingham: Open University Press.

Weiner, M. J. (1981) *English culture and the decline of the industrial spirit 1850–1980*, Cambridge: Cambridge University Press.

Weinzierl, R. and Muggleton, D. (2003) 'What is "post-subcultural studies" anyway?', in Muggleton and Weinzierl, *op. cit.*

Werndley, A. (2003) 'The isolated teenager convention in *Point Horror*', *Diegesis: Journal of the Association for Research in Popular Fictions*, No. 6, pp. 39–45.

Wernick, A. (1999) 'Bataille's Columbine: the sacred space of hate', www.ctheory. net/printer.aspx?id=119, accessed 27 June 2007.

West, L., Miller, N., O'Reilly, D. and Allen, R., eds (2001) 'Travellers' tales: from adult education to lifelong learning and beyond', *Proceedings of the 31st Annual Conference of SCUTREA*, University of East London, 3–5 July, pp. 58–61.

White, C. (2003) *True confessions: social efficacy, popular culture, and the struggle for schools*, Cresskill, NJ: Hampton Press.

Whiteley, S. (2004) 'Use, misuse and abuse: current issues in popular musicology', inaugural lecture, University of Salford, 11 February.

Wilcox, R. (2001) 'There will never be a "very special" Buffy: Buffy and the monsters of teen life', *Journal of Popular Film and Television*, reprinted in *Slayage*, Vol. 2, www.slayage.tv.

Wilcox, R. and Lavery, D., eds (2002) *Fighting the forces: what's at stake in Buffy the Vampire Slayer*, Lanham, NJ: Rowman and Littlefield.

Williams, K. (1989) 'The gift of an interval: Michael Oakeshott's idea of a university education', *British Journal of Educational Studies*, Vol. 37, No. 4, pp. 384–397.

Williams, R. (1983) *Keywords*, London: Fontana.

Willis, P. (1977) *Learning to labour: how working class kids get working class jobs*, Farnborough: Gower.

—— (2003) 'Foot soldiers of modernity: the dialectics of cultural consumption and the 21st century school', *Harvard Educational Review*, Vol. 73, No. 3, pp. 390–415.

Wilson, E. (1980) *Only halfway to paradise*, London: Tavistock.

Wilson, J. (1997) *Bad girls*, London: Yearling.

Wiseman, R. (2002) *Queen bees and wannabes: helping your daughter survive cliques, gossip, boyfriends and other realities of adolescence*, London: Piatkus.

Wisker, G. (1998) 'If looks could kill: contemporary women's vampire fictions', in Pearce and Wisker, *op. cit.*

Wollstonecraft, M. (1994) *Thoughts on the education of daughters*, Yeadon: Woodstock.

Yorks, L. and Kasl, E., eds (2004) *New directions for adult and continuing education: collaborative enquiry as a strategy for adult learning*, San Francisco: Jossey-Bass.

Young, T. (1993) '*Beavis and Butt-head*, ha ha ha', *Modern Review*, Vol. 1, No. 12 p. 9.

Zalcock, B. (1999) *Renegade sisters: girl gangs on film*, London: Creation.

Zero Hour [television series] (1999) 'Massacre at Columbine', broadcast 20 April.

Index